VEGAN MADE EASY

VEGAN
MADE
EASY

Editors Laura Bithell
Designer Alison Shackleton
Jacket Designer Laura Hall
Producer, Pre-production Heather Blagden
Producer Mandy Inness
Photography Brigitte Sporrer
Food styling Julia Skowronek
Indexer Vanessa Bird
Managing Editor Dawn Henderson
Special Sales Creative Project Manager
Alison Donovan

First published in Great Britain in 2019
by Dorling Kindersley Limited
80 Strand, London WC2R 0RL

Material in this publication was previously published
in *Vegan on the Go* (2017) and *Vegan Cakes and
Other Bakes* (2018).

A CIP catalogue record for this book is available
from the British Library.
ISBN 978-0-2414-1885-7

Printed and bound in China

A WORLD OF IDEAS:
SEE ALL THERE IS TO KNOW

www.dk.com

CONTENTS

VEGAN BASICS

store cupboard essentials, vegan
food swaps, equipment, and more

MAKING VEGAN EASY

With veganism on the rise, it's getting much easier to maintain a healthy plant-based diet. That said, following a plant-based diet can have its challenges. With the luxury of time, making a delicious, healthy vegan evening meal can be a piece of cake, but when it comes to a rushed lunch break or finding something to satisfy your sweet tooth, you can come unstuck. That's where this book comes in. It tackles two of the biggest challenges for vegans, eating on the go and baking your favourite cakes and other treats without eggs, milk, cream, or butter.

Even on hectic days, your stomach will be rumbling by lunchtime – but your phone rings and there's an email to send before you can quickly find something to eat, and before you know it you've grabbed that uninspiring, lonely vegan wrap from the local shop, again. Sound familiar? No wonder many vegans prefer to prepare their meals at home. In a German Vegetarian Association survey of 3,500 vegans and vegetarians, 75 per cent packed their own lunch several times each week. The kinds of recipes they wanted were balanced, simple, and quick, and the on-the-go recipes in this book aim to be just that. They are designed to take away the lunchtime stress by giving you plenty of exciting, healthy vegan options to prepare at home and pack up for the day.

Finding an indulgent vegan baked treat can be just as hard as sourcing your lunch. What do you do if you're strictly vegan but you still love the creamy taste of cheesecake and the buttery texture of a biscuit? Baking is a hot topic for those following a vegan diet – whether for some or all of the time – because purely plant-based cakes, biscuits, breads, and rolls are hard to find. The baking recipes in this book give you plenty of delicious options and give you the chance to have fun in the kitchen. They are all easy to make at home, and, where possible, avoid exotic ingredients. You can also easily pack many of them up into a lunchbox for a mid-afternoon treat. Most importantly, they taste just as good, if not better, than dairy- and egg-based bakes.

With delicious recipes designed for convenience, and handy tips on store cupboard essentials, plant-based baking substitutes, and more, being vegan has never been easier.

VEGAN FOOD SUPPLIES

It's always a good idea to keep a few basics stocked in your store cupboard, fridge, and freezer, especially if you're planning on-the-go meals ahead. If you're prepared, you will only need to purchase a few additional fresh ingredients each week, and getting your lunchbox ready will be as easy as pie. Our recipes have been kept nice and simple and the ingredients are not hard to obtain. Most can be found in supermarkets and, if not, at health food shops, organic shops, pharmacies, or a vegan mail order company.

IN THE CUPBOARD

Cans of vegetables, pulses, and fruits.

Preserves in jars such as gherkins, olives, tomatoes, and peppers.

Dried fruits and vegetables such as mushrooms, tomatoes, and chillies.

Herbs and spices (dried): among the most useful are chilli powder, curry powder, garam masala, smoked paprika, ginger, cumin, herbes de Provençe, turmeric, marjoram, nutmeg, oregano, paprika, pepper, allspice, salt, and cinnamon.

Yeast flakes for seasoning and to create a "cheesy" flavour (see p134 and p190).

Olive oil ideally cold-pressed, good-quality organic.

Flours for baking, binding, and thickening, such as plain flour and chickpea flour.

Nuts and seeds it's a good idea to keep chia seeds, cashews, hazelnuts, sesame seeds, and walnuts.

Pasta is an essential. It's a basis for so many dishes.

Quinoa, rice, or wild rice can also form the basis for lots of salads, side dishes, and fillings.

Textured soy or TVP (textured vegetable protein), finely or coarsely ground, diced, or as a steak.

Seasoning and sweeteners such as agave syrup, maple syrup, barbecue sauce, vinegar, vegetable stock or bouillon, tomato ketchup, soy sauce, miso, and tahini.

IN THE FREEZER

Fresh vegetables cleaned, blanched if necessary, and stored in portions, keep for several months.

Frozen vegetables usually contain more vitamins than fresh vegetables, since they are frozen immediately after harvesting. Pay attention to the producer's best before dates.

Lemon juice and **sauces** in little portions for dressings, sauces, or for flavouring; keep for a few weeks.

Pastry and dough pizza dough, puff pastry, shortcrust, and filo (home-made or shop-bought) will keep for a few months in the freezer.

IN THE FRIDGE

Fresh **herbs** will keep in the fridge for up to 1 week, wrapped in damp kitchen paper.

Vegan **margarine** should keep in the fridge for at least 3 weeks.

Non-dairy milk such as soya, rice, oat, almond, nut, or multigrain milks and drinks. For spicy dishes, use a sugar-free vegetable milk; for baking, use soya milk because it thickens in combination with vinegar and combines well with other ingredients. Unopened, it can be kept without chilling for several months; once opened, store in the fridge and use within 3–4 days.

Unopened soya, oat, or rice cream can be stored at room temperature for at least 6 months; once opened, store in the fridge and use within 2–3 days.

Soya yogurt without added sugar will keep in the fridge for around 2 weeks.

Unopened tempeh can be stored without chilling for several months; once opened, it will keep in the fridge for up to 8 weeks, but must then be used without further delay.

Tofu natural tofu (with no added flavours) and/or smoked tofu (already seasoned) will both keep unopened in the fridge for at least 2 weeks. Natural tofu stored in brine should be kept in a covered container, with the brine always covering the tofu.

Tomato purée will keep unopened and protected from the light for at least a few months, once opened store in the fridge and use it up within 1–2 weeks.

PACKING ON-THE-GO FOOD

A huge variety of lunchboxes are available. Choose one which is strong and airtight, so that nothing can leak out. Buy yourself a large, medium, and small box made from stainless steel, recycled plastic, or renewable raw materials. Also get an insulated container for soups or warm dishes and a vacuum flask for smoothies or other drinks – these will usually keep your lunch warm for up to 6 hours, or cool for up to 24 hours. Practical alternatives include thoroughly cleaned, recycled plastic containers with a tight-fitting lid, screw-top jars or preserving jars, as well as foil and cling film. Dressings are best transported separately, perhaps in a spare compartment in your lunchbox, or in a little glass jar.

Many offices are equipped with a small kitchen, including a microwave or hob for reheating, so using a microwaveable, or heat-resistant, container saves you from decanting your lunch onto a plate, thus creating extra washing up. Unless it is in an insulated container, food should always be kept in a cool place, so get yourself a little corner of the office fridge and kitchen cupboard to store your food and seasonings.

LIGHTNING-QUICK LUNCHBOX RECIPES

Sometimes you just need something super-quick to grab in the morning when you're trying to pack up your lunch or snack. The perfect thing is having leftovers from the previous day which you can just tip into a lunchbox, so try to cook more than you need for your evening meal. But even if you don't have leftovers to help you out, there are loads of other options.

Filled rolls or bread with toppings are particularly quick, just add in a few vegetable batons. If you get hungry between meals, nuts are perfect – the best thing is to put together your own nut mixture which you can then perk up with chocolate chips or whatever else you fancy. A fresh fruit salad is also easy to assemble – add a dash of lemon juice to prevent the fruit from turning brown. And perhaps you can treat yourself to something to nibble on – vegan nachos, crisps, and pretzels don't have to be just for watching television! Perhaps try some delicious dips to go with them (see p62, pp104–07, pp130–33, p134, and p146).

EASY MORNING MUESLI

Often there isn't even enough time for breakfast in the morning – and that's when muesli is the perfect thing to take with you on the go. Muesli is simple to make vegan by using soy yogurt or a non-dairy milk. You can buy ready-made muesli mixtures, or assemble a batch yourself, depending on what grains, nuts, fruits, and seeds take your fancy. With some protein-rich chia seeds added, it can become a proper power food.

Muesli with chia seeds and fruit

Peel **1 mandarin** and split into segments, slice up **1 small banana**, and chop **½ apple**. Mix the fruit with **150g (5½oz) soya yogurt**, **1 tbsp fine oat flakes**, and **1 tsp chia seeds**. Sweeten with **2 tbsp agave syrup**.

Overnight oats

The evening before, put **50g (1¾oz) fine oat flakes** into a jar with a screw-top lid. Add **240ml (8fl oz) hot water** and **20g (¾oz) frozen raspberries** and leave to soak overnight. Next morning, stir in **2 tbsp agave syrup** and **1 tbsp chopped cashews** (or other nuts).

SIMPLE SPREADS

Bread is the ultimate quick lunchbox saviour! These days, shops sell plenty of vegan spreads, but home-made spreads have the advantage that they can be varied to suit your own taste. Make spreads from pulses, nuts, seeds, vegetables, fruit, rice or rice cakes, and silken or smoked tofu. Add fresh or dried herbs and spices to enhance the flavours. Be creative and stock up on delicious ingredients which will save you time every morning. You will find more spread recipes in the book, too (see pp130–33).

Basic sunflower seed spread

Toast **100g (3½oz) sunflower seeds** in a pan without any oil. Put them in a food processor and grind, gradually adding **6–8 tbsp sunflower oil**. If desired, add a splash of water or lemon juice. Spice it up with dried **herbs, salt, pepper, and smoked paprika**, or just eat as it is with a bit of jam on your bread. The savoury version also works wonderfully as a dip.

QUICK SOUPS

Especially in winter, soups are a welcome and warming meal. If you have a microwave or even a hob at work, you can pretty much take your own supplies with a jar of tomato passata and/or instant vegetable stock, soup noodles, and some croutons. For a simple broth with croutons, a kettle would even suffice. You'll find more delicious soup recipes later (see pp94–99).

Alphabet spaghetti soup

Heat **1 tbsp oil** in a saucepan, finely slice a **small piece of leek** into rings and sauté briefly, then add **300ml (10fl oz) water** and **½ vegetable stock cube** and bring to the boil. As soon as the water is boiling, add **80g (2¾oz) alphabet pasta** and cook according to the instructions on the pack (around 6–7 minutes). Pour into a bowl and sprinkle with **1 tsp chopped parsley**, if desired.

Tomato soup

Finely chop **70g (2¼oz) mixed vegetables** (carrots, celery, leek). Heat **1 tbsp oil** in a saucepan, lightly brown the vegetables, add **300ml (10fl oz) tomato passata,** and thin with a little vegetable stock or water, then simmer for a few minutes until the vegetables are just cooked. Season with salt and pepper and, if desired, stir in **1 tbsp fresh or frozen herbs** and **1 tbsp** vegan cream.

SALADS — QUICK & HEALTHY

Salads are ideal for the vegan lunchbox. The basic ingredients are usually vegan anyway, they are a great way to use up leftover fruit and vegetables that you have at home, and they are often quick to prepare. Here are a couple of suggestions, but go ahead and make up your own creations, or find more salad recipes later in the book (see pp108–123).

Turbo tabbouleh

Bring to the boil **3 tbsp couscous** with double that quantity of **salted water**. Switch off the hob, cover and leave to steep for 10 minutes. In the meantime, wash and finely chop **4 cherry tomatoes, ½ courgette, 6 mint leaves,** and **6 sprigs of parsley**. Mix together a citrus dressing using the juice of **1 lime, 3 tbsp olive oil, salt,** and plenty of **black pepper**. Mix all the ingredients well.

Speedy sprouting salad

Mix **2 handfuls** of your chosen **beansprouts** (home-grown or bought) with **1 handful of seasonal lettuce leaves** and **1 orange**, split into segments. Blend **2 tbsp oil** and **2 tbsp vinegar** with the juice you retained from the **orange** and add this to the **salad**. Mix everything thoroughly and season to taste with **salt** and ground **mixed coloured peppercorns**.

Smoked tofu salad

Wash, dry, and roughly shred **2–3 handfuls of seasonal lettuce leaves**. Finely chop some leftover vegetables (**pepper, cucumber, olives**) and fold these in. Mix with a dressing made from **1 tbsp cider vinegar, 3 tbsp olive oil, salt, pepper,** and a **squeeze of lemon juice**. Chop **100g (3½oz) smoked tofu** into cubes, sauté in **1 tbsp olive oil** over a high heat and then add a **dash of soy sauce**. Fold into the salad along with **1 tbsp sesame seeds**.

Vegan sausage salad

Slice **150g (5½oz) vegan sausage, 4 gherkins,** and **3 radishes**. Peel, halve, and slice **1 small red onion** into fine rings. Halve and deseed **1 small pepper** and finely chop. Whisk **2 tbsp oil** with **1 tbsp vinegar** and **1 tsp mustard**, pour it over the other ingredients, mix everything together, and season to taste with **salt** and **pepper**. If desired, garnish with **2 tbsp cress**.

BAKING SUPPLIES

Once you're familiar with the best ingredients to use, including swaps for animal products, vegan baking can be as simple as conventional baking. It is super easy to rustle up a delicious cake with a very modest supply of high-quality, organic ingredients, which you can keep stocked in your store cupboard.

ESSENTIAL FOOD SUPPLIES

One advantage of vegan baking is that most of the ingredients keep for longer than animal products, which can go off easily. If you bake often, you should keep a good supply of the ingredients below.

Plain flour
Shelf life: if stored in an airtight container, away from the light and in a dry location at 16–20°C (60.8–68°F), up to 1 year

Fine cane sugar
Shelf life: if stored in an airtight container, away from the light and in a dry location at 16–20°C (60.8–68°F), up to 1 year or longer

Baking powder
Shelf life: if stored in an airtight container in a dry location and unopened, 1½ years or longer

Dry yeast
Shelf life: if stored in an airtight container in a dry location and unopened, up to 2 years

Soya milk
Shelf life: kept sealed, even if not chilled, several months

Flavourless oil, for example, rapeseed oil
Shelf life: kept sealed and airtight in a cool dark location, at least 1 year

Vanilla extract
Shelf life: kept sealed in a cool, dark place, 6 months to 1 year. Pure vanilla extract has an indefinite shelf life

Vegan margarine
Shelf life: 6–8 weeks

SIMPLE SWAPS

Nowadays most animal products can easily be replaced with plant-based equivalents, sometimes by simply combining two or three ingredients with each other.

Butter	Vegan margarine
Buttermilk	1 part soya milk + 1 part soya yogurt + 1 splash lemon juice
Cream	Soya cream, rice cream, coconut cream, or oat cream
Cream cheese	Mix 500g (1lb 2oz) soya yogurt with 400g (14oz) cashews at maximum power until you have a fine, creamy purée. Decant into a bowl, cover securely with cling film, and leave to ferment at room temperature for 24 hours.
Gelatine	Agar-agar
Honey	Agave syrup, maple syrup
Milk	Soya milk, oat milk, almond milk, spelt milk, rice milk, hemp milk, or other nut milks
Quark	Soya quark, silken tofu. Alternatively, line a sieve with a clean linen cloth and place it over a bowl. Add unsweetened soya yogurt, and twist the ends of the cloth together firmly at the top, fixing them in place with a rubber band. Place in the fridge overnight and squeeze out any excess liquid.
Sour cream	1 part soya yogurt + 1 part soya cream + 1 splash lemon juice, or alternatively, finely puréed silken tofu
Whipped egg whites	Ener-g Egg Replacer
Yogurt	Soya yogurt

INSTEAD OF 1 EGG

There are various options for replacing eggs, but the ingredients should always be chosen to suit the flavour of the relevant recipe.

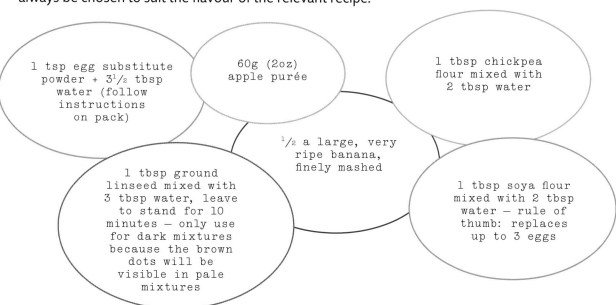

1 tsp egg substitute powder + 3$^{1}/_{2}$ tbsp water (follow instructions on pack)

60g (2oz) apple purée

1 tbsp chickpea flour mixed with 2 tbsp water

$^{1}/_{2}$ a large, very ripe banana, finely mashed

1 tbsp ground linseed mixed with 3 tbsp water, leave to stand for 10 minutes — only use for dark mixtures because the brown dots will be visible in pale mixtures

1 tbsp soya flour mixed with 2 tbsp water — rule of thumb: replaces up to 3 eggs

VEGAN BAKING TIPS & TECHNIQUES

With the right ingredients and techniques, you can make vegan bakes just as light, moist, and tasty as bakes using eggs, milk, cream, and butter.

Vinegar as a catalyst

Cider vinegar is best for vegan baking. You won't be able to taste the vinegar at all in the finished cake, but it helps the baking soda unleash its power and, when combined with soya milk, it improves the quality of the baked product. Whisk soya milk and vinegar together in a bowl; the acetic acid thickens the soya milk after about 5 minutes. Stir the mixture into your other ingredients to make light cakes and pastries with a fine texture.

Mixing with a spoon

With many vegan recipes, it is important not to "over stir" the mixture, so ingredients should be mixed gently with a spoon. The carbon dioxide in mineral water can potentially make the mixture lighter and fluffier, and the addition of leavening agents, such as yeast and bicarbonate of soda, also help the dough rise and lighten beautifully. Mixing with an electric whisk or stirring for too long or too vigorously would destroy the resulting air bubbles, making the dough too heavy and stopping it from rising properly. Mixtures should not be left to stand for too long after stirring; instead they should be baked promptly, as soon as the leavening agents have been allowed to work fully, so that the mixture rises well. Any fillings, such as fruit, should be washed and chopped before preparing the mixture so they can be added quickly.

Sweeten properly

Always use fine cane sugar. Coarse cane sugar is best avoided as it doesn't dissolve easily, particularly in shortcrust pastry. Coarse sugar can impede or even completely prevent the mix from rising. In dark mixtures prepared with lots of cocoa powder, coarse cane sugar crystals can remain visible – indicating that the sugar has failed to dissolve. This means the sugar won't evenly sweeten the baked item.

Gelling and setting

Agar-agar is a good plant-based gelling agent, most commonly available in powdered form. Since it has powerful bonding capabilities, it is used very sparingly: ½ tsp agar-agar is enough for about 250ml (9fl oz) liquid. The fine powder is stirred into cold liquid, which is briefly brought to the boil, simmered for a few minutes, then quickly stirred into the mixture that needs to set. The liquid will only set once it has cooled down completely. Alcohol reduces the setting properties, as do citrus fruits and their juices, due to their acidity.

Whipping cream

Always make sure your soya, rice, or coconut whipping cream is well chilled and beat it at top speed using an electric hand mixer for at least 3 minutes, until the cream is nice and stiff. Rice cream is less firm in consistency after whisking than soya or coconut cream so, if using this, we recommend you sprinkle in some cream stiffener about half way through whisking, before continuing to beat. If the cream is chilled again after beating, it will set even more firmly and is particularly good for piped decorations.

Oven temperatures

Unless otherwise specified, the temperatures provided in this book refer to non-fan settings. For fan ovens, the temperature should be lowered by about 20°C (68°F).

BAKING EQUIPMENT

Whether you're vegan or not, it is important to have the right baking equipment. Below are the "must-have" and "nice-to-have" pieces of equipment that will make your bakes perfect.

MUST-HAVE EQUIPMENT

Measuring jug, saucepans, frying pans, fine sieve, large and small spoons, paring knife or potato peeler, graters, pastry brush, chopping board, rolling pin, kitchen scales (ideally digital), toothpicks or skewer for testing. Also:

Mixing bowls
For preparing most recipes, two mixing bowls are enough. Often dry ingredients are combined in one bowl and liquid ingredients in a second bowl. For beating cream, we also recommend a mixing bowl with a lid with an opening for the beaters.

Baking tins
High-quality baking tins made of metal or silicone are crucial for the success of many baked items. We recommend a springform tin and, where required, a pie dish, a loaf tin, a 12-hole muffin tin or silicone tray, and a rectangular ovenproof (glass) dish, for bakes like brownies. If your baking tin isn't quite the right size, just adjust the quantities and baking times.

Baking paper
Environmentally friendly, washable baking paper, which can be reused again and again, or some simple coated baking paper. Different sizes are helpful.

Electric hand whisk
For preparing cream, frostings, or toppings, at least 450 watt.

NICE-TO-HAVE EQUIPMENT

The decision to purchase additional kitchen gadgets is entirely down to the individual, but the items here are often highly practical, save time, and can help to make baked goods look even more attractive.

Cake ring
This holds cakes in shape during filling or stacking and helps ensure accurate alignment where there are multiple layers to a cake.

Dough scraper, spatula, and palette knife
These help smooth out the surface on creamy layers and other spreadable substances and can be used to straighten up edges.

Piping bag with nozzles
Piping bags made from reusable material are easy to use and to clean.
Recommended nozzles are:
· a 14–16mm star nozzle
· a variety of 18mm nozzles for decorating cupcakes
· a flower nozzle
· a round nozzle.
Adapters make it easy to change nozzles quickly by screwing and unscrewing, but you can also make a simple piping bag yourself (see p369).

Zester or box grater
This makes it easy to remove and zest the peel on citrus fruit and shreds the zest evenly, making it ideal for decorative purposes.

Waffle iron
Use this for sweet and savoury waffles – ideally a classic heart-shaped iron. Oiling the surface makes cleaning easier.

Food processor for grinding or mixing
An optional luxury for preparing cakes made with raw ingredients or which do not involve baking. It grinds and mixes thoroughly in a single process.

BREAKFAST BITES

tasty breakfast treats to enjoy
at home or on the go

MUESLI BARS

Dried fruits and nuts give you ample fuel for the day ahead, while amaranth provides calcium, magnesium, iron, and zinc. Muesli bars are the perfect morning snack – a source of power in your lunchbox. They are quick to prepare and these sweet bars, with their hearty oat flakes, have everything you could want from a quick energy boost. You can vary the dried fruits as you fancy, as long as you use the same quantity, so the recipe will never get boring.

50g (1¾oz) macadamia nuts
50g (1¾oz) hazelnuts
50g (1¾oz) cashew nuts
250g (9oz) dried fruit (raisins, dates, goji berries, apricots)
5 tbsp vegan margarine
5 tbsp demerara sugar
150ml (5fl oz) agave syrup
2 tbsp lemon juice
30g (1oz) puffed amaranth
200g (7oz) jumbo oats
pinch of ground cinnamon

1 Preheat the oven to 180°C (350°F/Gas 4). Roughly chop all the nuts with a knife or in a food processor. Depending on the variety, either leave the dried fruit whole or chop it into little pieces.

2 Put the margarine, sugar, and agave syrup into a saucepan and bring to the boil over a high heat. Stir in the nuts, dried fruit, lemon juice, puffed amaranth, oats, and cinnamon.

3 Line a baking tray with greaseproof paper. Use a moistened spatula to spread the mixture over the tray in a 2cm (¾in) thick layer. Bake in the centre of the oven for around 15 minutes until the mixture is holding together well. Slice into 12 bars while still warm, then leave to cool and store in an airtight container.

Makes 2–3 glasses
Time: 10 mins prep
+ 1–2 hrs chilling

TIP
A large green smoothie provides you with vitamins and energy for the whole day.

SPINACH AND BANANA SMOOTHIE

Peel and coarsely chop the banana and the orange. Peel the apple, cut into quarters, remove the core, and chop roughly. Add all the fruit chunks and the spinach to a food processor. Peel and finely grate the ginger and add to the food processor with the lemon juice, baobab and moringa powders (if using), and linseed oil. Blend the ingredients until smooth, then pour in 500ml (16fl oz) water and mix everything briefly once again. Decant into little bottles and chill for 1–2 hours. Or you can chill it in a vacuum flask and serve 1 portion at a time.

1 very ripe banana
1 small orange
1 small apple
75g (2½oz) baby spinach
1.5cm (½in) piece of fresh root ginger
juice of 1 small lemon
1 tbsp baobab powder (optional; from a health food shop or online)
1 tsp moringa powder (optional; from a health food shop or online)
½ tsp linseed oil

ALMOND AND CINNAMON DRINK

Makes 2 glasses
Time: 5 mins prep
+ 1–2 hrs chilling

Whisk all the ingredients vigorously, either by hand in a bowl using a balloon whisk, or put them into a food processor and mix briefly. Pour the drink into little bottles and chill for 1–2 hours. Or you can chill it in a vacuum flask and serve 1 portion at a time.

500ml (16fl oz) almond milk, or other plant-based milk
1 tbsp apple syrup
pinch of ground star anise
pinch of salt
pinch of ground cardamom
1 tsp ground cinnamon

Makes 1 large plait
Time: 30 mins prep
+ 100 mins proving
+ 35 mins cooking

TRIPLE NUT PLAIT

Walnuts, almonds, and hazelnuts make a fabulous combination in this yeasted plait. It tastes better than anything you could buy from a bakery, not to mention the fact it's made without any animal products. Home-made is always best – just sit back and enjoy the results!

For the dough
500g (1lb 2oz) strong white flour, plus extra for dusting
½ tsp sea salt
70g (2¼oz) soft vegan margarine, plus extra for the baking tray
20g (¾oz) fresh yeast
80g (2¾oz) golden caster sugar
1 tsp vanilla sugar, or ½ tsp vanilla extract
260ml (9fl oz) almond milk, or other plant-based milk

For the filling
100g (3½oz) ground walnuts
100g (3½oz) ground almonds
100g (3½oz) ground hazelnuts
3 heaped tbsp wholemeal breadcrumbs
2 tbsp vegan margarine
8 tbsp agave syrup
2 tbsp vanilla sugar, or 2 tsp vanilla extract
½ tsp ground cinnamon
220ml (7½fl oz) almond milk, or other plant-based milk
200g (7oz) apricot jam

1 To make the dough, mix the flour and salt in a bowl. Add blobs of margarine and rub in with your fingers. Make a dip in the mix, crumble in the yeast and sprinkle over the caster sugar and vanilla sugar or extract. Heat the almond milk in a pan over a low heat and pour it in. Dust with a bit of flour, cover, and let this mix prove in a warm place for around 10 minutes. Knead for 10 minutes to create a smooth dough. Cover and leave to prove at room temperature for at least 1 hour. Knead it through once again and leave to prove for an additional 30 minutes.

2 Meanwhile, mix the walnuts, almonds, hazelnuts, and breadcrumbs for the filling in a bowl. Put the margarine into a large pan with the agave syrup, vanilla sugar or extract, cinnamon, and almond milk and bring to the boil, then stir well over a medium heat. Stir in the nut mixture and remove the pan from the heat.

3 Preheat the oven to 180°C (350°F/Gas 4). Grease a baking tray. Roll out the dough to create a 5mm (¼in) thick rectangle. Spread the jam evenly over it and top with the nut filling. Roll up the dough from a long edge and press together gently. Cut the roll lengthwise through the centre either once or twice, then twist each piece so that the cut edges face upwards. Either intertwine the dough pieces into a "cord" or plait them. Lay the plait on the baking tray and bake in the centre of the oven for 30–35 minutes until golden brown. Remove from the tray and leave to cool on a wire rack.

Makes 10
Time: 35 mins prep
+ 2 hrs proving
+ 20 mins cooking

CINNAMON SWIRLS
WITH CASHEW MAPLE ICING AND PECANS

1 For the icing, cover the cashews with cold water to soak.
To make the dough, mix both types of flour, the sugar, yeast, salt, and nutmeg in a bowl with a balloon whisk. Heat the apple purée, soya milk, and margarine in a saucepan over a low heat and stir. Remove the pan from the heat and leave the apple mixture to cool. Add the apple mixture to the flour mixture and knead everything for 10 minutes, until you have a smooth and supple dough. Cover and leave the dough to prove in a warm place for 1½ hours.

2 Knead the dough briefly once again on a floured work surface and roll it out to create a rectangle. For the filling, melt the margarine in a small pan over a medium heat. Stir in both types of sugar and the cinnamon and spread the mixture evenly over the dough. Roll up the dough from a long edge and cut the roll into 5cm (2in) thick slices. Line a baking tray with greaseproof paper. Gently press the dough swirls flat, lay them on the baking tray, cover, and leave to prove for another 30 minutes.

3 Preheat the oven to 180°C (350°F/Gas 4). Brush the dough with soya milk and bake in the centre of the oven for 18–20 minutes. Remove from the oven and leave to cool.

4 To make the caramelized pecans, let the sugar and 2½ tbsp water gently caramelize in a pan over a medium heat. Stir in the pecans, transfer the mixture to a piece of greaseproof paper, and leave to cool. Finely chop the nuts with a large sharp knife.

5 Drain the cashews in a sieve. Blitz them in a food processor with some maple syrup until smooth, adding a splash of water if required. Spread the cashew icing on the cinnamon swirls and sprinkle with chopped caramelized pecans.

For the icing and pecans
200g (7oz) cashews
50g (1¾oz) demerara sugar
100g (3½oz) pecans
maple syrup

For the dough
300g (10oz) strong white flour, plus
    extra for dusting
150g (5½oz) wholegrain spelt flour
3 tbsp golden caster sugar
7g sachet of dried yeast
1 tsp sea salt
pinch of freshly grated nutmeg
140g (5oz) apple purée
150ml (5fl oz) soya milk, or other
    plant-based milk, plus extra
    for brushing
80g (2¾oz) vegan margarine

For the filling
60g (2oz) vegan margarine
60g (2oz) demerara sugar
60g (2oz) white caster sugar
3 slightly heaped tsp
    ground cinnamon

Makes 10 bagels
Time: 25 mins prep + 85 mins proving + 15 mins baking

SESAME BAGELS

1 Add the flour and salt to a large bowl and create a well in the centre. Warm the margarine with 250ml (9fl oz) water in a small pan over a low heat until it has melted. Leave the mixture to cool a little until it's lukewarm. Crumble in the yeast and add the sugar. Cover the mixture and leave to stand for about 10 minutes, then combine with a balloon whisk and pour into the well in the centre of the flour. Knead everything until it forms a smooth dough. Shape the dough into a ball, cover, and leave to prove in a warm place for about 45 minutes, until doubled in size.

2 Dust your work surface with flour. Divide the dough as evenly as possible into 10 pieces and shape these into balls. Use the handle of a wooden spoon to make a hole in the centre of each ball to create a ring. Use your fingers to widen the hole in each dough ring to about 2–3cm (¾–1½in).

3 Line a baking tray with baking paper and place the bagels on it. Leave to prove for another 30 minutes. Brush the tops of the bagels with soya milk and scatter evenly with sesame seeds. Set the oven to 230°C (450°F/Gas 8); do not preheat. Put the bagels into the centre of the cold oven and bake for about 15 minutes. Remove and leave to cool on a wire rack.

400g (14oz) strong plain flour, plus extra for dusting
1 tsp salt
25g (scant 1oz) vegan margarine
1 cube fresh yeast
1 tsp fine cane sugar
3½ tbsp soya milk, for brushing
3 tbsp pale sesame seeds

TIP
If you make bagels regularly, you can buy a special tool that lets you quickly mould the bagels so they are all the same size and shape.

For the batter:
390g (13½oz) plain flour
40g (1¼oz) fine cane sugar
2 tbsp baking powder
½ tsp salt
750ml (1¼ pints) rice milk
90ml (3fl oz) orange juice, freshly
  squeezed
1–2 tsp vanilla extract
90ml (3fl oz) rapeseed oil
1 generous splash of rum

Also:
vegan oil spray (or vegan
  margarine), for greasing the iron
jams, fresh fruit, icing sugar or
  whipped soya cream (as desired),
  to serve

FLUFFY WAFFLES

These vegan soya-free waffles can be served with a fruit coulis, jam, or simply icing sugar for a breakfast treat or for afternoon coffee with friends.

1 To make the batter, combine the flour, cane sugar, baking powder, and salt in a bowl. In a separate bowl, whisk the rice milk with the orange juice and vanilla extract and leave to thicken for 5 minutes, then add the rapeseed oil and rum and stir all of the ingredients together until smooth.

2 Combine the liquid and dry ingredients to create a smooth batter. The batter shouldn't be left to stand for too long, so use it quickly.

3 Preheat the waffle iron and squirt it generously with an oil spray. Add a ladle of batter to the iron and cook . Repeat to make one waffle after another. Carefully remove the waffles from the iron and serve immediately with jam, fresh fruit, icing sugar, and/or soya cream.

TIP
These fabulously fluffy waffles, made without any soya flour or egg substitute, are even more flavoursome with the addition of vanilla powder to the batter. If serving to children, leave out the rum.

Makes 1 large portion
Time: 55 mins prep
+ 30 mins proving

SEMOLINA SLICE
WITH APPLE AND PEAR PURÉE

1 Peel the apples and the pear, cut into quarters, remove the core, and chop finely. Place in a saucepan with 1–2 tbsp water and bring to the boil over a high heat, then cover and simmer over a medium heat until the fruit is disintegrating. Lightly mash with a fork or potato masher, add sugar to taste and the cinnamon, and leave to simmer for a final 5 minutes. Set aside.

2 To make the semolina slices, bring the soya milk to the boil with the salt in a saucepan over a high heat. Gradually trickle in the semolina, stirring constantly with a balloon whisk. Simmer briefly, then transfer to a cake tin and leave to stand for about 30 minutes until cool.

3 Melt 1 tbsp of the margarine over a medium heat in a saucepan. Cut the semolina block into pieces. Add these to the pan and dollop on the remaining margarine. Fry the slices until they are golden brown and crispy underneath; this can take up to 15 minutes. Turn and fry until crisp on the other side. Sprinkle with sugar. If desired, scatter the raisins or Rum Raisins over the fruit purée. Store the purée and semolina slices separately. Both of these also taste great cold.

For the purée
2 small apples
1 large pear
10–20g (¼–¾oz) light brown sugar
1 tsp ground cinnamon
1 tbsp raisins or Rum Raisins (see Tip, below), for sprinkling (optional)

For the semolina slice
250ml (9fl oz) soya milk, or other plant-based milk
pinch of sea salt
150g (5½oz) wholewheat semolina
90g (3oz) vegan margarine
2–3 tbsp light brown sugar

Special equipment
20cm (8in) square or round cake tin

TIP
Instead of making semolina slices, you can make little balls or "dumplings". In this case, don't transfer the semolina into a tin, just remove it from the hob and leave to cool for 30 minutes. Fry the mixture in the margarine and use a fork or spoon to shape it into little balls. By the way, the apple and pear purée tastes particularly delicious with rum raisins. These are made by covering 1 tbsp raisins with rum, which you then leave to soak in a sealed container for 2–3 days.

JUICY
MANDARIN AND
CHIA SEED MUFFINS

These fruity muffins will really sweeten up your home or office! They are a handy size and the mandarins give them a truly indulgent juicy sweetness which is rounded off perfectly by the combination of wheat and nutty spelt flours.

50g (1¾oz) strong bread flour
75g (2½oz) plain flour
25g (scant 1oz) wholegrain spelt
  flour
½ tsp bicarbonate of soda
¾ tsp baking powder
1 tsp chia seeds
75g (2½oz) golden caster sugar
125g (4½oz) soya yogurt, or other
  plant-based yogurt
2 tbsp soya milk, or other plant-
  based milk
25g (scant 1oz) agave syrup
2 tbsp oil
½ tsp edible mandarin oil (from
  a health food shop or online,
  optional)
juice and grated zest of 2 unwaxed
  mandarins

1 Preheat the oven to 180°C (350°F/Gas 4). Put 6 paper cases into a muffin tray. Mix together the 3 types of flour, bicarbonate of soda, baking powder, chia seeds, and sugar in a bowl with a balloon whisk.

2 In another bowl, whisk the yogurt with the milk, agave syrup, oil and mandarin oil (if using). Stir in the mandarin juice and zest. Add the yogurt mixture to the flour mixture and combine everything with a spoon, just until all the ingredients are combined and you have a smooth mixture.

3 Distribute the mixture between the muffin cases so that they are each around two-thirds full. Bake the muffins in the centre of the oven for around 25 minutes until golden. Insert a wooden skewer: if no mixture sticks to it, the muffins are done. (Otherwise, continue to cook for a couple of minutes more, then test again.) Lift the muffins in their cases out of the tray and leave to cool on a wire rack.

BUCKWHEAT PANCAKES
WITH CARAMELIZED APPLE SLICES

The gluten-free batter for these pancakes is made from hearty buckwheat flour. The apple lends sweetness and moisture and it caramelizes really beautifully in the pan. You could also make a savoury version (see Tip, below).

1 Mix together the flour, baking powder, vanilla seeds, sugar, and salt in a bowl. Add the mineral water and stir everything until you have a smooth consistency. Peel, quarter, and core the apple, then slice thinly. Place the apple slices in a small bowl of water with the lemon juice.

2 Heat half the oil in the pan, add half the batter, spreading it out slightly if necessary, and top with half the apple slices. Cook over a medium heat until the edges are firm. Sprinkle over half the sugar. Turn the pancake and cook the other side until it is also golden brown, then remove from the pan. Cook the second pancake in the same way using the remaining ingredients. Leave to cool, then package up to take with you. Tastes great either warm or cold.

125g (4½oz) buckwheat flour
1 tsp baking powder
scraped-out seeds from
   ¼ vanilla pod
1 tbsp golden caster sugar
pinch of sea salt
300ml (10fl oz) ice-cold
   carbonated mineral water
1 tart apple
juice of ½ lemon
3 tbsp flavourless vegetable oil
25g (scant 1oz) demerara sugar

TIP
The apple slices can also be served separately to the pancakes. Alternatively, for a savoury meal, prepare the pancakes with your choice of chopped onion, vegetables (pepper pieces, sweetcorn), salt, or fresh herbs.

400g (14oz) wholemeal spelt flour
150g (5½oz) muesli of your choice
¾ tsp salt
250ml (9fl oz) almond milk, plus
   extra for brushing
1½ tbsp agave syrup
1 cube fresh yeast
30g (1oz) vegan margarine

MUESLI ROLLS

Muesli to go: this recipe takes your favourite muesli
and transforms it into an easy to transport bread roll.
Ideal for when you're on the move.

1 Combine the flour, muesli, and salt in a large bowl. Warm the
almond milk over a low heat and pour it into a separate bowl.
Stir in the agave syrup, crumble in the yeast, and stir everything
gently. Cover and leave in a warm place for about 10 minutes.

2 Melt the margarine in a pan and add to the flour and muesli
mixture. Stir the almond milk and yeast mixture once again then
add this to the dough mixture. Knead everything thoroughly to form
a smooth, pliable dough – if necessary add a bit more almond milk.
Cover and leave the dough to prove in a warm place for 45 minutes,
until doubled in size.

3 Shape 6 rolls from the dough, make a cross incision in the top
of each one, and leave to prove for a further 30 minutes.

4 Preheat the oven to 200°C (400°F/Gas 6). Brush the rolls
with some almond milk and bake in the centre of the oven
for 20–30 minutes. Remove from the oven and leave to cool slightly.

Makes 1 portion
Time: 10 mins preps
+ at least 20 mins soaking

CHIA AND CASHEW PUDDING
WITH APRICOT PURÉE

Healthy chia seeds are a quick and easy way to transform cashew cream into an excellent pudding. A sweet apricot purée adds a fruity finishing touch. If you also include some acai fruit powder, you are guaranteed a really nourishing breakfast snack.

1 To make the pudding, put all the ingredients except for the chia seeds into a food processor and purée until you have a smooth cashew cream. Add the chia seeds and 250ml (9fl oz) water and stir well. Transfer the mixture to a screw-top jar or other sealable container and leave to stand for at least 20 minutes in the fridge so that the chia seeds can swell.

2 Meanwhile, halve the apricots lengthways and remove the stones. Finely purée the apricots with the maple syrup in a food processor. Stir in the acai berry powder straight away (if using), or sprinkle it over the purée later as decoration.

3 Top the chia cashew pudding with the apricot purée and garnish with acai berry powder (if using) if you chose not to stir it into the purée in the previous step. Seal the containers and store in the fridge until ready to eat or transport.

For the pudding
1 tbsp cocoa powder
4 pitted dates
1 tbsp cashew nut butter
1 tsp agave syrup
finely grated zest of 1 small
    unwaxed orange
3 tbsp chia seeds

For the purée
150g (5½oz) apricots
1 tsp maple syrup
1 heaped tsp acai berry powder
    (from a health food shop,
    optional)

500ml (16fl oz) rice milk
1 tsp vanilla sugar, or ½ tsp vanilla
    extract
pinch of sea salt
125g (4½oz) pudding rice
wholemeal breadcrumbs, for
    the tin
50g (1¾oz) golden caster sugar
½ tsp ground cinnamon
30g (1oz) vegan margarine
420g (15oz) strawberries

Special equipment
20cm (8in) cake tin

CARAMELIZED RICE PUDDING CAKES WITH STRAWBERRIES

1 To make the rice, stir the rice milk in a saucepan over a medium heat with the vanilla sugar or extract and salt and bring to the boil. Reduce the heat, gradually pour in the pudding rice, stirring constantly, and simmer for 10 minutes. Sprinkle a 20cm (8in) cake tin with breadcrumbs and decant the rice into the tin so it forms a layer about 4cm (1½in) thick. Leave to cool, cover with cling film, and chill in the fridge for at least 12 hours.

2 Turn the rice out of the tin and chop into pieces. Mix the sugar and cinnamon on a plate and press the pieces into the mix on both sides. Melt the margarine in a pan over a medium heat and fry the rice slices on both sides until the sugar has caramelized. Leave to cool slightly, then either eat straight away or transfer into a storage container. Pack the strawberries up separately.

2 medium-tart apples
juice of 1 small lemon
150g (5½oz) coconut cream
scraped-out seeds from
    ½ vanilla pod
1 tbsp maple syrup
50g (1¾oz) puffed wholegrain
    quinoa
60g (2oz) aronia berries (sweet and
    sour berries), or blueberries
1 tbsp hazelnut brittle

AUTUMNAL APPLE DREAM

1 Peel, quarter, and core the apples, then grate coarsely into a bowl. Drizzle the apple with lemon. Beat the cream and fold into the fruit along with the vanilla seeds and maple syrup.

2 Layer up the apple cream mixture alternately with puffed quinoa and aronia berries in a screw-top jar. Finish with an apple and cream layer and sprinkle with hazelnut brittle. Seal the glasses or containers and chill until ready to eat.

TIP
For an (even) easier treat, use coconut yogurt or soya yogurt instead of the cream.

Makes 4 pancakes
Time: 15 mins prep
+ cooking time

AMERICAN PANCAKES

Delicious and fluffy, these pancakes are a guaranteed breakfast highlight.
They are traditionally eaten with maple syrup or fresh fruit.

1 In a bowl, combine the flour with the bicarbonate of soda
and salt. In a separate bowl, mix together the soya or almond
milk, soya yogurt, 2 tablespoons of water, and the rapeseed oil.

2 Use a spoon to swiftly fold the liquid ingredients into the dry
mixture until you have a smooth, stiff batter. Heat some oil in
a pan, put dollops of about 3 tablespoons of the batter into the oil,
and gently smooth them down into pancakes (don't press them
completely flat, they are supposed to be slightly thick). Cook the
pancakes over a moderate heat, adding some more oil if necessary.
Once the pancakes are pale brown on one side, flip them over and
cook on the other side.

3 Serve the pancakes straight away, with plenty of maple syrup
and fresh fruit, chocolate drops, or jam, as you prefer.

For the batter
140g (5oz) plain flour
1 tsp bicarbonate of soda
1 pinch of salt
110ml (3¾fl oz) soya milk or almond
   milk
115g (4oz) soya yogurt
1 tbsp rapeseed oil

Also:
flavourless oil, for cooking
maple syrup, fresh fruit, vegan
   chocolate drops, or jam, to serve

TIP
The pancakes can
be served as a
perfect hearty weekend
breakfast, layered up
with baked beans and some
tofu sausages on the side.
For a sweet option, try
the American style of
drenching the pancakes
in maple syrup and
garnishing with
banana.

**Makes 10 rolls
(or 1 x 25cm/10in loaf tin)**
Time: 10 mins prep + approx. 5 hrs
proving + 30 mins baking

250g (9oz) plain flour, plus extra
   for dusting
1 tsp dried yeast
50g (1¾oz) fine cane sugar
1 pinch of salt
seeds scraped from ½ vanilla pod
30g (1oz) vegan margarine, plus
   extra for greasing the tin
3½ tbsp soya milk, for brushing
40g (1¼oz) icing sugar, for dusting

BRIOCHE ROLLS

These soft, round rolls are a delicacy that taste best if
eaten fresh from the oven, either plain or with some
vegan margarine and jam.

1 In a large bowl, mix together the flour, dried yeast, cane sugar, and
salt. Fold in the vanilla seeds. Add 120ml (4fl oz)water and knead
for about 5 minutes. Then add the margarine and knead again – it
will take a while for the dough to absorb the fat. Cover and leave the
dough to prove in a warm place for 45 minutes, until it has doubled
in size.

2 To knock out the air from the dough, use your hands to gently
work the dough into a ball. Leave it covered in the fridge for at
least 3 hours, or ideally overnight. Then create 10 equal-sized rolls
from the dough and place them on a baking tray lined with baking
paper. Alternatively, grease a loaf tin and dust it with flour. Place the
dough in the tin and smooth it out. Cover the rolls or the bread with
a clean, damp tea towel and leave to rise for 1 hour until the dough
has doubled in volume.

3 Preheat the oven to 180°C (350°F/Gas 4). Brush the rolls or bread
with soya milk. Bake the rolls for 15–20 minutes, or the bread for
25–30 minutes, in the centre of the oven until golden. Leave to cool
slightly and dust with icing sugar.

SAVOURY SNACKS & LIGHT BITES

small lunches and snacks to
satisfy cravings between big meals

PESTO AND "RICOTTA" BALLS

So simple, so delicious: these have a fresh edge that will enhance any lunchbox. They are also great to serve at a party, and can be popped into a pretty glass to take along as a gift for your hosts.

1 litre (1¾ pints) soya milk
5 tbsp cider vinegar
bunch of Thai basil
5 tsp vegan basil pesto
½ tsp chilli powder
sea salt
freshly ground black pepper
olive oil, for marinating

1 Bring the soya milk to the boil in a pan over a high heat. As soon as it begins to boil, stir in the vinegar. Remove the pan from the heat and leave the mixture to cool – during this time the solid components will settle. Carefully pour away the liquid. Put the remaining solid ingredients into a sieve lined with a clean tea towel. Bring the corners of the towel together and then twist, so that as much liquid as possible is squeezed out.

2 Pull the leaves from the basil and chop them roughly. Mix together the soy "ricotta" in a bowl with the pesto and chilli powder and season to taste with salt and pepper. Form 10 little balls from the mixture and put them in a screw-top jar or preserving jar with the basil leaves. Completely cover with the oil and leave to infuse for 3–4 days.

TIP
If you can, leave the jar in the fridge in your office kitchen and just help yourself whenever you fancy. These are great with salad or bread, or layered up with sliced tomatoes in a lunchbox.

LITTLE POTATO CAKES
WITH YOGURT DIP

These delicious bites can be fried, or baked in the oven without any oil at all. Serve with this fresh yogurt dip, flavoured with a few chives. A little snack to pep you up and that you can enjoy with a completely clear conscience.

1 Peel the potatoes, cut into large chunks, and boil in salted water for around 15 minutes until soft. Drain and transfer to a bowl. While still warm, mash with a fork until fairly smooth. Add the flour, 1 tsp more salt, and the herbes de Provençe and work everything together to a smooth consistency.

2 Roll out the mix on a generously floured work surface until it is 5mm (¼in) thick, using a rolling pin which you have also liberally coated with flour. Dust a 6cm (2½in) diameter round cutter or glass with flour and stamp out discs. Heat the oil in a pan and fry the potato cakes on both sides until golden brown. Remove and drain on kitchen paper, then leave to cool.

3 To make the dip, stir together the yogurt and chives and season to taste with salt and pepper. Pack up the potato cakes and the dip separately to take with you.

For the cakes
200g (7oz) waxy potatoes
sea salt
120g (4¼oz) white spelt flour, plus extra for dusting
2 tsp herbes de Provençe
1–2 tbsp oil

For the dip
3–4 tbsp soya yogurt, or other plant-based yogurt
1 tbsp chopped chives
sea salt
freshly ground black pepper

TIP
The potato cakes can also be baked in the oven. Preheat the oven to 180°C (350°F/Gas 4), place them on a baking tray lined with baking parchment, and prick each several times with a fork. Bake in the centre of the oven for 10 minutes, then turn them over and bake for a further 10 minutes, or until they are a pale golden brown colour.

Makes 2 snack portions
Time: 10 mins prep
+ 25 mins cooking

200g (7oz) canned chickpeas
    (drained weight)
2 tbsp olive oil
2 tsp garam masala
1 tsp sea salt
1 tsp onion powder

ROASTED CHICKPEAS

1 Preheat the oven to 200°C (400°F/Gas 6). Drain the chickpeas, carefully pat them dry with kitchen paper, and transfer them to a bowl. Add the oil, garam masala, salt, and onion powder and gently mix with your hands until the oil and spices are evenly distributed.

2 Line a baking tray with greaseproof paper and spread the chickpeas over it so they lie in a single layer. Bake in the centre of the oven for 10 minutes, then turn. Increase the oven temperature to 220°C (425°F/Gas 7) and bake for a further 10–13 minutes. Leave to cool completely and they will crisp up.

Makes 2 snack portions
Time: 10 mins prep
+ 30 mins cooking

½ cauliflower, about 500g (1lb 2oz)
1 tbsp chilli oil
2 tbsp olive oil
pinch of chilli powder
2 tsp mild curry powder
pinch of ground allspice
½ tsp ground cumin
pinch of ground turmeric
3 slightly heaped tsp Thai chilli
    paste

SPICY OVEN-ROASTED CAULIFLOWER

1 Preheat the oven to 190°C (375°F/Gas 5). Split the cauliflower into florets and place in a bowl. Line a baking tray with greaseproof paper. Put both types of oil into a screw-top jar along with all the spices and the chilli paste. Close the lid and shake the jar vigorously until the ingredients combine to make a smooth paste.

2 Use your hands or a pastry brush to distribute the spicy paste all over the cauliflower florets. Spread the cauliflower over the baking tray and bake in the centre of the oven for 25–30 minutes. Use a toothpick to test whether it is cooked; it should pass through a floret with no resistance. The cauliflower is delicious warm or cold.

SPICY KALE CRISPS

Makes 1–2 snack portions
Time: 10 mins prep
+ 15 mins cooking

175g (6oz) curly kale
1 tbsp sesame oil
½ tsp soy sauce
pinch of chilli powder
pinch of yeast flakes

1 Preheat the oven to 170°C (340°F/Gas 3½). Line a baking tray with greaseproof paper. Wash the kale and dry it thoroughly, then remove and discard any coarse stalks. Shred the leaves into large pieces. Mix the oil and soy sauce in a small bowl. Brush the kale leaves on both sides with the oil mixture and lay them on the baking tray. The leaves should not overlap, so if necessary bake in batches.

2 Mix the chilli powder and yeast flakes in another small bowl and sprinkle over the kale leaves. Depending on their thickness, bake in the centre of the oven for around 15 minutes until crisp. Remove and leave to cool completely.

SMOKY COCONUT "BACON"

Makes 2 snack portions
Time: 10 mins prep
+ 20 mins cooking

125g (4½oz) coconut chips
1 tbsp maple syrup
1 tbsp soy sauce
1 tsp liquid smoke (optional; from a delicatessen or online)
½ tsp smoked paprika

1 Preheat the oven to 140°C (275°F/Gas 1). Put the coconut chips into a bowl. Whisk together the maple syrup, soy sauce, liquid smoke, and 1 tsp of water. Pour this over the coconut chips and gently mix everything with your hands until the liquid is evenly distributed. Sprinkle over the paprika and mix it in.

2 Line a baking tray with greaseproof paper and spread the coconut chips on it; they should not be overlapping. Bake in the centre of the oven for 15–20 minutes, turning 2–3 times during cooking. Remove and leave to cool completely.

TIP
The kale crisps can be eaten as a little nibble, but they also work wonderfully as a topping on a sandwich or burger.

Makes 2–3 snack portions
Time: 10 mins prep

2 ripe avocados (ideally, the
    Hass variety)
½ red chilli
1 small green chilli
1 garlic clove (optional)
juice and zest of ½ unwaxed lime
½ tsp sea salt
pinch of freshly ground white
    pepper

To serve
vegetable batons (such as peppers,
    carrots, or celery)
vegan nachos or crackers

GUACAMOLE

1 Halve the avocados and remove the stones. Scrape out the flesh from the skins with a spoon, put it into a small bowl, and mash with a fork. Deseed the red chilli and finely chop. Slice the green chilli into little rings. Peel the garlic (if using) and either chop very finely or crush in a garlic crusher.

2 Add the red chilli, garlic, and lime juice and zest to the avocado. Stir well and season to taste with salt and pepper. Decorate with green chilli rings. Then take along whatever you fancy dipping in it: vegetable batons, nachos, or crackers.

Makes 2 snack portions
Time: 10 mins prep
+ 24 hrs soaking
+ 1 hr cooking

125g (4½oz) dried chickpeas
sea salt
1 garlic clove
1 tbsp lemon juice
1 tbsp tahini
pinch of paprika, plus extra
    to serve
freshly ground black pepper
4 tbsp olive oil, plus extra to serve

HUMMUS

1 Leave the chickpeas to soak, covered in water, for 24 hours. Drain and put them into a pan, cover with slightly salted water, and simmer with the lid on over a gentle heat for around 1 hour, until they are soft. Drain in a sieve.

2 Peel and crush the garlic. Put the chickpeas into a blender with the garlic, lemon juice, tahini, ½ tsp more salt, the paprika, and some pepper and purée until smooth. Gradually add enough oil to make a smooth, velvety consistency. Tip the hummus into a lunchbox. Use a spoon to draw a spiral in the surface, drizzle in a little more oil, and garnish with paprika. This goes well with flatbreads.

TIP
Soaked, freshly cooked chickpeas have a better flavour and firmer consistency than the canned variety. But if you're in a hurry, feel free to use canned chickpeas; you will need double the quantity.

Makes 2–3 snack portions
Time: 15 mins prep
+ 30 mins cooking

CARROT HEART SUSHI

1 Wash the rice in a sieve under cold running water until the water runs clear. Let it drain thoroughly. Transfer to a saucepan and cover with cold water. Bring to the boil, cover, and simmer over a low heat for around 15 minutes. Turn off the heat and leave the rice to swell for a further 15 minutes.

2 Meanwhile, peel the carrots. Along both sides of the length of the carrots, cut down towards a central point so that each carrot is teardrop shaped. Now, along the curved broad edges, cut a notch centrally down the length of each carrot. Finally, on each side, carve out a curve. You are aiming to sculpt carrots whose cross-sections are heart-shaped. Cook the carrots in a pan of salted water for 5–10 minutes, until al dente.

3 Mix together the vinegar with the syrup or sugar and ¾ tsp salt. Mix this sweetened vinegar with the still-warm rice, then leave it to cool. Let the carrots drain, then pat them dry.

4 Lay out 1 nori sheet on a bamboo mat. With moistened fingers, spread out half of the rice on the sheet, leaving a 2cm (¾in) border along the upper edge. Lay 1 carrot on the lower edge and carefully roll up the sheet. Brush the bare strip of nori with water and press it down. Follow the same process with the second sheet of nori and the remaining rice and carrot. Slice the rolls into pieces using a very sharp, dampened knife and sprinkle with sesame seeds (if using). Pack up the sushi, soy sauce, wasabi, and ginger separately to take with you.

For the sushi rolls
125g (4½oz) sushi rice
2 carrots
sea salt
1½ tbsp rice vinegar
1½ tsp rice syrup, or sugar
2 nori sheets (see Tip, below)
toasted sesame seeds, for
    sprinkling (optional)

To serve
soy sauce
wasabi
pickled sushi ginger

Special equipment
bamboo mat, for rolling (from an
    Asian store)

TIP
You can buy sheets of nori in various sizes. The length of your carrots should correspond to the size of the nori sheet. If you'd like a bit more umami flavour, cook the carrots the previous day and marinate them overnight in soy sauce. Pat dry before using.

Makes 3–4 snack portions
Time: 35 mins prep
+ 30 mins cooking

SMOKED TOFU AND CRUNCHY VEG SUSHI

Asian dishes are particularly well-suited to the lunchbox. Here we roll up some cucumber, parsnip, smoked tofu, and avocado with wasabi paste giving an astringent kick. Practical for transporting, eating, and dipping. And, best of all: it's good for you!

For the sushi rolls
125g (4½oz) sushi rice
¼ cucumber
1 small parsnip
50g (1¾oz) smoked tofu
¼ avocado
2½ tsp rice vinegar
½ tbsp golden caster sugar
¼ tsp sea salt
½ tbsp rapeseed oil
½ tbsp soy sauce
3 nori sheets
wasabi paste

To serve
soy sauce
sweet chilli sauce

Special equipment
bamboo mat, for rolling (from an
    Asian store)

1 Wash the rice in a sieve under cold running water until the water runs clear. Let it drain thoroughly. Transfer to a saucepan and cover with cold water. Bring to the boil, cover, and simmer over a low heat for around 15 minutes. Turn off the heat and leave the rice to swell for a further 15 minutes.

2 Meanwhile, peel the cucumber and parsnip and slice into even, thin strips. Slice the smoked tofu into thin strips. Carefully scoop out the flesh of the avocado from the skin with a spoon in a single piece and slice into strips.

3 Stir together the vinegar, sugar, and salt in a bowl. Mix this sweetened vinegar with the still-warm rice, then leave it to cool. Heat the oil in a pan and briefly brown the smoked tofu and parsnip over a medium heat. Add the soy sauce.

4 Lay out 1 nori sheet on a bamboo mat. Spread out half the rice so that it is around 5mm (¼in) thick and make a dip along the centre with your thumb. Put a little wasabi paste into the lower half of the dip. Fill the entire dip evenly with half the cucumber, parsnip, smoked tofu, and avocado. Carefully roll it up, press gently together, and brush with a bit of water. Do the same with the second nori sheet and the remaining fillings. Slice the rolls into pieces using a very sharp, dampened knife. Package up the little sushi rolls and the dipping sauces separately to take along with you.

AUBERGINE SCHNITZEL
WITH GARLIC CREAM

Absolutely ravenous? Craving a filling snack? These aubergines with their crisp and spicy paprika-and-oat coating are just the thing and certainly a far cry from the usual dull lunch time fare. The garlic cream is super-quick to prepare and is wonderful for greedy dipping!

1 To make the schnitzel, chop off both ends of the aubergine. Cut it lengthways into 2cm (¾in) thick slices. Salt the slices on both sides, lay them on a thick layer of kitchen paper, weigh them down with a chopping board, and leave for 10 minutes to remove the liquid from the vegetable.

2 Meanwhile, spread the flour onto a flat plate (reserving 1 tbsp) and season with salt and pepper. Gradually stir the remaining flour (1 tbsp) into the cold cream. Season the cream with salt, 1 tsp pepper, paprika, and yeast flakes. Spread the panko breadcrumbs on another plate.

3 Pat dry the slices of aubergine. First turn the slices in the flour, then draw them through the cream, and finally toss them in the panko crumbs. Heat the oil in a pan and sauté the aubergine schnitzel in batches over a medium heat until golden brown on both sides. Let them drain on a wire rack.

4 To make the cream, peel and finely chop the garlic and stir it into the Vegan mayonnaise. Package up the schnitzels and cream separately to take with you. The schnitzels taste great either warm or cold. Serve with a crispy flatbread and/or a crunchy salad with a great dressing (see pp104–5).

Makes 2 small portions
Time: 25 mins prep

For the schnitzel
1 large aubergine
sea salt
100g (3½oz) plain flour
freshly ground white pepper
200g (7oz) chilled oat cream, or other plant-based cream
½ tsp sweet smoked paprika
2 tsp yeast flakes
100g (3½oz) panko, or breadcrumbs
3½ tbsp olive oil

For the garlic cream
1 garlic clove
100g (3½oz) Vegan Mayonnaise (see p104)

INDIAN VEGETABLE PANCAKES

These unbeatable little pancakes are made from semolina and vegetables.
Served with a fruity mango chutney, they are a delicious Indian inspired snack.

1 small onion
1 small red pepper
2 sprigs of coriander
80g (2¾oz) semolina
150ml (5fl oz) cold vegetable stock
½ tsp sea salt
½ tsp curry powder
pinch of chilli powder
pinch of ground cardamom
2 tbsp rapeseed oil
1 tbsp cucumber relish
500g (1lb 2oz) Mango Chutney (see p91, or ready-made)

1 Peel and finely chop the onion. Cut the pepper into quarters, then chop into little cubes. Finely chop the coriander. Stir together the semolina, stock, salt, curry powder, chilli, and cardamom in a bowl. Add the chopped onion and pepper with the coriander and stir until everything is combined.

2 Heat 1 tbsp oil in a pan. Add half the batter to the pan and spread out gently. Cook the pancake over a medium heat for 2–3 minutes until slightly brown. Turn and cook for another 2–3 minutes. Add the remaining oil to the pan and cook the rest of the batter to make a second pancake. Stir together the cucumber relish and the mango chutney to make a dip. Pack up the pancakes and dip separately to take with you. To serve, spread the pancake with the dip – it tastes great either warm or cold.

TIP

Try another Indian classic: red lentil pancakes. To make the batter, stir 150g (5½oz) ground red lentils with 170ml (6fl oz) water and season with 1tsp garam masala, ½ tsp curry powder, and ½ tsp sea salt. Leave to steep for a good 15 minutes. Heat 2½ tbsp rapeseed oil in a pan and cook little pancakes in batches over a medium heat until golden brown. Mango chutney goes wonderfully with these, too.

Makes 30 straws
Time: 20 mins prep
+ 20 mins baking

For the party straws:
5 ready-made puff pastry sheets (15 × 15cm/6 x 6in each); see pp364–65, chilled
40g (1¼oz) vegan cheese, grated
1 heaped tsp caraway
1 heaped tsp coarse sea salt
1 heaped tsp dried rosemary

Also:
3½ tbsp soya milk, for brushing

PARTY STRAWS

Ready in a flash, these herby straws will be gobbled up instantly by party guests!

1 Cut each puff pastry sheet into 6 equal-sized strips. Brush each of the 30 strips with soya milk. Scatter equal quantities of cheese and caraway over half of the pastry strips and scatter the other half with sea salt and rosemary.

2 Preheat the oven to 180°C (350°C/Gas 4). Twist the pastry strips and place them on a baking tray lined with baking paper. Bake in the centre of the oven for 15–20 minutes, until golden. Remove and eat when they are lukewarm or cold.

TIP

It's important to work quickly with the puff pastry and while it is still cold. You can also make a sweet version of these party straws by sprinkling them with cinnamon sugar.

Makes 2 snack portions (8 cakes)
Time: 30 mins prep
+ 12 hrs infusing

BROCCOLI CAKES
WITH MANGO AND AVOCADO SALSA

1 To make the salsa, halve the tomatoes, remove the stalks and seeds, and chop finely. Peel the mango and avocado and remove the stones, then chop finely. Slice the chilli lengthways, remove the seeds, and slice into short, thin strips. Peel the onion and chop finely. Mix the prepared ingredients in a bowl with the coriander. Add the lime juice, agave syrup, and salt to taste. Leave the salsa to infuse in the fridge for 12 hours.

2 For the cakes, wash and chop the broccoli florets, and peel and chop the onion. Put in a food processor with the coriander leaves, purée until smooth, then decant into a bowl.

3 Use a balloon whisk to combine the chickpea flour with the spices, salt, pepper, and linseed in a bowl. Add the dry mixture to the broccoli mixture and work everything together with your hands until you have a firm consistency. Divide the mix into 8 portions and shape each into a small, flat cake.

4 Heat the oil in a pan and fry the cakes on both sides over a medium heat until golden brown. Package up the broccoli cakes and the salsa separately. These taste great either warm or cold.

For the salsa
2 tomatoes
½ small mango
½ small avocado
1 small red chilli
1 small red onion
1 tbsp finely chopped coriander leaves
1 tbsp lime juice
1 tsp agave syrup
½ tsp sea salt

For the cakes
100g (3½oz) broccoli florets
1 small red onion
1 tbsp finely chopped coriander leaves
3 tbsp chickpea flour
pinch of curry powder
pinch of ground cumin
pinch of ground ginger
pinch of chilli powder
½ tsp sea salt
pinch of freshly ground black pepper
1 tbsp ground linseed
5 tbsp olive oil

TIP
People who aren't keen on avocado can just make a pure mango salsa. Simply leave out the avocado and use double the quantity of mango.

**Makes 2–3 snack portions
(8–10 rollmops)**
Time: 30 mins prep
+ 2–3 days marinating

AUBERGINE ROLLMOPS

You definitely won't find these in anyone else's lunchbox! These unusual aubergine rolls are the ultimate proof that vegetable snacks are unbelievably versatile and exceptionally delicious. The spicy marinade gives the aubergine the most amazing flavour. Whether eaten with bread, straight from the jar, or as an embellishment for a salad or other dish, you can keep a pot of these in your office for every eventuality.

For the marinade
175ml (6fl oz) white wine vinegar
3 tbsp golden caster sugar
25g (scant 1oz) sea salt
6–8 juniper berries
black peppercorns (optional)
3–4 bay leaves

For the rollmops
2 aubergines
sea salt
1 onion
3 gherkins
1 tbsp medium-strength mustard,
   such as Dijon
1 tsp sea salt
1 tsp freshly ground pepper

1 To make the marinade, bring 500ml (16fl oz) water to the boil in a saucepan with the vinegar, sugar, salt, juniper, peppercorns to taste (if using), and bay leaves, then remove from the heat and set aside.

2 For the rollmops, trim off the aubergine stalks. Cut lengthways into 5mm–1cm (¼–½in) thick slices. Salt the slices on both sides. Lay them on a thick layer of kitchen paper and leave for 10 minutes, weighed down with a wooden board in order to remove the liquid.

3 Bring some generously salted water to the boil in a large saucepan and boil the aubergine pieces for 5 minutes over a medium heat. Remove the slices from the water using a slotted spoon and leave to drain. Peel the onion and slice into thin strips. Likewise cut the gherkins into strips.

4 Spread the aubergine slices with mustard, season with 1 tsp more sea salt and the pepper, and top each piece with strips of gherkins and onion. Roll them up and secure each using a toothpick. Layer the rollmops in a large screw-top jar. Cover with the warm marinade and leave to infuse for 2–3 days.

MEDITERRANEAN
STUFFED TOMATOES

Really ripe tomatoes are used in this little feast, which can be quickly rustled up for your everyday lunchbox. The tomatoes are stuffed with a creamy filling whisked together from home-made cashew cheese, non-dairy cream, nutritious argan oil, rocket, and black olives – all of which are packed full of flavour. Pop the lids on and they're ready!

4 tomatoes
60g (2oz) rocket
6 pitted black olives
100g (3½oz) Hot Cashew "Cream Cheese" (see p134)
2 tbsp spelt cream, or other plant-based cream
½ tsp argan oil
pinch of sea salt
pinch of freshly ground black pepper
pinch of dried oregano
pinch of dried rosemary

1 Cut a little lid off the stalk-end of each tomato. Hollow out the tomatoes using a spoon, discard the seeds, and chop the flesh. Chop the rocket very finely. Chop the olives.

2 Use a hand-held blender to purée the Hot Cashew "Cream Cheese", cream, and oil. Fold in the chopped tomatoes, rocket, and olives, then season to taste with salt, pepper, oregano, and rosemary. Distribute between the hollowed-out tomatoes. Replace the tomato lids. This dish tastes great with some rustic bread.

GREEK BOWLS

All these Greek treats work on their own as well as working well together. Gyros made from soy chunks served with tzatziki in the traditional manner; delicious vine leaves, stuffed with a fresh lemony rice; and a little mezze bean side dish with the all-essential garlic and spices.

Makes 1 large portion
Time: 25 mins prep
+ 12 hrs infusing
+ 30 mins draining

For the gyros
300ml (10fl oz) hot vegetable stock
75g (2½oz) coarse soy crumbs (from a health food shop)
4 tbsp olive oil, plus more for frying
1 generously heaped tbsp gyros seasoning

For the tzatziki
½ cucumber
1 tsp sea salt
1 small garlic clove
90g (3oz) soya yogurt, or other plant-based yogurt
1 tbsp extra virgin olive oil
1 tbsp lemon juice
½ tbsp dried dill
freshly ground black pepper

SOY GYROS WITH TZATZIKI

1 To make the gyros, pour the stock over the soy chunks in a bowl and leave to steep for 10 minutes. Drain in a sieve and leave to cool. Squeeze out the soy chunks well and mix with the 4 tbsp oil and gyros seasoning in a bowl. Leave to infuse in a freezer bag or airtight container in the fridge for 12 hours.

2 Heat a generous amount of oil in a pan and fry the soy chunks, initially over a high heat, then continue to cook over a lower heat until well browned all over. Set aside.

3 To make the tzatziki, halve the cucumber lengthways, remove the seeds, and grate finely. Mix with the salt and leave to drain in a sieve for 30 minutes, then squeeze out thoroughly. Peel and crush the garlic. Combine the grated cucumber in a bowl with the garlic, yogurt, oil, lemon juice, and dill. Season to taste with pepper. Pack up the gyros and tzatziki separately if transporting in a lunch box, and reheat the gyros briefly before serving.

TIP
If you like, you can replace the dill in the tzatziki with finely chopped mint leaves.

STUFFED VINE LEAVES WITH LEMON RICE

1 Toast the pine nuts in a dry pan until golden brown, then chop finely and set aside. Peel and finely chop the onion. Heat 4 tbsp oil in a pan and sauté the onion over a medium heat. Add the rice and fry briefly, then pour in half the stock and simmer over a low heat for about 18 minutes, stirring frequently, and gradually adding the remaining stock during this time. Towards the end of the cooking time, stir in the lemon zest and juice and pine nuts.

2 Wash the vine leaves under cold running water and remove the stalks. Lay the leaves onto your work surface with their rough sides facing upwards. Put 1 heaped tbsp rice onto each and fold over the right and left sides of each leaf. Roll up the leaves firmly, starting at the stalk end. Lay the little rolls snugly together in a small pan. Drizzle with the remaining 4 tbsp oil, sprinkle with salt, and pour in water to cover. Weigh them down with a small plate, then cover, bring to the boil, and simmer over a low heat for 25 minutes. Carefully remove the vine leaves and leave to cool. Serve with lemon slices.

MEZZE GREEN BEANS

1 Cut the ends off the beans. Cover with water in a pan and add the salt and bay leaf. Cook over a medium heat for 5–8 minutes until al dente, then drain in a sieve, blanch in cold water, and leave to drain.

2 Heat the oil in a pan and sauté the beans over a high heat; continue to cook over a medium heat until golden brown. Switch off the heat. Add the vinegar to the beans. Peel and crush the garlic over the beans. Mix everything well and leave to infuse slightly. Finally, season to taste with sea salt and pepper. Some crunchy fresh bread tastes great with this dish.

Makes 12
Time: 35 mins prep
+ 25 mins cooking

20g (¾oz) pine nuts
1 small onion
8 tbsp olive oil
100g (3½oz) risotto rice
300ml (10fl oz) vegetable stock
finely grated zest and juice of
    1 unwaxed lemon plus extra
    lemon slices to serve
12 preserved vine leaves
1 tsp sea salt

TIP
While you are cooking you might as well make a larger quantity — the vine leaves will keep, covered in olive oil, for several days.

Makes 1 lunchbox
Time: 20 mins prep
+ infusing

250g (9oz) green beans
1½ tsp sea salt
1 bay leaf
2 tbsp olive oil
1 tbsp balsamic vinegar
2 garlic cloves
freshly ground black pepper

TIP
The Arabic word mezze roughly translates as "small meal". Here this consists of green beans which are given a wonderfully intense flavour by sautéing them briefly, then adding garlic, balsamic vinegar, and salt.

LITTLE QUINOA BALLS
WITH MINT SAUCE

These golden spheres are not just visually delightful, they are also rich in healthy protein. The refreshing mint and yogurt sauce, with its delicate hint of lemon, adds the perfect finishing touch to this unbelievably delicious dish, which can be enjoyed either warm or cold.

For the quinoa balls
150g (5½oz) quinoa
225ml (7½fl oz) vegetable stock
1 small onion
1 small red pepper
½ bunch of spring onions
1 tbsp olive oil, plus extra for frying
125g (4½oz) wholemeal
    breadcrumbs
2 tsp gluten-free flour, or other
    flour
½ tsp herb salt, or sea salt plus
    ½ tsp mixed herbs
pinch of ground Indian Tellicherry
    pepper (from a delicatessen),
    or black pepper
½ tsp curry powder
pinch of sugar

For the sauce
3 sprigs of mint
1 garlic clove (optional)
finely grated zest and juice of
    ½ small unwaxed lemon
200g (7oz) soya yogurt, or other
    plant-based yogurt
sea salt
freshly ground white pepper

1 Rinse the quinoa in a sieve until the water runs clear. Bring it to the boil in the stock and simmer over a medium heat until the quinoa has absorbed the stock. In the meantime, peel and finely chop the onion. Quarter the peppers, remove the seeds, and chop into little cubes. Trim the spring onions and slice into fine rings. Heat the 1 tbsp oil in a sauté pan and sauté the onion, pepper, and spring onions over a medium heat until transparent. Leave to cool slightly.

2 For the sauce, pick the leaves from the mint stalks and chop finely. Peel and finely chop the garlic, if using. Stir together the mint, garlic, lemon zest and juice, and yogurt until smooth. Season with salt and pepper.

3 Mix together the quinoa, vegetable mixture, breadcrumbs, flour, and herb salt. Add the pepper, curry powder, and sugar and combine everything well. Use your hands to shape the mixture into little balls (see Tip, below). Heat some oil in a pan and fry the little balls over a medium heat until they are golden brown all over. Remove from the pan and leave to drain on some kitchen paper. Pack up the little balls and the sauce separately to take with you – they taste great warm or cold. Naan breads or salad go really well with these.

TIP
The easiest way to shape these balls is with slightly dampened hands. Try to make the balls nice and round and about the size of a table tennis ball.

Makes 2–3 snack portions
(5 rolls)
Time: 30 mins prep
+ 12 hrs marinating

SOBA NOODLE SUMMER ROLLS
WITH TOFU AND CORIANDER

1 Drain the tofu and dry it thoroughly using kitchen paper. Cut into batons and lay in a flat dish. Stir together the curry paste and orange juice in a small bowl. Pour evenly over the tofu batons, cover, and leave to marinate in the fridge for 12 hours. Let the tofu drain thoroughly. Heat the oil in a pan and brown the batons on all sides over a high heat. Drain on some kitchen paper and season well with salt and pepper. Leave to cool.

2 In the meantime, boil the soba noodles for 6 minutes in salted water, or according to the packet instructions, then drain in a sieve and plunge into cold water to stop the cooking. Drain again. Peel the cucumber and carrot and slice into fine sticks. Pick the leaves from the coriander.

3 In a flat dish, leave 1 spring roll wrapper to soak for 1–2 minutes in very warm water. Carefully spread this out on a clean work surface. Spread one-fifth of the vegetables centrally across the sheet, top this with one-fifth of the soba noodles, and finally one-fifth of the tofu batons and some coriander leaves. Fold the left and right edges of the rice paper over the ends of the filling. Pull the lower edge upwards and roll the package up from the bottom. Do exactly the same for the 4 other sheets and the remaining filling ingredients.

4 To make the dip, whisk together the peanut butter, soy sauce, oil, and agave syrup. Toast the sesame seeds in a dry pan, then crush slightly using a mortar and pestle and stir most of them into the dip. Garnish with the remaining sesame seeds and coriander leaves. Pack up the rolls and dip separately to take with you.

For the rolls
150g (5½oz) tofu
1 heaped tbsp red Thai curry paste
1 tbsp orange juice
about 2 tbsp olive oil
sea salt
freshly ground black pepper
50g (1¾oz) green tea soba noodles (or regular soba noodles)
¼ cucumber
1 carrot
small bunch of coriander
5 spring roll wrappers, each 22cm (8½in) in diameter

For the dip
2 level tbsp crunchy peanut butter
1 tbsp soy sauce
1½ tbsp sesame oil
1 tsp agave syrup
1 tsp sesame seeds
1 tsp coriander leaves

TIP
You can vary the vegetables as you fancy. Instead of coriander, mint tastes very refreshing, particularly in the summer.

Makes 2 small portions
Time: 30 mins prep

BAKED SWEET POTATOES
WITH LENTIL AND AVOCADO SALAD AND A GRAPEFRUIT DIP

If you are a bit adventurous, this recipe will be right up your street. Baked sweet potatoes are served with a lentil and avocado salad and the whole thing is topped with a dip made from vegan cream cheese, grapefruit, and spices.

For the sweet potatoes and salad
2 small sweet potatoes
150g (5½oz) beluga lentils
100ml (3½fl oz) vegetable stock
1 avocado (ideally the Hass variety)
1 small red onion
½ red chilli
1 tbsp white wine vinegar
2 tbsp extra virgin olive oil
sea salt
freshly ground black pepper

For the dip
100g (3½oz) vegan cream cheese
finely grated zest and juice of
   ¼ unwaxed grapefruit
pinch of cayenne pepper
pinch of chilli flakes

1 Preheat the oven to 200°C (400°F/Gas 6). Wash and pat dry the sweet potatoes, prick with a fork, place on a baking tray lined with foil, and bake in the centre of the oven for 25 minutes.

2 Meanwhile, cook the lentils in the stock according to the packet instructions until they are just done. Halve the avocado and remove the stone. Scoop out the avocado from the skin using a spoon and chop it finely. Peel and finely chop the onion. Deseed and finely chop the chilli. Drain the lentils in a sieve, then mix in a bowl with the avocado, onion, and chilli. Stir together the vinegar, oil, salt, and pepper to make the dressing. Pour the dressing over the lentils and gently stir to coat them.

3 For the dip, mix the cream cheese with the grapefruit zest and juice, cayenne pepper, and chilli flakes and stir until smooth. Season with salt and pepper to taste.

4 Pack up the sweet potatoes (wrapped in foil), salad, and dip separately to take with you. To serve, optionally reheat the potatoes and cut them lengthways, or split into halves. Top with the salad and serve with the dip.

SWEETCORN FRITTATAS
WITH MANGO CHUTNEY

Sweet meets spicy, with crispy baked sweetcorn and a sweetly refreshing and tart mango chutney. Subtle hints of chilli and ginger add a bit of extra spice to this delicious and filling combination.

1 To make the frittatas, grate the courgette finely and mix in a bowl with ½ tsp salt. Leave to drain in a sieve. Similarly, drain the sweetcorn, put this in a bowl, too, and crush some of the kernels roughly with a fork.

2 Mix the cornflour, chickpea flour, and bicarbonate of soda in a bowl using a balloon whisk. Stir together the stock, tomato purée, and spring onion greens and add this to the flour mixture. Squeeze as much liquid as you can out of the courgette before adding it to the flour mixture with the sweetcorn. Work everything together to create a dough-like consistency. Season with salt and pepper and divide into 6 portions. Shape each into a small flat cake. Heat the oil in a pan and fry the frittatas in batches over a medium heat until golden brown on both sides. Leave to drain on kitchen paper.

3 Peel the mango ready to make the chutney. Remove the stone and finely chop the fruit. Peel the onion and ginger and chop finely. Heat the oil in a small pan and sauté the onion over a medium heat, then add the ginger and continue to cook briefly. Add the mango, vinegar, sugar, curry powder, lemon juice, chilli powder, and 2 tbsp water and simmer for about 5 minutes, stirring continuously until the mixture is slightly mushy but still with distinct chunks of fruit. Decant into a warm, clean screw-top jar, seal firmly, and leave to cool. Pack up the frittatas and chutney separately to take with you. The frittatas taste great either warm or cold.

TIP
The chutney tastes really delicious with a few chopped mint leaves.

For the frittatas
1 courgette
sea salt
100g (3½oz) canned sweetcorn
40g (1¼oz) cornflour
75g (2½oz) chickpea flour (from a health food shop)
½ tsp bicarbonate of soda
3½ tbsp vegetable stock
1 tbsp tomato purée
2 tbsp chopped spring onion greens
freshly ground black pepper
olive oil

For the chutney
½ mango
1 red onion
2.5cm (1in) piece of fresh root ginger
1 tbsp olive oil
2 tbsp white wine vinegar
2 tbsp demerara sugar
1 tsp mild curry powder
2 tbsp lemon juice
pinch of chilli powder, or to taste

SOUPS & SALADS

creamy soups and delicious salads
from all over the world

Makes 1 large or 2 small
portions
Time: 30 mins prep
+ 2 hrs chilling

GAZPACHO

Southern Spain and Portugal encapsulated in soup form! This highly nutritious cold soup is traditionally prepared from uncooked vegetables and white bread. Tomato, onion, paprika, and cucumber combine beautifully, with ginger playing a role, too, in this less traditional recipe. Gazpacho is perfect for hot summer days – transport it in an insulated container for a cooling and filling meal.

3 thick slices of white bread
7 ripe tomatoes, about 500g
    (1lb 2oz) in total
1 small onion
1 garlic clove (optional)
1.5cm (½in) piece of fresh root
    ginger
1 red pepper
½ cucumber
250ml (9fl oz) tomato juice
1 tbsp lime juice
2½ tbsp olive oil, plus extra
    if needed
1 tbsp red wine vinegar
1 tsp sweet smoked paprika
½ tsp sea salt
freshly ground black pepper
pinch of sugar
1 tbsp finely chopped basil leaves

1 Remove the crusts from the white bread and cut into rough cubes. Soak in lukewarm water. Cut a cross in the base of each tomato, place in a bowl, pour over boiling water, then blanch in iced water to cool them down. The skins should just peel off. Peel, quarter, and remove the core and seeds. Peel and finely chop the onion, garlic (if using), and ginger.

2 Cut the pepper in half lengthways and remove the core and seeds. Peel the cucumber, cut in half lengthways, and remove the core. Chop about one-quarter of the pepper and cucumber into very small cubes and set aside. Chop the rest roughly.

3 Squeeze out the bread cubes thoroughly. Put them in a food processor with the tomatoes, onion, garlic, ginger, roughly chopped vegetables, tomato juice, lime juice, oil, and vinegar and purée well. Season to taste with paprika, salt, pepper, and sugar. Add as much oil or water as you need to make the soup the desired consistency. Chill for around 2 hours (or overnight). Pack up the soup and finely chopped vegetables separately and scatter the vegetables and basil over the soup just before serving. Or simply stir everything together before transporting.

Makes 2 large or 4 small portions
Time: 30 mins prep
+ 20 mins cooking

SQUASH SOUP
WITH CARAMELIZED GINGER

1 Peel the potatoes, onion, garlic, and about one-third of the ginger and coarsely chop them all into cubes. Halve the squash and remove the soft centre and seeds. Coarsely chop the squash, including the skin. Heat the oil in a pan and sauté all the chopped ingredients over a medium heat. Pour over the stock and cook everything for about 10 minutes, until soft.

2 Purée the vegetable chunks in the soup using a hand-held blender. Stir in the coconut milk, salt, pepper, nutmeg, and cinnamon and simmer everything for a further 5–10 minutes over a low heat.

3 Meanwhile, carefully melt the sugar in a heavy-based pan over a medium heat, without stirring. Peel the remaining ginger, slice it into julienne strips, and lightly caramelize these in the sugar. Remove from the pan and leave to cool.

4 Leave the soup to cool and then chill. Pack up the soup, ginger strips, sour cream, and parsley separately. To serve, briefly warm the soup, stir in a blob of sour cream, and then sprinkle over some parsley and strips of ginger.

2 potatoes
1 onion
1 garlic clove
3cm (1¼in) piece of fresh root ginger
1 small Hokkaido squash, about 500g (1lb 2oz) in total
oil, for frying
600ml (1 pint) hot vegetable stock
100ml (3½fl oz) coconut milk
½ tsp sea salt
pinch of freshly ground black pepper
pinch of freshly ground nutmeg
pinch of ground cinnamon
40g (1¼oz) demerara sugar
2 tsp vegan sour cream
3 tbsp roughly chopped flat leaf parsley leaves

TIP
If you don't have any way of heating the soup at work, you can heat it at home and transport it in a vacuum flask to keep warm.

Makes 2 large or 4 small
portions
Time: 20 mins prep
+ 10 mins cooking

500g (1lb 2oz) broccoli
1 small onion
1 tbsp rapeseed oil
½ tbsp vegan margarine
1 tbsp plain flour
1½ tbsp white wine
500ml (16fl oz) vegetable stock
100g (3½oz) oat cream, or other
    plant-based cream
½ tsp sea salt
pinch of freshly ground white
    pepper
pinch of freshly ground nutmeg
2 tsp flaked almonds

BROCCOLI CREAM SOUP

1 Remove the broccoli stalk, split it into florets, and cut these into equal-sized pieces. Peel and finely chop the onion. Heat the oil in a large, high-sided pan and sauté the onion over a medium heat. Add the margarine and broccoli, dust with the flour, and sauté for around 2 minutes until the flour has combined with the other ingredients (it must not go brown). Deglaze the pan with the wine and gradually pour in the stock, stirring continuously. Pour in the cream and cook for 5–10 minutes until the broccoli is soft. Purée with a hand-held blender and season the soup to taste with salt, pepper, and nutmeg.

2 Toast the flaked almonds in a dry pan. To serve, briefly heat the soup and then scatter over the flaked almonds, or just stir these into the soup before transporting.

Makes 2 large or 4 small
portions
Time: 10 mins prep
+ 20 mins cooking

6 carrots, about 500g (1lb 2oz) in
    total
½ parsnip, about 100g (3½oz)
½ sweet potato, about 250g (9oz)
1.5cm (½in) piece of fresh root
    ginger
500ml (16fl oz) vegetable stock
½ tsp sea salt
pinch of freshly ground white
    pepper
pinch of ground coriander
pinch of freshly ground nutmeg
2 tsp sesame seeds
50g (1¾oz) vegan sour cream

CREAMED CARROT SOUP

1 Peel the carrots and slice thinly, then peel the parsnip and sweet potato and chop into roughly 1cm (½in) cubes. Peel the ginger and chop finely. Bring the stock to the boil in a saucepan; tip in the carrots, parsnip, sweet potato, and ginger; cover; and cook over a low heat for around 20 minutes until soft.

2 If desired, take a few carrot slices out of the pan and set aside. Use a hand-held blender to purée the remaining vegetables in the stock. Then return the reserved carrot slices to the pan. Season the soup to taste with salt, pepper, coriander, and nutmeg; leave to cool; then chill.

3 Toast the sesame seeds in a dry pan. If you wish, you can stir the sesame seeds into the soup before transporting. Pack up the sour cream separately to take with you. To serve, briefly heat the soup, then sprinkle over the sesame seeds (unless you have already added them) and add a blob of sour cream.

Makes 1 large or 2 small portions
Time: 20 mins prep
+ 12 hrs marinating

GREEK FARMER'S SALAD

1 For the "feta", peel the onion and garlic (if using) and chop them finely. Add them to a bowl and combine with the lemon juice, oil, vinegar, salt, pepper, herbes de Provençe, and chilli powder to create a marinade. Slice the tofu into 1cm (½in) cubes and put it in a freezer bag with the marinade. Press the air out of the bag and seal it tightly shut. Marinate the tofu in the fridge for 12 hours.

2 For the salad, peel the cucumber, slice it in half, remove the seeds, and cut into bite-sized pieces. Similarly chop the tomato into bite-sized pieces, removing the core in the process. Peel and halve the onion and slice it into thin rings, or chop it finely. Halve the peppers, remove the seeds, then chop into bite-sized strips. Roughly chop the oregano. Add all the prepared salad ingredients to a bowl with the olives.

3 Stir together the lemon juice, agave syrup, oil, vinegar, salt, and pepper to create a delicious vinaigrette and use it to dress the salad. Scatter over the "feta" cubes. This tastes great with some fresh flatbread, ideally warmed, on the side.

For the "feta"
1 small red onion
1 garlic clove (optional)
squeeze of lemon juice
100ml (3½fl oz) extra virgin olive oil
1 tbsp herb vinegar
1 tsp sea salt
1 tsp ground mixed coloured peppercorns
1 tbsp herbes de Provençe
pinch of chilli powder
250g (9oz) smoked tofu

For the salad
½ cucumber
1 large beef tomato
1 red onion
2 small yellow peppers
2 tbsp oregano leaves
50g (1¾oz) black olives, stones removed
1 tsp lemon juice
½ tsp agave syrup
1 tsp extra virgin olive oil
1 tsp white wine vinegar
½ tsp sea salt
pinch of freshly ground black pepper

TIP
You can use the "feta" marinade oil again, by adding more herbs and spices to freshen it up once more before marinating another batch of tofu.

PANZANELLA —
ITALIAN BREAD SALAD

This tastes like a little piece of Italy. A traditional salad, it is really filling thanks to the bread pieces, which are coated with good-quality olive oil before being baked. Cucumber and cherry tomatoes bring a wonderful freshness. Simple and good, the only thing missing from this lunchbox is a view of Italy!

5 slices of baguette, about 150g (5½oz) in total
8 tbsp extra virgin olive oil
½ small cucumber, about 100g (3½oz)
5 cherry tomatoes, about 150g (5½oz) in total
2 spring onions
3–4 sprigs of basil
2 tbsp balsamic vinegar
squeeze of lemon juice
sea salt
freshly ground black pepper

1 Preheat the oven to as high as it will go. Cut the baguette into bite-sized cubes and put them in a bowl. Add 4 tbsp of the oil and mix together well with your hands.

2 Line a baking tray with greaseproof paper and spread the bread out over it. Bake in the centre of the oven for about 10 minutes, until crisp (keep an eye on it, as you don't want it to burn). Remove from the oven and leave to cool.

3 Meanwhile, chop the cucumber into bite-sized chunks. Halve the tomatoes. Trim the spring onions, then slice into rings. Pick off and shred the basil leaves. Mix together the cucumber, tomatoes, spring onions, basil, and cubes of bread.

4 Stir together the remaining oil with the vinegar, lemon juice, salt, and pepper to make the dressing. Transport the dressing and salad separately and ideally combine them 20 minutes before you are ready to eat, so the bread can absorb the dressing.

Each dresses 1 portion of salad
Time: 10 mins prep each
+ infusing

DRESSINGS AND DIPS

These create endless options for your lunchbox. With just a little experimentation, you can pair up each of the dressings below in new ways with a huge variety of seasonal salads. Creamy dips such as Vegan Mayonnaise and Tartare Sauce (see right), are the perfect finishing touch for potatoes, roast vegetables, burgers, wraps, or falafel.

1 small shallot
3 tbsp vinegar (white wine, red wine, or herb vinegar)
½ tsp sea salt
pinch of freshly ground white pepper
pinch of sugar
touch of Dijon mustard
9 tbsp extra virgin oil (such as sunflower, safflower, or olive oil)

VINAIGRETTE

Peel and finely chop the shallot. Stir together with the vinegar, salt, pepper, sugar, and mustard in a bowl. Gradually add the oil, stirring continuously and mix until everything is emulsified.

TIP
For vinaigrette, the ratio of vinegar to oil should be 1:3, so the dressing isn't too acidic.

150g (5½oz) vegan sour cream
1 tbsp Dijon mustard
½ bunch of flat leaf parsley
1 tsp linseed oil
1 tbsp olive oil
pinch of sea salt
pinch of freshly ground black pepper
1 tsp agave syrup, or to taste

SOUR CREAM AND PARSLEY DRESSING

Mix the sour cream with the mustard in a bowl. Pick the leaves from the parsley stalks, chop them finely, and fold into the cream mixture. Gradually stir in the linseed and olive oils. Season the dressing to taste with salt, pepper, and agave syrup.

½ bunch of chives
250g (9oz) soya yogurt, or other plant-based yogurt
juice of ½ lemon
1 tbsp walnut oil
sea salt
freshly ground black pepper
pinch of sugar, or to taste

SPEEDY YOGURT AND WALNUT DRESSING

Snip the chives finely. Stir the soya yogurt, lemon juice, and oil together with a balloon whisk until smooth, then fold in the chives. Season the dressing to taste with salt, pepper, and sugar.

VEGAN MAYONNAISE

Process the soya milk with 100ml (3½fl oz) oil in a food processor until smooth. Add the vinegar, salt, and mustard and process everything again. Slowly trickle in the remaining oil with the processor running. Then add the potatoes, until you have a creamy consistency. Season to taste with pepper, sugar, curry powder, and lemon juice (if using). Store in the fridge until ready for use.

TIP
The mayonnaise will keep in the fridge for 7–10 days. It tastes great with Little Potato Cakes (see p57) or Spicy Kale Crisps (see p61) and is the perfect finishing touch for sandwiches and burgers.

250ml (9fl oz) soya milk, or other plant-based milk
200ml (7fl oz) extra virgin olive oil
2 tbsp white wine vinegar
1 tsp sea salt
1 tbsp medium-strength mustard
100g (3½oz) floury potatoes, cooked and mashed
pinch of freshly ground white pepper
pinch of sugar
pinch of curry powder (optional)
1 tsp lemon juice (optional)

TARTARE SAUCE

Stir together the mayonnaise, cucumber relish, capers, chervil, and tarragon in a small bowl until well combined. Snip the chives finely and fold into the tartar sauce. Season to taste and chill.

TIP
The tartare sauce can be tweaked by adding finely-chopped onion. It tastes really great with Spicy Oven-roasted Cauliflower (see p58), with Little Quinoa Balls (see p84), or with wraps.

1 × recipe Vegan Mayonnaise (see above)
2 tbsp cucumber relish (from a jar)
1 tsp capers, rinsed and finely chopped
pinch of dried chervil
pinch of dried tarragon
½ bunch of chives
sea salt
freshly ground black pepper

THOUSAND ISLAND DRESSING

Deseed and very finely chop the pepper and chilli. Finely chop the cucumber. Pick the leaves from the parsley stalks, then chop them finely. Stir together the mayonnaise, yogurt, ketchup, and cream in a bowl. Add the sambal oelek, lime juice, salt, and pepper to taste. Fold the pepper, chilli, cucumber, and parsley into the mayonnaise mixture. Leave the dressing to infuse for 30 minutes, then adjust the seasonings, if you want. Chill until ready to use.

¼ green pepper
¼ red chilli
1 cucumber
½ bunch of flat leaf parsley
100g (3½oz) Vegan Mayonnaise (see above)
150g (5½oz) plant-based yogurt
3 tbsp tomato ketchup
2 tbsp oat cream
4 drops of sambal oelek, or to taste
2 tsp lime juice, or to taste
½ tsp sea salt
½ tsp freshly ground white pepper

VEGAN MAYONNAISE

SOUR CREAM AND PARSLEY DRESSING

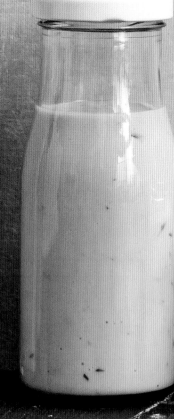

THOUSAND ISLAND DRESSING

SPEEDY YOGURT AND WALNUT DRESSING

VINAIGRETTE

TARTARE SAUCE

ANDALUCIAN ASPARAGUS SALAD

Makes 1 large or 2 small portions
Time: 25 mins prep

Two varieties of regal asparagus spears are found in this Andalucian salad: an unusual combination with zesty oranges, sweet dates, and delicately bitter olives. This is a fruity and piquant spring salad, which makes for a tasty, interesting, and aesthetically pleasing lunchbox.

1 Chop the seitan into 1cm (½in) pieces. Remove the woody ends from all the asparagus spears. Peel the lower one-third of the stem of each green asparagus spear. Slice all the asparagus spears diagonally to make 4cm (1½in) long pieces. Set the asparagus tips aside.

2 Finely chop the dates. Finely grate 1 orange, or use a zester to make fine strips. Cut both oranges in half and squeeze the juice into a bowl.

3 Heat the oil in a pan and sauté the seitan and the asparagus pieces (not the tips) for a short while over a medium heat. Stir in the olives and orange zest. Add the vinegar, soy sauce, and orange juice. Mix in both types of paprika, the salt, pepper, allspice, and finally the lime juice. Let cook over a low heat for 5 minutes. Finally, fold in the asparagus tips and dates and cook briefly. The salad tastes great warm or cold.

100g (3½oz) seitan
250g (9oz) white asparagus spears
250g (9oz) green asparagus spears
5 pitted dates
2 small unwaxed oranges
2 tbsp extra virgin olive oil
50g (1¾oz) pitted black olives
1 tbsp balsamic vinegar
1 tbsp soy sauce
½ tsp hot paprika
1 tsp sweet smoked paprika
½ tsp sea salt
pinch of freshly ground black pepper
pinch of ground allspice
1 tbsp lime juice

COURGETTE "SPAGHETTI" SALAD
WITH WILD GARLIC PESTO

Vegetable noodles are a fantastic way of enjoying gluten-free spaghetti. This spaghetti salad is served with home-made wild garlic pesto and doesn't even need to be cooked, which makes it super-simple and really practical, especially when you find yourself short of time.

For the salad
400g (14oz) courgettes
200g (7oz) cherry tomatoes

For the pesto
50g (1¾oz) pine nuts
60g (2oz) wild garlic
5 tbsp extra virgin olive oil
2 tsp yeast flakes
½ tsp lemon juice
1 tsp sea salt
pinch of freshly ground black pepper
pinch of sugar

1 To make the salad, use a spiralizer to cut the courgettes into long thin "spaghetti" shapes. Alternatively, use a potato peeler to make long thin slices and then cut these up into fine strips with a knife. Put the courgette "spaghetti" into a bowl. Halve the tomatoes and mix them in with the courgettes.

2 To make the wild garlic pesto, lightly toast the pine nuts in a dry pan until they begin to release their aroma. Add the wild garlic, oil, yeast flakes, lemon juice, salt, pepper, and sugar. Purée the ingredients to your desired consistency (fine or coarse) using a hand-held blender.

3 Either mix together the pesto and courgette spaghetti salad before transporting, or pack them up separately to take with you. Serve the salad cold.

KALE, QUINOA, AND SWEETCORN SALAD

Kale, like all other varieties of cabbage, is high in vitamin C. Here it is served in a winning combination with quinoa, sweetcorn, and almonds. A superfood salad which is in a class of its own.

50g (1¾oz) quinoa
100ml (3½fl oz) vegetable stock
200g (7oz) kale
1 onion
4 tbsp extra virgin olive oil
1–2 spring onions, green parts only
20g (¾oz) blanched almonds
2 tsp sesame seeds
100g (3½oz) canned sweetcorn
3 tbsp lemon juice
1 tsp herb or white wine vinegar
3 tbsp sesame oil
1 tbsp agave syrup
sea salt
freshly ground black pepper

1 Rinse the quinoa in a sieve until the water runs clear, then simmer in the stock according to the packet instructions (usually about 15 minutes). Meanwhile, remove the coarse stalks from the kale and roughly shred the leaves. Peel and finely chop the onion.

2 Heat 1 tbsp of the olive oil in a sauté pan and sauté the onion over a high heat for 1 minute. Add the kale and continue to sauté for 5 minutes. Pour off any liquid, set the pan aside, and leave to cool.

3 Drain the cooked quinoa into a sieve, rinse with cold water, and leave to drain. Slice the spring onions into rings. Roughly chop the almonds. Toast the sesame seeds in a dry pan until golden brown. Drain the sweetcorn in a sieve. Mix together the lemon juice, vinegar, sesame oil, remaining 3 tbsp of olive oil, and agave syrup to make the dressing and season to taste with salt and pepper.

4 Combine the kale and onion mixture with the quinoa, spring onions, almonds, sesame seeds, and sweetcorn in a bowl. Stir in the dressing and adjust the seasoning once again.

MEXICAN PEPPER SALAD

1 To make the salad, quarter the peppers, remove the seeds, then chop into bite-sized pieces. Quarter the tomatoes, remove the core and seeds, then chop into small cubes. Peel and finely chop the onion. Snip the chives finely. Drain the sweetcorn and beans in a sieve, rinse under cold water, and leave to drain. Carefully mix all the prepared ingredients together in a bowl.

2 For the dressing, whisk all the ingredients in a little bowl with a balloon whisk. Add the dressing to the salad and carefully mix together.

TIP
Nachos and Guacamole go wonderfully with this (see p62).

Makes 2 portions
Time: 20 mins prep

For the salad
3 peppers; ideally 1 red, 1 yellow, and 1 green
2 beef tomatoes
1 onion
½ bunch of chives
140g (5oz) canned sweetcorn
125g (4½oz) canned kidney beans

For the dressing
finely grated zest and juice of ½ unwaxed lime
1 tbsp white wine vinegar
2 tbsp extra virgin olive oil
½ tsp sea salt
pinch of freshly ground black pepper
pinch of chilli powder
pinch of sugar

Makes 1 portion
Time: 15 mins prep
+ 12 hrs infusing

TUSCAN BEAN SALAD

1 Drain the beans in a sieve, then transfer to a bowl. Peel and finely chop the shallot. Heat 3 tbsp oil from the sun-dried tomatoes in a small saucepan and sauté the shallot until it is transparent. Add the tomato purée and continue to cook briefly. Fold the shallot mixture into the beans.

2 Slice the sun-dried tomatoes into thin strips. Fold into the beans with the parsley, mint, and capers. Adjust the flavour to taste by adding salt, pepper, oregano, basil, vinegar, and agave syrup. Leave the salad to infuse for 12 hours. If necessary adjust the seasoning again, then transfer to your lunchbox.

240g (8½oz) canned haricot or cannellini beans
1 shallot
60g (2oz) sun-dried tomatoes in oil
1½ tbsp tomato purée
3 tbsp chopped parsley leaves
1 tbsp chopped mint leaves
½ tbsp capers, rinsed
½ tsp sea salt
pinch of freshly ground white pepper
pinch of dried oregano
pinch of dried basil
1½ tbsp white wine vinegar
½ tsp agave syrup

Makes 2 large portions
Time: 30 mins prep

ASIAN NOODLE SALAD

Do you ever fancy indulging in a spot of overseas travel in your lunch break? The mie noodles, pak choi, and beansprouts in this oriental salad will whisk you straight off to Asia! A fresh, healthy, and completely vegan alternative to ordering a take-away.

For the salad
250g (9oz) vegan mie noodles (from an Asian store)
sea salt
100g (3½oz) pak choi
½ red pepper
½ onion
75g (2¾oz) beansprouts
1 tbsp rapeseed oil
1 tbsp sesame seeds
2 sprigs of coriander

For the dip
1 tbsp peanut butter
½ tbsp rice vinegar
½ tsp lime juice
1 tsp agave syrup
pinch of ground coriander
½ tsp sea salt
pinch of freshly ground white pepper

1 To make the salad, cook the noodles in lightly salted water according to the packet instructions. Drain in a sieve, refresh under running cold water, leave to drain thoroughly, then set aside in a large bowl. Halve the pak choi, then slice into thin strips. Remove the seeds from the pepper, and slice into strips. Peel the onion and slice thinly. Put the beansprouts into a sieve and rinse under cold water, then leave to drain.

2 Heat the oil in a wok and sauté the pak choi, pepper, and onion over a medium heat. Add the beansprouts and sauté them briefly too – the vegetables should remain nice and crunchy. Add the vegetables to the noodles in the bowl. Toast the sesame seeds in a dry pan until golden brown. Pick the leaves from the coriander sprigs and chop them finely. Add the sesame seeds and coriander to the salad ingredients.

3 To make the dip, put the peanut butter into a small bowl along with the vinegar, lime juice, and agave syrup and stir until smooth. Add the ground coriander, salt, and pepper to taste. Pack up the salad and the dip separately to take with you. To serve, add the dip to the salad and mix all the ingredients carefully.

Makes 1 medium or 2 small portions
Time: 15 mins prep

INDIAN CHICKPEA AND POMEGRANATE SALAD

A brand-new way to use this wonderful, tart-sweet fruit. The pomegranate seeds are combined exquisitely with chickpeas and an Indian-style mint and yogurt dressing. A valuable addition to any vegan lunchbox!

For the salad
1 spring onion
½ red pepper
½ onion
1.5cm (½in) piece of fresh root ginger
½ pomegranate
400g can of chickpeas
25g (scant 1oz) pine nuts

For the dressing
1 tbsp soya yogurt, or other plant-based yogurt
1 tbsp chopped mint leaves
½ tsp sea salt
pinch of freshly ground white pepper
pinch of ground cumin
½ tsp garam masala
pinch of sugar

1 To make the salad, trim the spring onion and slice into fine rings. Remove the seeds from the pepper, then cut into thin strips. Peel and finely chop the onion and ginger. Remove the seeds from the pomegranate. Tip the chickpeas into a sieve and rinse with cold water before leaving to drain. Put all the prepared ingredients into a bowl.

2 For the dressing, mix together the yogurt, mint, salt, pepper, cumin, garam masala, and sugar. Add the dressing to the salad in the bowl and carefully mix together. Toast the pine nuts in a dry pan until golden brown. Pack up the salad and pine nuts separately to take with you, or just combine them ahead of time.

Makes 1 large or 2 small portions
Time: 20 mins prep
+ 30 mins infusing

ARABIAN LENTIL SALAD

Lentils are one of the best sources of protein. In this salad they are also a guaranteed winner in terms of flavour, thanks to the accompanying Arabian-style spices. Dates balance things out with some added sweetness, while harissa lends the dish a mildly spicy flavour – all the ingredients work in perfect harmony to create a real lunchtime treat.

1 To make the salad, tip the lentils into a sieve, rinse under cold water, and leave to drain. Peel the cucumber, slice it in half lengthways, remove the seeds, then chop into cubes. Quarter the tomato, remove the core and seeds, then chop finely. Slice the celery thinly. Pick the leaves from the herb stalks and chop finely. Cut the dates into small pieces. Peel and finely chop the shallot and garlic. Heat the oil in a pan and sauté the shallot over a medium heat, then add the garlic. Leave the mixture to cool, then mix with the prepared ingredients in a bowl.

2 To make the dressing, stir together the lime juice, oil, salt, pepper, cumin, allspice, agave syrup, and harissa. Add the dressing to the salad in the bowl. Leave to infuse for at least 30 minutes, then taste again and adjust the seasoning, if desired, with more salt and pepper.

For the salad
400g can of green lentils
½ cucumber
1 very large tomato
2 celery sticks
¼ bunch of flat leaf parsley
¼ bunch of mint
5 pitted dates
1 shallot
1 small garlic clove
1 tbsp olive oil

For the dressing
juice of 1 small lime
1½ tbsp extra virgin olive oil
½ tsp sea salt
pinch of freshly ground black pepper
pinch of ground cumin
pinch of ground allspice
1 tsp agave syrup
½ tsp harissa

TIP
This salad is ideal for preparing in advance for your lunchbox, because it really improves in flavour when left to infuse.

ORIENTAL
CAULIFLOWER AND POTATO SALAD

200g (7oz) waxy potatoes
sea salt
½ small cauliflower
½ small aubergine
1 small garlic clove
1 red chilli
50g (1¾oz) cashew nuts
2 sprigs of coriander
1½ tbsp rapeseed oil
120ml (4fl oz) coconut milk
pinch of freshly ground black
   pepper
pinch of ground cumin
pinch of ground cinnamon
pinch of ground allspice

1 Scrub the potatoes and cook them with the skins on in salted water for 20–25 minutes. Drain, leave them to cool slightly, then peel and cut into thick slices.

2 Meanwhile, split the cauliflower into florets. Cut off the aubergine stalk and cut into cubes. Peel and finely chop the garlic. Slice the chilli in half lengthways, remove the seeds, then chop finely. Toast the cashews in a dry pan until golden brown, leave to cool, then chop roughly. Pick the leaves from the coriander stalks and chop finely.

3 Heat the oil in a large high-sided pan and sauté the garlic over a medium heat. Add the cauliflower, aubergine, and chilli and continue to cook until the vegetables are al dente. Add the coconut milk and season with salt, pepper, cumin, cinnamon, and allspice. Fold in the potatoes and transfer the mixture to a bowl. Scatter cashews and coriander over the salad and leave to cool completely.

SANDWICHES, WRAPS & ROLLS

from sandwiches to burgers —
spreads, toppings and wraps

Makes 1 large or 2 small
portions
Time: 10 mins prep
+ 15 mins cooking

6 slices of wholemeal bread
2½ tbsp home-made Ajvar
  (see below)
2½ tbsp vegan margarine

COLOURFUL LITTLE TOAST SPIRALS

Transform even inferior sliced bread into an ingenious snack. These colourful little rolls with their Serbian vegetable relish are the perfect solution if you find yourself getting peckish between meals. Add a couple of vegetable batons and just use the remaining Ajvar as a dip.

Preheat the oven to 200°C (400°F/Gas 6). Remove the crusts from the slices of bread and roll them flat with a rolling pin. Spread the Ajvar on top and roll them up. Melt the margarine in a pan and brush it over the toast rolls. Lay them next to each other in a casserole dish and bake in the centre of the preheated oven for 15 minutes. These go wonderfully with a salad, vegetable batons, or antipasti.

Makes about 250g (9oz)
Time: 10 mins prep
+ 25 mins cooking
+ 20 mins cooling

3 large red peppers
½ large red chilli
½ aubergine (halved lengthways)
1 tbsp sunflower oil
1 tsp cider vinegar
pinch of sea salt
pinch of freshly ground white
  pepper
pinch of hot paprika
½ tsp agave syrup

QUICK AJVAR

1 Preheat the oven to 220°C (425°F/Gas 7). Line a baking tray with greaseproof paper. Slice the peppers and chilli in half lengthways and remove the seeds. Remove the stalk from the aubergine. Lay the peppers, chilli, and aubergine skin side up on the baking tray. Bake in the centre of the oven for about 25 minutes, until the skins have turned dark and are blistering. Remove the tray from the oven and cover the vegetables with a clean, damp kitchen towel. Leave to cool for around 20 minutes.

2 Peel the peppers, chilli, and aubergine and chop into large pieces. Put these into a food processor with the oil, vinegar, salt, pepper, paprika, and agave syrup and purée until creamy. Decant into a screw-top jar and store in the fridge.

TIP
To preserve your ajvar, put the sealed jar in an ovenproof dish. Half-fill a large roasting tin with boiling water and place the dish in it. Cook for 25 minutes in an oven preheated to 200°C (400°F/Gas 6). Allow it to cool in the oven. It keeps for 3–4 months.

SPICY
TOMATO TARTARE
ON CRUNCHY CIABATTA

This can be packed up really quickly: toasted ciabatta in the box, delicious home-made tomato tartare with black olives in a storage jar, and your snack is complete. Just unpack, assemble, and enjoy. Crunchy bread and aromatic tartare sauce that melts in the mouth. And so simple!

1 If desired, skin the tomatoes: to do this, score a cross into the skins on the opposite side from the stalks, place in a bowl, pour over boiling water, and leave briefly. Plunge into cold water so they don't start to cook; the skins should just peel off. Quarter them, remove the seeds, and finely chop the flesh. Finely chop the olives.

2 Mix the tomatoes and olives with the salt, pepper, lemon zest, 1 tsp of the lemon juice, 1 tbsp of the oil, the vinegar, agave syrup, and basil. Taste and add extra lemon juice and possibly more salt and pepper, if you like.

3 Heat the remaining 1½ tbsp of oil in a large pan and toast the ciabatta slices in it on both sides until golden brown. Remove from the pan and leave to cool. Pack up the ciabatta and tomato tartare separately to take with you. To serve, simply spread the tomato tartare on the slices of bread.

4 ripe tomatoes
40g (1¼oz) pitted black olives
½ tsp sea salt
pinch of freshly ground mixed
    coloured peppercorns
finely grated zest and juice of
    ½ unwaxed lemon
2½ tbsp extra virgin olive oil
½ tsp balsamic vinegar
½ tsp agave syrup
1–2 tbsp chopped basil leaves
4 slices of ciabatta

Each makes 1 jar
Time: 10 mins prep
+ cooking + draining and infusing

200g (7oz) smoked tofu (ideally
strongly smoked)
240g (8½oz) canned kidney beans
½ tsp English mustard
pinch of ground ginger
1 large onion
3–4 tbsp olive oil
2 tsp dried marjoram
1 tsp chopped parsley leaves
sea salt
freshly ground black pepper

SMOKY PÂTÉ

1 Crumble the smoked tofu into little pieces and put it into a food processor. Pour the kidney beans into a sieve, let them drain thoroughly, then add these to the food processor along with the mustard and ginger.

2 Peel and finely chop the onion. Heat the oil in a pan and sauté the onion over a medium heat. Add to the food processor and purée well to a creamy consistency. Fold in the marjoram and parsley and season to taste with salt and pepper.

500g (1lb 2oz) soya yogurt
2 tbsp vegan sour cream
2 tbsp good-quality pumpkin
seed oil
1 tsp sea salt
pinch of freshly ground black
pepper
3 tbsp pumpkin seeds

SOY LABNEH AND PUMPKIN SEED SPREAD

1 Put the yogurt into a sieve lined with a clean tea towel. Stand this over a bowl and leave in the fridge to drip for 12 hours. Squeeze it and put the resulting soy labneh into a bowl. Purée it with the sour cream, oil, salt, and pepper using a hand-held blender.

2 Set aside a few pumpkin seeds for decorating, then finely chop the remainder and toast them in a dry pan. Leave to cool slightly, then fold them into the labneh. Decant into a screw-top jar or other well-sealed container and sprinkle with the remaining pumpkin seeds.

TIP
To go with all these spreads, just pack up your choice of fresh bread, Little Potato Cakes (see p57), or Courgette Cake (see p193).

SPICY "CREAM CHEESE" WITH GHERKINS

1 Put the yogurt into a sieve lined with a clean tea towel. Stand this over a bowl and leave in the fridge to drip for 12 hours. Squeeze it and put the resulting soy cheese into a bowl. Add the sour cream, margarine, both types of paprika, garlic powder, salt, pepper, tomato purée, and capers. Use a hand-held blender to purée everything in the bowl until smooth.

2 Finely chop the gherkins. Remove the seeds from the pepper. Peel the onion then finely chop both this and the peppers. Fold the chopped ingredients into the cream cheese. Add chilli powder to taste and leave to infuse for 4–5 hours.

500g (1lb 2oz) soya yogurt
80g (2¾oz) vegan sour cream
70g (2¼oz) soft vegan margarine
2 tbsp mild paprika
¼ tbsp hot paprika
½ tsp garlic powder
1 tsp sea salt
1 tsp freshly ground white pepper
1 tsp tomato purée
15g (½oz) capers, rinsed
2 gherkins
½ small red pepper
1 small onion
pinch of chilli powder

SANDWICH SPREAD

Bring the stock to the boil in a small saucepan. Peel and finely chop the onion and put in a bowl. Crumble in the rice cakes and mix in the hot stock, oil, tomato purée, chives, salt, pepper, marjoram, and sweet smoked paprika.

125ml (4½fl oz) vegetable stock
1 onion
14 rice cakes
1 tbsp sunflower oil
2½ tbsp tomato purée
2 tbsp chopped chives
½ tsp sea salt
pinch of freshly ground black pepper
½ tsp dried marjoram
pinch of sweet smoked paprika

SPICY RED LENTIL SPREAD

Rinse the lentils in a sieve and leave to drain thoroughly. Bring to the boil with the stock in small saucepan, cover and cook for 15 minutes, then leave to cool. Mix the lentils and any remaining stock with the spices, salt, oil, and liquid smoke (if using), then purée until really smooth using a hand-held blender.

50g (1¾) red lentils
150ml (5fl oz) vegetable stock
½ tsp ground turmeric
½ tsp curry powder
½ tsp ground coriander
pinch of chilli flakes
½ tsp sea salt
½ tbsp olive oil
2 drops of liquid smoke (optional; from a delicatessen or online)

HOT "CREAM CHEESE" SPRING SANDWICH

Bring a touch of springtime to your lunchbox with radishes, cress, cucumber, and this delicious hot cashew "cream cheese". Quick and easy to prepare, this is a non-dairy spread that works really well. Of course it tastes great at other times of year too... any time, really.

For the hot cashew "cream cheese"

200g (7oz) cashew nuts
2 tsp lemon juice
2 tbsp olive oil
2 red chillies
2 tbsp yeast flakes
1 tsp sea salt
pinch of freshly ground black pepper
½ tsp sweet smoked paprika
5 drops of chilli sauce (optional)

For the sandwiches

¼ cucumber
½ bunch of radishes
½ small punnet of cress
handful of salad leaves
4 slices of wholemeal bread

1 To make the hot cashew cream cheese, soak the cashews in cold water for 12 hours. Drain in a sieve, then purée thoroughly in a food processor with 100ml (3½fl oz) water, the lemon juice, and oil. Transfer to a bowl. Halve the chillies lengthways, remove the seeds, and chop finely. Stir into the cashew mixture with the yeast flakes, salt, pepper, paprika, and chilli sauce (if using) until well combined.

2 To make the sandwiches, peel the cucumber and slice it and the radishes thinly. Snip the cress with some scissors. Shred the salad leaves into little pieces.

3 Toast the slices of bread and spread with the "cream cheese" mixture. Distribute the salad leaves between 2 slices of toast, top with the sliced cucumber and radishes, and sprinkle with the cress. Place the remaining slices of toast on top. If you like, split the toasts in half, then pack them into a well-sealed container.

TIP
Dress the salad with vinaigrette before adding it to the sandwiches. Stir together 1 tsp finely chopped shallot with 1 tsp white wine vinegar, 1½ tbsp extra virgin olive oil, a pinch each of salt, pepper, and sugar, and ¼ tsp Dijon mustard.

BARBECUE "PULLED" JACKFRUIT SANDWICH

The classic street food sandwich, with spicy veggies and barbecue sauce, make a delicious, healthy lunch. The role of "pulled pork" is played by jackfruit – a popular ingredient in Asian cuisine.

1 Put the jackfruit into a sieve, let it drain well, then rinse under cold water and let it drain once again. Carefully shred into rough pieces. Heat the oil in a pan and sauté the jackfruit for 3–4 minutes over a medium heat, then season with salt. Peel and crush the garlic and sauté this briefly too. Add the barbecue sauce, stir, then cover and leave to simmer over a low heat for 1 hour. Give it a stir every so often and, if necessary, splash in some water. Season to taste with salt and pepper, remove from the hob, and leave to infuse for 12 hours.

2 Briefly toast the sliced bread under the grill or in the toaster then spread with a little bit of barbecue sauce. Top 2 pieces of bread with 1 lettuce leaf each. Arrange the tomato, onion, and some jackfruit "pulled pork" on top, then drizzle with barbecue sauce. Top with the remaining lettuce leaves and cover with the other slices of bread. Wrap the sandwiches in cling film to take with you.

560g can of green jackfruit in water or brine (see Tip, below)
2 tbsp olive oil
sea salt
2 garlic cloves
150g (5½oz) vegan barbecue sauce, plus extra for the sandwich
freshly ground black pepper
4 slices of bread
4 lettuce leaves
1 tomato, sliced
1 small red onion, finely sliced

TIP
You can buy canned jackfruit in Asian stores. It's very important for this recipe to get young, green jackfruit in water or brine, and not preserved in syrup!

TEMPEH MAYO BAGEL

If you have fond memories of the taste of tuna fish, you will love this bagel. The nori seaweed flakes contribute a similar flavour, with tempeh further complementing the overall effect. This fermented soy product is like a little fountain of health, that shouldn't just be limited to the dishes of its country of origin: Indonesia. There's no limit to the creativity you can exercise when filling these bagels – but one thing is certain: a few colourful beansprouts will always make it prettier and tastier.

For the tempeh mayo
200g (7oz) tempeh, in a block
½ celery stick
½ small onion
130g (4¾oz) Vegan Mayonnaise
    (see p105)
1 tsp dried dill
2 tbsp lemon juice
sea salt
freshly ground black pepper
1 tsp Dijon mustard
1 tsp agave syrup
2 tsp nori seaweed flakes (from an
    Asian store)

For the bagels
2 bagels
4 lettuce leaves (optional)
handful of beansprouts (optional)

1 To make the salad, steam the tempeh over simmering water for 20–30 minutes. Leave to cool, then finely crumble with your fingers, or in a food processor. Chop the celery finely. Peel the onion and chop this finely, too.

2 Combine the celery, onion, Vegan Mayonnaise, dill, lemon juice, salt, pepper, mustard, agave syrup, and nori flakes in a bowl and mix well. Fold in the tempeh and leave the salad to infuse in an airtight container for 12 hours.

3 To finish off, halve and toast the bagels. Lay 2 lettuce leaves on each of the lower halves, top with the tempeh salad and beansprouts, then cover with the upper bagel halves. Wrap in cling film or greaseproof paper to take with you.

SPINACH TOFU SCRAMBLE WRAP
WITH ROCKET

For the spinach
1 small onion
1 garlic clove
½ tbsp vegan margarine
100g (3½oz) frozen spinach, defrosted
1 tbsp oat cream, or other plant-based cream

For the tofu scramble
1 small onion
1 large tomato
½ red pepper
250g (9oz) tofu
3 tbsp olive oil
¾ tsp ground turmeric
1½ tsp curry powder
2 tbsp soy sauce
2 tbsp soya milk, or other plant-based milk
sea salt
freshly ground black pepper
2 tbsp chopped chives

For the wraps
2 large wraps
40g (1¼oz) rocket

Who needs eggs when you've got tofu? This is a kind of non-dairy version of scrambled egg that works wonderfully in this wrap with the accompanying spinach and crunchy red pepper. Neatly rolled up, it is the perfect lunch to pack up and take away.

1 To make the spinach mixture, peel the onion and garlic, then chop the onion and crush the garlic. Melt the margarine in a pan and sauté the onion over a medium heat. Add the spinach and let it wilt with the lid on. Stir in the cream and garlic and let everything thicken slightly.

2 To make the tofu scramble, peel and chop the onion. Halve the tomato, remove the stalk and seeds, and chop the flesh. Deseed, and chop the pepper. Crumble the tofu with your fingers. Heat the oil in a pan and fry the onion and tofu crumbs over a high heat for 1 minute, then reduce the heat to medium and continue to fry until golden brown. Turn the mixture, add the turmeric and curry powder, and continue to cook everything for a further 3–4 minutes. Pour in the soy sauce and cook for an additional 3–4 minutes. Next add the tomato and soya milk. Season everything to taste with salt and pepper and let it simmer gently for a bit longer. Remove the pan from the heat and finally fold the chives into the mixture.

3 To assemble, warm the wraps and lay them out on a work surface. Spread the spinach along the centre of each wrap and top with the tofu scramble and some rocket. Fold in the left and right sides of the wrap over the filling. Then, fold up the lower half, press down lightly, and firmly roll up the wrap from the lower edge. If desired, cut each wrap in half and wrap in foil to take with you.

SWEET POTATO BURGERS
WITH BARBECUE SAUCE

It's hard to imagine a more satisfying and substantial meal than these sweet potato burgers with barbecue sauce! They will make you full and happy. A delicious patty made from sweet potatoes mixed with an exciting combination of spices, all stacked up with crunchy vegetables.

For the patties
1 large sweet potato
sea salt
1 shallot
½ bunch of chives
pinch of freshly ground black
    pepper
½ tsp sweet smoked paprika
1 tbsp dried marjoram
pinch of ground cumin
pinch of ground allspice
1 tsp Dijon mustard
2 tbsp plain or gluten-free flour
40g (1¼oz) fresh breadcrumbs
2½ tbsp rapeseed oil

For the burgers
2 large burger buns
vegan barbecue sauce
handful of salad leaves
small piece of cucumber, sliced
1 tomato, sliced
handful of coriander leaves

1 To make the patties, peel the sweet potato, chop into little pieces, and cook for 10–15 minutes in salted water, until tender. Drain in a sieve. Peel and finely chop the shallot. Snip the chives finely. Use a potato masher to mash up the sweet potato with the shallot and chives in a large bowl until evenly combined. Stir in ½ tsp salt, pepper, the paprika, marjoram, cumin, allspice, and mustard. Add the flour and mix everything thoroughly again.

2 Spread the breadcrumbs out on a plate. Shape 2 even patties from the potato mixture and turn them in the breadcrumbs. Heat the oil in a pan and fry the patties over a medium heat on both sides until golden brown. Remove from the pan and leave to drain on some kitchen paper.

3 Split the burger buns in half, toast them, and spread the cut surface with barbecue sauce. Top the lower halves with salad leaves, then a patty, cucumber and tomato slices, and some coriander. Wrap in cling film. If desired, add some extra barbecue sauce.

PITTA BREADS WITH "EGG SALAD"

This is an oriental-inspired delicacy made with crispy smoked tofu, crunchy fresh cabbage, and spices – all the magic of 1,001 nights wrapped up in a flatbread.

1 To make the salad, cut the smoked tofu into very small cubes. Heat the oil in a pan and sauté the smoked tofu initially over a high heat and then over a medium heat until it is crisp and firm. Set aside.

2 Cut the plain firm tofu into 1cm (½in) cubes, then peel and finely chop the red onion. Slice the spring onions into rings. Slice the cabbage into thin strips and chop. Drain the chickpeas thoroughly in a sieve. Combine the plain firm tofu, red onion, spring onions, cabbage, and chickpeas in a bowl.

3 Stir in the mayonnaise. Season the salad to be as spicy as you like using the black salt (if using), salt, pepper, curry powder, and turmeric. Fold in the smoked tofu and chopped chives. Open up the pitta pockets. Package up the bread and salad separately, then fill the pittas with the salad when you are ready to eat.

150g (5½oz) smoked tofu
3 tbsp olive oil
250g (9oz) plain firm tofu
1 small red onion
2 spring onions
175g (6oz) green cabbage
90g (3oz) canned chickpeas
150–200g (5½–7oz) Vegan
    Mayonnaise (see p105)
1 slightly heaped tsp black salt
    kala namak (optional)
1½ tsp sea salt
½ tsp freshly ground black pepper
3 tsp curry powder
1 tbsp ground turmeric
1 tbsp chopped chives
2 pitta breads

TIP
Your lunch will be even tastier if you warm the flatbreads briefly in the oven just before filling.

Makes 4
Time: 40 mins prep

For the kofta
125g (4½oz) red lentils
120ml (4fl oz) vegetable stock
1 tbsp wholemeal breadcrumbs
2 tbsp plain flour
pinch of sea salt
pinch of hot paprika
pinch of smoked paprika
1 tbsp spring onions, sliced
  into rings
olive oil, for frying

For the hummus
200g (7oz) canned chickpeas
juice of 1 small lemon
100g (3½oz) frozen spinach, thawed
3½ tbsp extra virgin olive oil
2 tsp tahini
1 tsp ground cumin
1 tsp sea salt
½ tsp curry powder
pinch of chilli powder
2 small garlic cloves, crushed

For the sandwiches
4 small cherry tomatoes
1 large focaccia
2 handfuls of mixed salad leaves
1 small red pepper, sliced

FOCACCIA
WITH SPINACH HUMMUS AND RED LENTIL KOFTA

1 To make the lentil kofta, simmer the lentils in the stock over a medium heat in a covered pan for 10–15 minutes, until soft.

2 Meanwhile, to make the hummus, drain the chickpeas and add them to a bowl with all the other hummus ingredients. Use a hand-held blender to purée everything until smooth and creamy. Set aside.

3 Drain the lentils in a sieve and leave to cool slightly, then purée thoroughly with a hand-held blender. Put them in a bowl and add the breadcrumbs, flour, salt, both types of paprika, and the spring onions and work everything together to a firm consistency. Use your hands to shape around 16 little balls from the mixture. Heat the oil for frying in a pan and cook the kofta in batches over a medium heat, turning, until brown all over. Leave to drain on some kitchen paper.

4 Either halve or quarter the tomatoes, depending on size. Spilt the bread into 4 sections and, if desired, warm it in the oven, then slice each section open horizontally. Distribute the hummus, salad leaves, peppers, tomatoes, and 4 lentil kofta between each of the bread quarters. Wrap in cling film to take with you.

TIP
Roasted garlic also works well with these sandwiches. Preheat the oven to 180°C (350°F/Gas 4), cut the stalk end from 1 small bulb of garlic and peel off the outer skin. Mix 3 tbsp olive oil with 1 tsp herbes de Provence and a pinch of sea salt. Brush an ovenproof dish with oil, put in the garlic, drizzle the rest of the oil over it and bake for 30 minutes, until soft. Squeeze out the cloves and use to stuff the sandwich.

VEGETABLE WRAPS

Savoy cabbage is wrapped around tempeh here, with a bit of shredded red cabbage for crunch and segments of orange for juicy zest. These little rolls are a great, refreshing alternative to the usual soggy and uninspiring doughy wraps you can buy in the shops. Pack the dressing separately for dipping your rolls.

1 Wash the Savoy cabbage leaves and cut out the thick central stalks. Heat the stock in a pan and blanch the leaves over a medium heat for 2 minutes. Take them out and plunge them in cold water, then pat them dry and set aside.

2 Slice the tempeh into thin strips. Peel the onion and slice finely. Heat the oil in a pan and sauté the tempeh strips over a high heat. Add the sliced onion and continue to sauté until transparent. Season with salt and pepper.

3 Cut the red cabbage into thin strips and transfer to a bowl. Sprinkle with salt and then toss thoroughly. Peel and segment the orange, reserving any juice that comes out as you do so. Mix the orange segments and juice with the red cabbage. Fold in the chives.

4 To make the dressing, stir the soya yogurt in a bowl with the parsley, oil, salt, pepper, and cinnamon. Spread out the cabbage leaves on your work surface and put a bit of the red cabbage salad and tempeh along the centre of each. Fold in the sides of the leaves over the filling and then carefully roll up from the bottom. Finally, tie them up with string so that the rolls don't come apart while you are transporting them. Wrap them in greaseproof paper, foil, or cling film in your lunchbox. Pack the dressing separately.

For the wraps
4 large Savoy cabbage leaves
250ml (9fl oz) vegetable stock
50g (1¾oz) tempeh
1 small red onion
1 tsp coconut oil
sea salt
freshly ground white pepper
100g (3½oz) red cabbage
½ orange
1 tbsp chopped chives

For the dressing
100g (3½oz) soya yogurt, or other
   plant-based yogurt
½ tbsp chopped parsley
   leaves
dash of walnut oil
pinch of sea salt
pinch of freshly ground white
   pepper
pinch of ground cinnamon

Makes 5
Time: 30 mins prep
+ 30 mins steaming

For the vegan sausages
160g (5¾oz) gluten powder, or
   gluten flour
10g (¼oz) fine oat flakes
20g (¾oz) chickpea flour
1 tsp hot paprika
1 tsp smoked paprika
10g (¼oz) yeast flakes
2 tsp garlic powder
¾ tsp sea salt
½ tsp freshly ground black pepper
140g (5oz) medium firm tofu
110ml (3¾fl oz) vegetable stock
2 tbsp olive oil, plus extra for frying
2 tbsp soy sauce

For the hotdogs
5 hotdog rolls
tomato ketchup
10 pickled cucumber slices
toppings: mustard, Vegan
   Mayonnaise (see p105), fried
   onions (all optional)

Makes 5
Time: 20 mins prep

For the curry sauce
1 large onion
5 tbsp olive oil
160g (5¾oz) tomato ketchup
100ml (3½fl oz) vegetable stock
4 heaped tsp mild curry powder,
   plus extra to serve
½ tsp chilli powder
sea salt
freshly ground black pepper
1 heaped tsp sugar

For the sausages
5 Vegan Sausages (see above)

HOME-MADE HOTDOGS

1 To make the sausages, mix together the gluten powder or flour, oat flakes, chickpea flour, hot paprika, smoked paprika, yeast flakes, garlic powder, salt, and pepper in a bowl. Purée the tofu, stock, oil, and soy sauce in a food processor until smooth. Add this paste to the flour mixture in the bowl and swiftly knead everything together. Split the mixture into 5 portions and shape each into a roughly 15cm (6in) long sausage.

2 Wrap up each of the sausages tightly in aluminium foil, twisting the ends together like a Christmas cracker. Lay these parcels in a steamer and cook over simmering water for 30 minutes. Leave to cool and unwrap from the foil. Heat a little oil in a frying pan and sauté the sausages over a medium heat for 4–5 minutes, turning to brown all over.

3 To serve, heat the hotdog rolls and fill each with some ketchup, 1 sausage and 2 slices of cucumber. If you like, drizzle over some mustard or vegan mayonnaise and sprinkle with fried onions.

HOME-MADE CURRYWURST

1 Make the sausages following steps 1 and 2 above. To make the curry sauce, peel and finely chop the onion. Heat the oil in a pan and sauté the onion over a medium heat. Add the ketchup and stock. Reduce the heat, stir in the curry powder, chilli powder, salt, pepper and sugar and let everything simmer gently.

2 To serve, cut the sausages into bite-sized pieces, drizzle with curry sauce, and dust with curry powder.

TIP
The sausages freeze well or can be kept in the fridge for 2–3 days.

ASIAN
GLASS NOODLE SALAD WRAPS

Glass noodle salad with a twist: packaged up in a delicious wrap. The filling provides everything you could want from the perfect glass noodle salad, enhanced with some added cashews. The end result is a Far Eastern delicacy in your lunchbox.

1 Slice the courgette into spaghetti-like strips with a spiralizer. Alternatively, use a potato peeler to create thin slices lengthways and then cut these into thin strips with a knife. Put the courgette and the noodles to soak in a large bowl of warm water for 10 minutes, until the noodles are soft. Transfer to a sieve and let the noodles and courgette drain, before returning them to the bowl. Set aside.

2 Slice the spring onions and half onion thinly. Quarter the pepper, remove the seeds, and cut into thin strips. Peel and finely chop the garlic and ginger. Toast the cashew nuts in a dry frying pan until golden brown.

3 Heat the oil in a pan. Sauté the spring onions, onion, and pepper over a high heat. Add the garlic and ginger and continue to cook briefly. Pour in the soy sauce and coconut milk and add the coriander. Fold in the cashew nuts.

4 Mix the pan of vegetables with the courgette and glass noodle mixture in the bowl and add salt, pepper, and lime juice to taste. Divide the iceberg lettuce into individual leaves and shred slightly. Briefly heat the wraps and lay them out on your work surface. Spread with sweet and sour sauce, top with lettuce leaves and the glass noodle salad, then roll them up firmly. Wrap in greaseproof paper, foil, or cling film to take with you.

1 courgette
75g (2½oz) glass noodles
½ bunch of spring onions
½ onion
1 red pepper
1 small garlic clove
1cm (½in) piece of fresh root ginger
20g (¾oz) cashew nuts
2½ tbsp sunflower oil
2 tbsp soy sauce
3½ tbsp coconut milk
1 tbsp chopped coriander leaves
sea salt
freshly ground black pepper
1½ tbsp lime juice
¼ head Iceberg lettuce
2 wraps
50g (1¾oz) vegan sweet and sour sauce

TIP
Roll a wrap in a piece of greaseproof paper and cut it through diagonally. It looks really professional and is easier to eat without making a mess!

Makes 1 large or
2 small burritos
Time: 15 mins prep
+ 15 mins cooking

RICE AND BEAN BURRITOS
WITH SALSA

1 To make the rice, heat the oil in a pan and sauté the rice over a medium heat. Add 130ml (4½fl oz) water, the salsa, and salt. Bring to the boil over a high heat, then cover, reduce the heat to a simmer, and cook for 10–15 minutes until done.

2 In the meantime, peel and finely chop the onion. Drain the beans in a sieve. Heat the 2 tbsp of oil in a pan and sauté the onion and beans over a high heat. Reduce the heat to medium and add the garlic and onion powders, salt, and sriracha sauce to taste. Pour in 80ml (2¾fl oz) water and let everything simmer for 2–3 minutes. Mash the bean mixture with a potato masher to produce a lumpy purée. If it seems too dry, add a little more water. Adjust the seasoning again.

3 Remove the stone and peel from the avocado half and slice it. Warm the tortilla, or tortillas, and lay it on your work surface. Spread the rice in a thick layer in the centre and top with the beans. Lay avocado segments on top and drizzle over sriracha sauce before scattering with parsley. Fold in the left and right sides of the tortilla over the filling. Then, fold up the lower half and press down lightly before rolling up firmly from the lower edge. If you like you can heat a bit of oil in a pan and fry the burrito over a high heat; this will help it hold together and add flavour. Wrap in foil and pack up for lunch.

For the rice
1 tbsp olive oil
100g (3½oz) jasmine rice
100g (3½oz) vegan hot salsa
½ tsp sea salt

For the beans
½ onion
200g (7oz) canned kidney beans
2 tbsp olive oil, plus extra for frying
½ tsp garlic powder
½ tsp onion powder
pinch of sea salt
sriracha sauce, to taste (hot chilli sauce from an Asian store, or another kind of chilli sauce)
½ avocado
1 very large (see Tip, below) or 2 small tortillas
parsley for sprinkling (optional)

TIP
The tortillas you can buy at the supermarket are often very small. Much larger tortillas can be bought at Middle Eastern grocery stores. In place of sriracha sauce, you can also use other vegan hot sauces.

HASH BROWN DELUXE SANDWICH

Hash browns are far more than just a traditional American breakfast food. In this recipe, we include them in a really chic sandwich with a fantastically flavoursome dressing. It will work wonders on your lunch break.

1 To make the hash browns, peel and coarsely grate the potatoes, put them into a clean tea towel, and thoroughly squeeze out any liquid. Mix with the salt, pepper, and nutmeg in a bowl. Heat ½–1 tsp oil in a pan, add half the potato mixture, use a spatula to press it down into a thin layer, and fry over a medium heat for 3–4 minutes. Once the edge is crispy, carefully turn the hash brown over and fry the other side until golden brown. Remove and set aside to drain on some kitchen paper. Do the same with the remaining oil (½–1 tsp) and the remaining grated potato.

2 To make the dressing, add the mayonnaise to a small bowl and mix with the cucumber relish, sea salt, paprika, garlic and onion powders, the vinegar, and a little more pepper, adjusting the quantities to taste.

3 Toast the rolls or sliced bread, as you prefer. Spread the lower halves of the rolls or 2 slices of toast with the dressing and top with the lettuce, tomato, pickled cucumbers, fried onions, and the hash browns. Cover with the tops of the rolls, or the remaining toast slices. Wrap the sandwiches in cling film.

For the hash browns
500g (1lb 2oz) potatoes
½ tsp sea salt
freshly ground black pepper
pinch of freshly grated nutmeg
1–2 tsp rapeseed oil

For the dressing
2 tbsp Vegan Mayonnaise
  (see p105)
2 tbsp cucumber relish
  (from a jar)
½ tsp sea salt
½ tsp sweet smoked paprika
½ tsp garlic powder
½ tsp onion powder
½ tsp cider vinegar

For the sandwich
2 wholemeal rolls, or 4 slices of
  wholemeal bread
handful of salad leaves
1 tomato, sliced
1½ tbsp sweet and spicy pickled
  cucumbers or gherkins
2 tsp bought crispy fried onions

PASTA & GRAINS

filling "on-the-go" meals — rice, noodles, spaghetti, and more

Makes 1 large or 2 small portions
Time: 25 mins prep

SPAGHETTI POMODORI E OLIO

High-quality olive oil, delicate pine nuts, a hint of lemon, and juicy tomatoes are what make this classic dish so irresistible. Proper Italian fare for your lunchbox – *buon gusto*!

1 Cook the spaghetti in salted water according to the packet instructions until it is al dente. Meanwhile, quarter the tomatoes, remove the stalk and seeds, and chop finely. Peel and finely chop the garlic and parsley. Stir the oil together with 1 tbsp water and the stock. Combine the oil mixture with the tomatoes, garlic, and parsley then add salt, pepper, lemon juice, and agave syrup.

2 Dry-roast the pine nuts in a pan until golden brown, then chop roughly. Drain the spaghetti in a sieve, return to the hot pan, and put over a medium heat. Fold in the tomato mixture and warm everything through for around 1 minute, stirring constantly. Transfer the spaghetti to your lunchbox and sprinkle with the pine nuts.

150g (5½oz) wholewheat spaghetti
sea salt
2 tomatoes
1 garlic clove
½ small bunch of flat leaf parsley
1 tbsp extra virgin olive oil
1 tsp powdered vegetable stock
freshly ground black pepper
squeeze of lemon juice
½ tsp agave syrup
20g (¾oz) pine nuts

Makes 4
Time: 20 mins prep
+ 30 mins cooking

STUFFED POLENTA
WITH GREEN MOJO

1 To make the filling, put the soy chunks in a bowl, pour over the stock, and leave to soak for 5 minutes. Drain in a sieve and leave to cool slightly. Use your hands to squeeze out as much of the liquid as possible.

2 In a small bowl, mix together the marjoram, thyme, hot and sweet paprika, parsley, oregano, nutmeg, onion powder, and salt. Add 4 tbsp of the olive oil and stir everything together to create a thin paste. Spread this paste over the soy chunks and work together using your hands. Set aside.

3 To make the polenta, bring the stock and soya milk to the boil in a large saucepan. Add the polenta, stirring all the time until you have a smooth mixture. Stir in the margarine. Switch off the heat, cover, and leave the polenta to swell for 10 minutes.

4 In the meantime, preheat the oven to 180°C (350°F/Gas 4). To finish off preparing the filling, heat 2 tbsp more olive oil in a pan and sauté the soy chunks over a high heat. Set aside and leave to cool. Halve the courgette, then cut into thin slices. Quarter the pepper, remove the seeds, and chop into cubes.

5 Season the polenta very generously, divide between four 40cm (16in) squares of foil, and spread it out slightly. Top each with one-quarter of the vegetables, tomatoes, and the soy chunks. Drizzle with the remaining 2 tbsp of oil. Close each piece of foil to create a parcel or roll so that the polenta is folded up over the filling and no air can escape. Lay the parcels on a baking tray and bake in the centre of the oven for around 30 minutes.

6 Meanwhile, make the mojo sauce. Roughly chop the parsley. Use a food processor to purée the parsley, cumin, oil, lemon juice, and a little salt to a smooth consistency. Pack up the polenta parcels and the mojo separately to take with you.

For the filling
75g (2½oz) coarse soy chunks (from a health food shop)
250ml (9fl oz) hot vegetable stock
1 tsp dried marjoram
1 tsp dried thyme
½ tsp hot paprika
½ tsp sweet paprika
pinch of dried parsley
pinch of dried oregano
pinch of freshly grated nutmeg
1 tsp onion powder
sea salt
8 tbsp olive oil
1 small courgette
1 red pepper
12 cherry tomatoes

For the polenta
200ml (7fl oz) vegetable stock
200ml (7fl oz) soya milk, or other plant-based milk
200g (7oz) fine polenta (cornmeal)
1 tbsp vegan margarine
freshly ground black pepper

For the mojo
small bunch of curly parsley
1 tsp ground cumin
150ml (5fl oz) extra virgin olive oil
squeeze of lemon juice

Makes 1 large or 2 small portions
Time: 25 mins prep
+ 20 mins cooking

SPAGHETTI FRITTATAS

These little noodle nests are truly predestined for the lunchbox. Our spaghetti frittatas combine all the best features of a delicious, creamy pasta dish. They are baked until crisp to make them even tastier and best of all: you can eat them with your fingers.

For the frittatas
150g (5½oz) wholewheat spaghetti
sea salt
30g (1oz) smoked tofu
1 small onion
30g (1oz) pitted green olives
1 tbsp olive oil
100g (3½oz) soya cream, or other
   plant-based cream
60g (2oz) vegan pizza cheese,
   shredded
pinch of herb salt, or sea salt plus
   a pinch of mixed herbs
freshly ground black pepper
pinch of dried oregano
vegan margarine, for the tin
4 basil leaves, to garnish

1 Cook the spaghetti in salted water, according to the packet instructions, until al dente. Meanwhile, cut the tofu into little cubes. Peel and finely chop the onion and olives.

2 Heat the oil in a large high-sided pan and sauté the tofu over a high heat. Add the onion and olives and cook briefly. Pour in the cream and 30g (1oz) of the cheese. Season with herb salt, pepper, and oregano and simmer over a low heat until the cheese has melted.

3 Preheat the oven to 220°C (425°F/Gas 7). Grease 4 muffin tin moulds with the margarine. Drain the spaghetti briefly in a sieve, then mix with the cheese mixture. Distribute the pasta mix between the muffin moulds: the best way to do this is to use a large fork to twist the spaghetti.

4 Scatter the remaining cheese over the spaghetti and bake the frittatas in the centre of the oven for 20 minutes. Remove and leave to cool slightly before releasing from the moulds. Pack them up and serve garnished with some basil leaves. The frittatas taste great either warm or cold.

Makes 1 large or 2 small portions
Time: 35 mins prep
+ 30 mins infusing

GRILLED
MINI PEPPERS
WITH RAINBOW BULGUR

These little peppers are called pimientos de Padrón and they originate from Galicia in Spain. They can be baked in the oven and are a delight to eat, not just with this colourful bulgur salad, but also on their own. This beautiful dish is enhanced with a Middle Eastern-style dressing.

1 Preheat the oven to 200°C (400°F/Gas 6). Wash the Padrón peppers, pat them dry with kitchen paper, and lay them in a single layer in an ovenproof dish. Drizzle with oil and season with salt and pepper. Chop the rosemary (if using), and scatter over the peppers. Bake in the centre of the oven for 20 minutes.

2 Meanwhile, peel and finely chop the onion for the bulgur salad. Heat the oil in a pan and sauté the onion and bulgur over a medium heat. Pour in the stock, stir everything well, and let the bulgur swell by leaving it, covered, over a low heat for around 10 minutes. Remove the pan from the hob and leave to cool.

3 Trim the spring onions and slice finely. Quarter the yellow pepper, remove the seeds, and chop it into bite-sized pieces. Halve the tomatoes. Finely chop the dates and the parsley.

4 To make the dressing, stir together all the ingredients in a little bowl. Mix the bulgur with the spring onions, yellow pepper, tomatoes, dates, parsley, and the dressing. To serve, lay the Padrón peppers on the bulgur, or serve alongside. This is perfect for preparing the evening before, as the flavour of the bulgur improves the longer it marinates in the dressing.

For the peppers
300g (10oz) pimientos de Padrón (small green peppers)
2 tbsp olive oil
sea salt
freshly ground black pepper
sprig of rosemary (optional)

For the bulgur
1 small onion
1 tbsp oil
80g (2¾oz) bulgur wheat
250ml (9fl oz) vegetable stock
½ bunch of spring onions
1 large yellow pepper
3 cherry tomatoes
5 pitted dates
3–4 sprigs of flat leaf parsley

For the dressing
finely grated zest and juice of ½ small unwaxed lemon
1½ tbsp argan oil
1 tsp light balsamic vinegar
1 tsp tomato purée
½ tsp harissa
½ tsp ras el hanout
1 tsp agave syrup

POTSTICKER NOODLES

So simple, so good: rice noodles, pak choi, and deliciously aromatic ginger, curry paste, and sesame oil all mingle splendidly in this Asian concoction. Broccoli joins the assembled ranks of delicious ingredients to add a nice crunch – and a little green goodness – to the noodles.

For the sauce

5 tbsp soy sauce
1 tbsp rice vinegar
1 tbsp red curry paste
½ tsp sesame oil
pinch of chilli powder
2 tbsp finely chopped spring onion greens

For the noodles

½ small pak choi, about 80g (2¼oz)
1 tbsp coconut oil
80g (2¼oz) broccoli florets
sea salt
freshly ground black pepper
80g (2¼oz) broad rice noodles (from an Asian supermarket)
½ tsp finely grated fresh root ginger

1 To make the sauce, add all the ingredients to a screw-top jar. Close the lid firmly and shake vigorously until the ingredients are well combined. Set aside.

2 Finely chop the pak choi. Heat the oil in a pan and sauté the broccoli until it is just cooked. Season with salt and pepper and set aside.

3 Cook the noodles in salted water according to the packet instructions. Add the pak choi shortly before the end of the cooking time. Drain the noodles and pak choi in a sieve, plunge into cold water, then drain again, and return to the pan. Add the sauce and heat everything through again. Fold in the broccoli and ginger, then transfer to your lunchbox.

TIP

"Potstickers" are filled dumplings made from rice flour. For our "potsticker" pasta, the filling is simply mixed in with the rice noodles. It's quicker and easier, but just as tasty.

FRIED RICE
WITH PINEAPPLE AND CASHEW NUTS

Fruity pineapple, sweetcorn, and golden-brown toasted cashew nuts give this delicately bronzed jasmine rice everything it needs to be a truly memorable culinary experience.

1 Cook the rice in salted water according to the packet instructions. Drain in a sieve and leave to cool. Toast the cashews in a small dry frying pan until golden brown, then remove from the heat and set aside. Chop the pineapple rings into bite-sized pieces. Melt the margarine in the pan over a medium heat, sauté the pineapple, then set aside.

2 Halve the pepper, remove the seeds, then chop into small chunks. Peel the carrot and slice thinly using a vegetable peeler. Drain the sweetcorn in a sieve. Heat 2 tbsp oil in a wok or frying pan. Sauté the pepper and carrot over a high heat, then continue to cook over a medium heat until golden brown and al dente. If the carrot browns too much before it is cooked, add a little water (any added liquid should evaporate completely). Season the vegetables with salt, pepper, and paprika.

3 Add the remaining 2 tbsp oil and increase the heat. Stir in the rice and sauté briefly over a high heat until crisp, then continue to brown over a medium heat. If the mixture dries out too much, add a little more oil. Fold in the sweetcorn, pineapple, and cashews and heat through. Transfer the rice dish to a lunchbox. Wash and slice the spring onions and scatter them over the rice. Sprinkle with paprika.

100g (3½oz) jasmine rice
sea salt
60g (2oz) cashew nuts
2 canned pineapple rings
2 tbsp vegan margarine
1 small red pepper
1 carrot
80g (2¾oz) canned sweetcorn
4 tbsp olive oil, plus extra if needed
good pinch of freshly ground white pepper
1½ tsp hot paprika, plus extra for sprinkling
2 spring onions, green sections only

TIP
The recipe also tastes great with broccoli and flaked almonds — you can eat it warm or cold, and as leftovers the next day.

ARABIAN RICE

This is modelled after *kabsa*, an Arabian rice dish usually served with meat.
In this recipe we use seitan instead, and it proves to be the perfect companion
for the rice, Middle Eastern spices, and crunchy flaked almonds.

250g (9oz) long grain rice
1 carrot
½ red pepper
1 shallot
1 garlic clove
150g (5½oz) seitan
1½ tbsp olive oil
1 tsp tomato purée
finely grated zest and juice of
    ½ unwaxed orange
500ml (16fl oz) vegetable stock, plus
    extra if needed
50g (1¾oz) flaked almonds
½ tsp *pul biber* (Aleppo pepper, or
    Turkish chilli flakes)
pinch of saffron threads
pinch of ground cinnamon
pinch of ground cumin
pinch of ground cardamom
sea salt
freshly ground black pepper
freshly grated nutmeg
handful of raisins (optional)

1 Put the rice in a sieve and rinse until the water runs clear. Leave to drain and set aside. Peel and finely chop the carrot. Quarter the pepper, remove the seeds, then finely chop. Peel and chop the shallot and garlic.

2 Chop the seitan into bite-sized pieces. Heat the oil in a pan and sauté the seitan over a high heat on all sides. Stir in the tomato purée, carrot, pepper, shallot, garlic, and orange zest and juice. Add the rice, plus sufficient stock to cover the rice well. Simmer over a medium heat for about 20 minutes until cooked, stirring occasionally and adding more stock if necessary.

3 Meanwhile, toast the flaked almonds in a dry pan. Season the rice with *pul biber*, saffron, cinnamon, cumin, and cardamom and add a pinch each of salt, pepper, and nutmeg. Stir in the raisins (if using). Decant into 2 lunchboxes and sprinkle with the almonds. If possible serve the *kabsa* hot, but the dish also tastes great served cold or at room temperature.

Makes 2 large portions
Time: 10 mins prep
+ 40 mins cooking

GRANNY'S PEARL BARLEY STEW

Everyone knows that granny makes the best stew. But where granny used bacon back in the day, here we have a vegetable version which uses delicate cubes of smoked tofu. This is a warming, filling soupy bowlful, with little round grains of pearl barley and hearty root vegetables. Just perfect on a cold day: bolstering and warming, like a hug in a bowl.

2 carrots
1 small piece of celeriac
300g (10oz) waxy potatoes
1 leek
2 tbsp oil
100g (3½oz) pearl barley
1 litre (1¾ pints) vegetable stock
2–3 sprigs of lovage, or parsley
   or celery leaves if you can't
   find lovage
200g (7oz) smoked tofu
sea salt
freshly ground black pepper

1 Peel the carrots, halve lengthways, and then slice. Peel the celeriac and potatoes and chop into bite-sized cubes. Wash the leek well and remove the root and the outer leaves. Slice into rings.

2 Heat 1 tbsp of the oil in a pan and sauté the carrots, celeriac, potatoes, and leek. Add the pearl barley and continue to sauté for a short while. Pour over the vegetable stock and add the lovage. Cook everything over a medium heat for 40 minutes. Give it a stir every so often and make sure there is enough liquid, adding water if necessary.

3 In the meantime, chop the tofu into rough cubes. Heat the remaining 1 tbsp of oil in a pan and sauté the tofu over a medium heat until golden brown on all sides.

4 Remove the lovage from the stew and stir in the tofu. Season to taste. Leave to cool, then chill. Reheat briefly before serving.

SPICY QUINOA CHILLI

Protein-rich quinoa is a truly versatile ingredient. Here it takes the leading role in a spicy chilli, with supporting parts being played by pepper, tomatoes, sweetcorn, kidney beans, and spices. Chilli is an obvious choice for the lunchbox: it is the perfect dish to prepare a day in advance, because it usually tastes even better once the flavours have infused for a day or so.

1 Run the quinoa under a tap in a sieve until the water flows clear, then cook it in the simmering stock for about 15 minutes, or according to the packet instructions. Drain in a sieve, rinse with cold water, and set aside. Slice the pepper and chilli in half lengthways and remove the seeds. Chop the pepper into bite-sized cubes and finely chop the chilli. Peel the onion and garlic and chop finely.

2 Heat the oil in a large pan and sauté the pepper, chilli, onion, and garlic over a medium heat. Add the tomato purée and briefly sauté this with the other ingredients. Add the tomatoes and simmer everything for 5 minutes.

3 Drain the sweetcorn and beans in a sieve, rinse with cold water, and fold into the sauce with the quinoa. Let everything continue to simmer for 5 minutes. Adjust the flavour by adding lime juice, salt, pepper, chilli powder, oregano, cumin, and maple syrup to taste. Leave to cool, then chill. Briefly reheat before serving.

100g (3½oz) quinoa
250ml (9fl oz) vegetable stock
½ green pepper
1 red chilli
1 small onion
1 garlic clove
1½ tbsp olive oil
2½ tbsp tomato purée
400g can of chopped tomatoes
140g can of sweetcorn
½ × 400g can of kidney beans
1 tbsp lime juice
pinch of sea salt
pinch of freshly ground white pepper
1 tsp chilli powder, or to taste
pinch of dried oregano
pinch of ground cumin
1 tsp maple syrup

TIP
A baguette goes really well with this, or try a baked sweet potato. To prepare the potato, preheat the oven to 180°C (350°F/Gas 4), scrub the sweet potato, pat it dry, place it on a baking tray, and sprinkle with 1 tbsp sea salt. Bake in the centre of the oven for 40–45 minutes. To serve, slice into the sweet potato, press the halves apart but do not separate, then fill with the quinoa chilli.

MACARONI "CHEESE" SALAD

Why not use this ever-popular comfort food dish as the inspiration for conjuring up a cold pasta salad? It doesn't need any "cheese" – the cashews and mustard help create a vegan version which is a total winner.

1 Cook the macaroni in salted water according to the packet instructions, until al dente. Drain in a sieve, refresh under running cold water, then leave to drain. Set aside.

2 To make the sauce, peel the sweet potato and carrot and chop into 2cm (¾in) cubes. Peel and quarter the onion. Boil the sweet potato, carrot, and onion in the stock until tender (about 10 minutes). Drain and reserve about 250ml (9fl oz) of the stock. Peel the garlic (if using) and use a food processor to purée the garlic, sweet potato, carrots, and onion with the reserved stock, cashews, mustard, salt, lemon juice, pepper, paprika, and margarine until smooth.

3 Halve the tomatoes. Trim the spring onions and chop them finely. Drain or defrost the peas and sweetcorn and pat them dry with kitchen paper. Mix together the macaroni, sauce, tomatoes, spring onions, peas, and sweetcorn.

For the macaroni
250g (9oz) macaroni
sea salt
4 cherry tomatoes
½ bunch of spring onions
50g (1¾oz) frozen peas
50g (1¾oz) frozen or canned
  sweetcorn

For the sauce
1 small sweet potato, about
  100g (3½oz)
1 small carrot
1 small onion
375ml (13fl oz) vegetable stock
1 small garlic clove (optional)
30g (1oz) cashew nuts
½ tsp Dijon mustard
½ tsp sea salt
squeeze of lemon juice
pinch of freshly ground black
  pepper
½ tsp sweet smoked paprika
1½ tbsp vegan margarine

TIP
This sauce is also excellent for topping grilled dishes, or used as a dip.

Makes 1 large or 2 small portions
Time: 20 mins prep
+ 15 mins cooking

POTATO "RISOTTO"

Sometimes it's good to do things a bit differently – this lunchbox risotto is made from potatoes instead of rice. The olives, capers, and sun-dried tomatoes provide a culinary lunch time escape to the Mediterranean – dreaming about your summer holidays while you eat is definitely to be encouraged!

400g (14oz) new potatoes
1 small red pepper
1 shallot
1 small garlic clove
2 tbsp olive oil
3 tbsp vegan margarine
25g (scant 1oz) capers, rinsed
40g (1¼oz) pitted black olives
50g (1¾oz) sun-dried tomatoes
  in oil
2 tbsp white wine
1 tsp balsamic vinegar
400ml (14fl oz) vegetable stock
sea salt
freshly ground black pepper
pinch of dried basil
pinch of dried rosemary
pinch of dried thyme
pinch of sugar
2 tbsp chopped chives

1 Peel the potatoes and cut into small cubes. Quarter the pepper, remove the seeds, and chop into small cubes. Peel and finely chop the shallot and garlic.

2 Heat the oil and margarine in a sauté pan and sauté the potatoes, pepper, shallot, and garlic over a medium heat. Finely chop the capers, olives, and tomatoes, add them to the pan and cook briefly. Deglaze with the wine and vinegar, scraping at the base of the pan, then pour in the stock and cook, stirring, for 15 minutes.

3 Season with salt, pepper, the herbs, and sugar, and fold in the chopped chives. Decant into a lunchbox to take with you.

Makes 1 large or 2 small
portions
Time: 20 mins prep

FENNEL, BANANA, AND FUSILLI SALAD
WITH ORANGE YOGURT DRESSING

Boring meals are history! In this delicious fennel and banana salad, flamboyant flavours come together to create a genuine taste sensation. Distinctive fennel really comes into its own here, while banana, apple, pasta, and a slightly sweet dressing prove the ideal partners.

1 To make the salad, cook the fusilli according to the packet instructions (usually 8–10 minutes) in salted water. Meanwhile, remove the tough core from the fennel, cut off the stalks, then finely grate the bulb. Peel and slice the banana. Peel the apple, remove the core, and grate it finely. Drain the pasta in a sieve and plunge into cold water to stop the cooking, then drain again. Fold in the fennel, banana, and apple.

2 For the dressing, mix together the yogurt, orange juice, oil, vinegar, curry powder, salt, and pepper in a small bowl. Toast the pine nuts in a dry pan until golden brown, then leave to cool. Pick the leaves from the parsley stalks and chop them finely. Fold the dressing, pine nuts, and parsley into the pasta mixture. Add lemon juice to taste and a little more salt and pepper, if you like.

For the salad
100g (3½oz) fusilli
sea salt
1 fennel bulb
1 large banana
½ apple

For the dressing
200g (7oz) soya yogurt, or other plant-based yogurt
6 tbsp orange juice
2 tbsp extra virgin olive oil
3 tbsp orange vinegar, or white wine or herb vinegar
½–1 heaped tbsp mild curry powder
1½ tsp sea salt
½ tsp freshly ground black pepper
50g (1¾oz) pine nuts
small bunch of parsley
squeeze of lemon juice

PIZZA, SAVOURY TARTS & BREADS

moreish recipes — freshly baked
loaves, homemade quiches and more

Makes a 28cm (11in) quiche / 8 slices
Time: 15 mins prep
+ 1 hr chilling
+ 30 mins cooking

ASPARAGUS QUICHE

Quiche is wonderfully versatile. The pastry here is quick to make and all you need to do is pop in the filling. This recipe combines green and white asparagus with tasty silken tofu and soya cream to create a really luxurious treat – instant pleasure in your lunchbox.

1 To make the pastry, put the flour and salt in a bowl and chop in the margarine. Briefly rub it together with your fingertips until the mixture resembles breadcrumbs. Sprinkle in the sugar and 8 tbsp water and stir with a knife until the mixture comes together in clumps and leaves the bowl clean. Form the pastry into a disc, wrap in cling film, and leave for 1 hour in the fridge.

2 For the filling, chop the woody ends from both types of asparagus. Peel the lower one-third of the green asparagus spears. Cut the chilli in half lengthways, remove the seeds, then slice into narrow strips. Preheat the oven to 180°C (350°F/Gas 4). Grease a 28cm (11in) springform tart tin.

3 Roll out the pastry on a floured work surface until it is large enough to line the tin. Carefully roll it over the rolling pin and lay it in the tin, pushing down gently in the corners to form a pastry case. Stir together the tofu, cream, cornflour, oil, oregano, and basil in a bowl until you have a smooth creamy consistency, then season to taste with salt and pepper. Spread the cream over the pastry then arrange the different coloured asparagus and the chilli strips in an alternating pattern on top.

4 Bake the quiche in the centre of the oven for 25–30 minutes until golden. Let it cool slightly in the tin on a wire rack. To serve or pack for lunch, remove the quiche from the tin and cut into pieces.

For the pastry
325g (11oz) plain flour, plus extra for dusting
1 tsp sea salt
150g (5½oz) vegan margarine, plus extra for the tin
pinch of sugar

For the filling
6 white asparagus spears
6 green asparagus spears
1 large or 2 small mild red chillies
300g (10oz) silken tofu
100g (3½oz) soya cream, or other plant-based cream
1 heaped tsp cornflour
1 tbsp olive oil
1 tsp dried oregano
1 tsp dried basil
freshly ground black pepper

Special equipment
28cm (11in) springform tart tin

Makes 4
Time: 20 mins prep
+ 30 mins proving
+ 20 mins cooking

HERB, OLIVE, AND TOMATO FILLED
HOME-MADE ROLLS

These are the perfect finger food: home-made rolls with a Mediterranean-style filling baked inside. Loads of herbs balance a spectacular, rich mixture of tofu, tomatoes, and olives. Tuck right in and enjoy – this is what is known as the ideal lunch.

For the dough
400g (14oz) strong white flour
1 tsp sea salt
7g (¼oz) sachet of dried yeast
1½ tbsp caster sugar
1 tsp mixed seeds (such as poppy
   seed, or caraway seed for flavour)
1–2 tbsp crushed linseeds, plus 1½
   tbsp for sprinkling
3½ tbsp olive oil
2 tbsp soya cream, or other plant-
   based cream
1 tsp herbes de Provençe

For the filling
1 shallot
175g (6oz) basil tofu, or tofu rosso,
   or a mixture
1 tsp dried basil
1 tsp herbes de Provençe
½ tsp dried oregano
½ tsp sea salt
pinch of freshly ground black
   pepper
5 sun-dried tomatoes in oil
1 tbsp olive oil
40g (1¼oz) soya cream, or other
   plant-based cream
15 pitted Kalamata olives

1 To make the dough, mix together the flour, salt, dried yeast, sugar, and seeds in a bowl using a balloon whisk. Add the oil and 200ml (7fl oz) lukewarm water and knead everything by hand for around 10 minutes until you have a smooth dough, kneading vigorously to get lots of air into it. Cover and leave to prove in a warm place for 30 minutes.

2 Meanwhile, peel and roughly chop the shallot. Purée the shallot in a food processor with the tofu, basil, herbes de Provençe, oregano, salt, pepper, and sun-dried tomatoes. Then add the olive oil and soya cream and work everything to a spreadable texture which is not too crumbly. Depending on how large they are, either halve or quarter the olives and fold them into the mixture. If necessary, adjust the seasoning to taste with extra salt and pepper.

3 Preheat the oven to 200°C (400°F/Gas 6). Line a baking tray with greaseproof paper. Split the dough into 4 equal-sized pieces and press each piece by hand into a flat disc. Place one-quarter of the filling on each disc, fold over the edges of the dough, press firmly together, and smooth out slightly. Turn the roll over and reshape the upper surface to neaten it up.

4 Place the bread rolls on the greaseproof paper, brush liberally with soya cream, and sprinkle with linseed and herbes de Provençe. Bake for around 18 minutes in the centre of the oven. Leave to cool completely on a wire rack.

Makes 2 small pizzas
Time: 10 mins prep
+ 20 mins proving
+ 20 mins cooking

CHIA AND ALMOND PIZZA

The little superfood seeds used in this recipe guarantee a real treat for your taste buds. Instead of cheese we use almond butter with yeast flakes, which is beautifully creamy and also incredibly healthy. This gluten-free pizza with almonds will elicit a chorus of "Mmmmm!" and surpass everything you would expect from a really good pizza.

For the dough

2 tbsp ground chia seeds (from a health food shop)
200g (7oz) ground almonds
½ tsp sea salt
gluten-free flour, for dusting

For the topping

100g (3½oz) tomato passata
2 tbsp tomato purée
½ tsp olive oil
sea salt
freshly ground white pepper
½ tsp pizza seasoning (see Tip)
1 small onion
½ small courgette
1 small red pepper
1½ tbsp almond butter
1½ tsp yeast flakes
50g (1¾oz) rocket

1 To make the dough, stir the chia seeds together with 4 tbsp water and leave to soak for about 20 minutes. Combine the almonds and salt and knead together with the chia seeds to create a smooth dough. Preheat the oven to 200°C (400°F/Gas 6). Line a baking tray with greaseproof paper.

2 Divide the dough in half and roll out each piece on a floured work surface using a rolling pin. Lay the discs of dough onto the baking tray and bake in the centre of the oven for 12–15 minutes until golden.

3 Meanwhile, make the sauce by stirring together the tomato passata, tomato purée, and oil, then season with salt, pepper, and pizza seasoning. Peel the onion, then slice it and the courgette thinly. Quarter the pepper, remove the seeds, and chop into thin strips. Combine the almond butter, yeast flakes, and 3 tbsp water and stir until smooth.

4 Spread the tomato sauce on the pizza base and top with the vegetables. Dollop on the almond butter mixture and cook the pizzas for 5–7 minutes until done. Leave to cool before packing. Pack the rocket separately. Ideally reheat the pizza briefly before serving and garnish with the rocket.

TIP
You can quickly make your own pizza seasoning from 1 tbsp each dried rosemary, oregano, basil, thyme, and yeast flakes.

Makes a 25cm (10in) loaf
Time: 10 mins prep
+ 30 mins proving
+ 1 hr cooking

COURGETTE CAKE

Fancy taking cake to work for a snack? And what a cake! With courgettes, carrot, and exquisite macadamia nuts, this vitamin-rich loaf is the ideal companion when you're out and about. And it's really versatile, too: you can spread it with either sweet or spicy toppings. It's great with whatever flavour you are craving.

1 Grate the courgettes and carrot. Chop the nuts and mix them with the flour, salt, cinnamon, baking powder, sugar, and lemon juice in a bowl. Add the courgette and carrot followed by 150ml (5fl oz) water and stir until everything is combined evenly. Cover and leave the mixture to prove for around 30 minutes.

2 Preheat the oven to 180°C (350°F/Gas 4). Grease the tin, pour in the mixture, and bake in the lower part of the oven for around 1 hour. Test the loaf by inserting a wooden skewer into the centre. If there is no mixture clinging to it when you pull it out, the cake is ready; if there is, bake it for a few minutes more, then test again. Leave to cool in the tin for 10 minutes, then turn out onto a wire rack and leave to cool completely.

1 large or 2 small courgettes
1 small carrot
75g (2½oz) macadamia nuts
225g (8oz) plain flour
pinch of sea salt
pinch of ground cinnamon
1 tsp baking powder
80g (2¾oz) golden caster sugar
juice of ½ lemon
vegan margarine, for the tin

Special equipment
25cm (10in) long loaf tin

TIP
For a sweet version, stir together 75g (2¹/₂oz) icing sugar and 2 tbsp lemon juice to make a glaze and pour it over the cake; or brush the top with melted vegan chocolate and sprinkle with chopped nuts. Kids love this cake, sliced, with jam and peanut butter. For a savoury version, spread a slice of the cake with a savoury spread (see pp130—31) and eat it with lettuce, cucumber, and tomatoes.

Makes 1 medium-sized loaf
Time: 40 mins prep
+ 2¼ hrs proving
+ 30 mins baking

SOFT POTATO BREAD

This potato bread is soft and moist, and tastes equally great with sweet or savoury toppings. It also stays fresh for several days.

For the yeast starter mix:
150ml (5fl oz) soya milk
2 heaped tsp bread spices (see below)
50g (1¾oz) spelt flour
1 sachet dried yeast
1 tbsp agave syrup

For the main dough:
100ml (3½fl oz) soya milk
3 tbsp soya yogurt
1 squeeze lemon juice
400g (14oz) spelt flour, plus extra for dusting
1½ tsp salt
300g (10oz) potatoes, peeled and cooked

1 To make the starter mix, warm the soya milk in a pan with the bread spices and then set aside. Combine the flour and dried yeast in a bowl. Stir the agave syrup into the spiced soya milk then mix everything into the dry ingredients until well combined. Cover and leave to prove in a warm place for about 15 minutes, then stir until smooth again.

2 For the main dough, whisk together the soya milk, soya yogurt, and lemon juice then warm over a low heat. Remove from the heat. Combine the flour and salt in a bowl. Mash the potatoes and add them to the flour. Stir in the soya milk, yogurt, and lemon juice mixture. Then add the starter mix and knead everything until you have a smooth dough, possibly adding a bit of soya milk or flour, if required. Cover and leave to prove in a warm place for about 1 hour, until doubled in size.

3 Knead the dough vigorously and shape it into an oval loaf. Place this on a baking tray lined with baking paper, dust with flour, and leave to prove again for about 1 hour. Preheat the oven to 200°C (400°F/Gas 6). Make 4 incisions in the top of the loaf and bake in the centre of the oven for 30 minutes. If the bread begins to darken too quickly, cover it with foil. Remove and leave to cool.

TIP
If the bread sounds hollow when you tap on the base, it is ready. You can make your own delicious bread spice by finely grinding fennel, coriander, caraway, cardamom, aniseed, and blue fenugreek in a pestle and mortar.

TARTE FLAMBÉE

With a crisp, thin base topped with delicious pointed cabbage, this vegan tarte flambée is just as good as the original!

1 To make the dough, combine the flour, salt, and sugar in a bowl. Add the soya drink and olive oil and knead everything vigorously until you have a homogeneous, soft dough. Cover and leave the dough to prove in a warm place for at least 2 hours.

2 Meanwhile, for the topping, halve the pointed cabbage, cut out the stalk in a V-shaped wedge, and slice the cabbage into roughly 1cm (½in) wide strips. Peel the onions and carrots, cut in half, and slice into thin strips. Dice the smoked tofu.

3 Heat the rapeseed oil in a large non-stick pan over a high heat and sear the tofu until it is nice and crisp. Reduce the heat and add the pointed cabbage, carrots, and onions. Cook over a moderate heat, stirring frequently, being sure not to let the vegetables colour too much. Season with the salt, pepper, nutmeg, and caraway.

4 Preheat the oven to 200°C (400°F/Gas 6). Knead the dough vigorously again, divide into two portions, and roll these out as thinly as possible. Lay the pieces on a baking tray lined with baking paper and cover with a thin layer of crème fraîche. Spread the topping out evenly then drizzle over the remaining crème fraîche. Bake the tarte flambée in the centre of the oven for 20–25 minutes, until slightly crisp and golden brown. Scatter the pine nuts over the tart about 10 minutes before the end of the baking time. Remove from the oven and enjoy while still warm.

For a 30 x 40cm (12 x 15½in) baking tray
Time: 15 mins prep
+ 2 hrs proving + 25 mins baking

For the dough:
250g (9oz) plain flour
½ tsp salt
1 pinch of fine cane sugar
100ml (3½fl oz) mild-tasting soya drink
2 tbsp olive oil

For the topping:
300g (10oz) pointed cabbage
3 onions
1 carrot
200g (7oz) smoked tofu or smoked tempeh
2 tbsp rapeseed oil
1 tsp salt
½ tsp freshly ground white pepper
1 pinch of grated nutmeg
½ tsp caraway

Also:
200g (7oz) vegan crème fraîche
20g (¾oz) pine nuts

For a 30 x 40cm (12 x 15½in)
baking tray
Time: 20 mins prep
+ 1 hr proving + 45 mins baking

ONION TART

This tart is easy to make, filling, and tastes fabulous!

1 To make the dough, put 200ml (7fl oz) lukewarm water into a large bowl, crumble in the yeast, and use a balloon whisk to dissolve it in the water. Add the flour, olive oil, salt, and sugar and knead everything until you have a homogeneous dough. If the dough is too sticky, add a bit more flour. Wrap the dough in cling film and put it in the fridge for at least 1 hour.

2 For the topping, peel the onions and garlic. Slice the leek and onions into very fine rings, mince the garlic and dice the peppers. In a high-sided pan, melt the margarine over a moderate heat and sauté the leek, onions, and garlic. Add the diced pepper, dust with flour, and continue to sauté briefly. Gradually add the vegetable stock, oat cream, and almond butter and thicken slightly, stirring constantly. Season to taste with the yeast flakes, caraway, and salt and pepper.

3 Preheat the oven to 200°C (400°F/Gas 6). Line a baking tray with baking paper and roll out the dough on it. Prick the dough with a fork, then top with the leek and onion mixture. Bake the onion tart in the centre of the oven for 40–45 minutes until golden; it is ready if the crust sounds hollow when tapped. Remove and enjoy while still warm.

For the dough:
½ cube fresh yeast
350g (12oz) spelt flour with a high gluten content, plus extra for dusting
2 tbsp olive oil
1 tsp salt
1 pinch of fine cane sugar

For the filling:
8 onions
1 garlic clove
1 long leek
1–2 red peppers
4 tbsp vegan margarine
200ml (7fl oz) vegetable stock
300g (10oz) oat cream, well chilled
5 tsp almond butter
8 tbsp yeast flakes
1 tbsp caraway
1 tsp salt and freshly ground black pepper

TIP
If you really feel this dish could do with some "bacon", replace the peppers with 200g (7oz) chopped mushrooms, drizzle with 2 tbsp olive oil and soy sauce, and season with pepper. Spread on the tart before baking.

Makes 20 rolls
Time: 10 mins prep
+ 10 mins proving
+ 25 mins baking

SPEEDY WHOLEGRAIN ROLLS

When you need a recipe that is both quick to make and healthy, these Kamut® rolls are just perfect.
Kamut® is a nutrient-rich, ancient variety of wheat, which is once again being cultivated today.

For the dough:
1 cube fresh yeast
750g (1lb 10oz) Kamut®, freshly
   milled, or wholewheat flour
1 tsp sea salt
½ tsp ground allspice
1 tsp ground turmeric

Also:
3½ tbsp soya milk, for brushing
pumpkin seeds, poppy seeds, or
   sesame seeds, for sprinkling
   (optional)

1 Crumble the yeast into a bowl containing 500ml (16fl oz) lukewarm water, cover, and leave in a warm place for 10 minutes. Combine the flour, sea salt, allspice, and turmeric in a separate bowl. Whisk the yeast and water and add to the flour mixture. Knead everything until it forms a smooth dough.

2 Preheat the oven to 200°C (400°F/Gas 6) and line a baking tray with baking paper. Form around 20 equal-sized rolls from the dough, place them on the baking tray, brush with soya milk, and sprinkle with the seeds of your choice, if using. Bake the rolls in the centre of the oven for about 25 minutes. Remove and leave to cool slightly.

TIP
If you spray the rolls with water halfway through the baking time, this makes the crust nice and crunchy. These rolls are perfect for freezing.

For a 30 x 40cm (12 x 15½in) baking tray
Time: 45 mins prep
+ 55 mins proving + 35 mins baking

SAVOY CABBAGE TART

The combination of savoy cabbage, lentils, and tomatoes on a yeast dough is quite simply brilliant. You've just got to give it a try!

For the dough:
½ cube fresh yeast
350g (12oz) spelt flour with a high gluten content
1 tsp salt
1 pinch of fine cane sugar
2 tbsp olive oil

For the topping:
85g (3oz) dried brown lentils
400g (14oz) savoy cabbage
2 onions
2 garlic cloves
100g (3½oz) tomato purée
3½ tbsp red wine or vegetable stock
500g can chopped tomatoes
1 pinch of herbal salt and freshly ground black pepper
½ tsp sweet paprika
1 pinch of grated nutmeg
juice of ½ lemon

Also:
3½ tbsp olive oil, for frying

1 To make the dough, crumble the yeast into a bowl containing 200ml (7fl oz) lukewarm water. Cover and leave to prove in a warm place for about 10 minutes, then whisk until smooth with a balloon whisk. Combine the flour, salt, and sugar in a large bowl. Add the olive oil and the water and yeast mixture and work until you have a smooth dough. Cover and leave to prove in a warm place for 30–45 minutes, until doubled in size.

2 Meanwhile, for the topping, cook the lentils according to the packet instructions, strain off the water, and leave to drain. Remove the stalk from the savoy cabbage and slice into diamonds. Peel and finely dice the onions and garlic. Heat the olive oil in a large pan, add the savoy cabbage, and sauté over a high heat. Add the onions, garlic, and tomato purée and cook briefly. Quickly deglaze with red wine and add the tomatoes. Season to taste with the herbal salt, pepper, paprika, nutmeg, and lemon juice. Finally, fold in the lentils.

3 Preheat the oven to 200°C (400°F/Gas 6) and line a baking tray with baking paper. Knead the dough again vigorously and roll it out on the baking tray. Spread the cabbage and lentil mixture on top and bake in the centre of the oven for 30–35 minutes. Remove and enjoy while still warm.

SPINACH QUICHE

Macadamia nuts introduce a bit of bite and, along with the slightly astringent rocket, they combine beautifully with the delicate spinach and tomato filling.

1 To make the pastry, combine the flour, margarine, salt, sugar, and 8 tablespoons of water in a bowl until it forms a dough. Wrap the pastry in cling film and chill in the fridge for 1 hour. Grease a springform tin, roll out the pastry, and place it in the tin. Shape the pastry so that the sides come up to create a border.

2 Preheat the oven to 200°C (400°F/Gas 6). For the filling, melt the margarine in a large high-sided pan. Add the spinach and sauté over a low heat. Peel the onion and garlic, dice finely, and add to the spinach. Halve the cherry tomatoes and add these, too. Pour in the cream and add the vegan cheese.

3 Season the filling to taste with salt, pepper, and the nutmeg and pour it into the pastry case. Bake the quiche in the centre of the oven for 50–60 minutes until golden. Chop the macadamias and scatter over the quiche about 10 minutes before the end of the cooking time. Remove the quiche and release from the tin to serve, scatter with the rocket, and drizzle with olive oil.

For the pastry:
325g (11oz) spelt flour with a high gluten content
150g (5½oz) vegan margarine, plus extra for greasing the tin
1 tsp salt
1 pinch of cane sugar

For the filling:
20g (¾oz) vegan margarine
450g (1lb) spinach leaves (frozen)
1 onion
1 garlic clove
200g (7oz) cherry tomatoes
300g (10oz) spelt cream (available online)
100g (3½oz) vegan cheese, grated
1 tsp salt
½ tsp freshly ground black pepper
1 pinch of freshly grated nutmeg
25g (scant 1oz) macadamia nuts

Also:
100g (3½oz) rocket
2 tbsp olive oil, to drizzle

Makes 2 pides
Time: 25 mins prep
+ 45 mins proving + 15 mins baking

For the dough:
250g (9oz) plain flour
½ sachet dried yeast
1 pinch of fine cane sugar
1 tsp salt

For the topping:
200g (7oz) spinach leaves (frozen)
200g (7oz) broccoli florets (frozen)
100g (3½oz) peas (frozen)
1 pinch of salt
1 small onion
1 small red pepper
125g (4½oz) oat cream
freshly ground black pepper, to
    taste
2 tbsp pine nuts

Also:
3½ tbsp soya milk
50g (1¾oz) sesame seeds

PIDES

"Pide", a type of Turkish flatbread, is a delicious alternative to pizza and is just as versatile as its Italian relative when it comes to toppings. The main difference is the shape.

1 To make the dough, combine the flour with the yeast, sugar, and salt in a bowl. Add 150ml (5fl oz) water and knead into a smooth dough. Cover and leave to prove in a warm place for 30–45 minutes, until doubled in size.

2 Preheat the oven to 200°C (400°F/Gas 6) and line a baking tray with baking paper. Halve the dough and roll out each piece on the baking tray until they are about a finger-width thick. The dough should be oval, with the ends tapering to a point.

3 For the topping, briefly blanch the spinach, broccoli, and peas in slightly salted boiling water, then drain. Peel the onion and slice into thin rings, then deseed the pepper and chop it into cubes. Spread both pides with the oat cream and top with the vegetables, seasoning to taste. Scatter with the pine nuts, then gently fold up the edges of the dough. Brush the edges of the pides with some soya milk, scatter with the sesame seeds, and bake in the centre of the oven for 15 minutes. Remove and enjoy while still warm.

SPICED MUFFINS

Savoury muffins are a great snack, and also a fabulous dish to take to a celebration or garden party. The delicious spelt flour with smoked tofu offers something quite new in terms of flavour.

100g (3½oz) smoked tofu
1 red onion
3 tbsp rapeseed oil, for frying
200g (7oz) spelt flour
1 tsp baking powder
1 tsp salt
½ tsp freshly ground black pepper
1 tsp sweet paprika
150g (5½oz) vegan margarine
3½ tbsp unsweetened soya milk

1 Finely dice the tofu and the red onion. Heat the rapeseed oil over a moderate heat in a non-stick pan. Sauté the tofu and onion.

2 Preheat the oven to 180°C (350°F/Gas 4). Put paper cases into the moulds of a muffin tray. In a large bowl, combine the flour with the baking powder and the spices. Add the margarine in little blobs and rub it in with your fingers. Gradually incorporate the soya milk followed by the onion and tofu mixture.

3 Transfer the mixture into the muffin cases and bake in the centre of the oven for 20–25 minutes, until an inserted skewer comes out clean. Remove from the oven. You can eat the muffins warm or cold.

TIP
Instead of smoked tofu, you could also dice 100g (3½oz) sweet potato, marinade it in soy sauce, and sauté with the onions. For a really wonderful smoky aroma, try using smoked paprika.

CIABATTA ROLLS

Makes 8–10 rolls
Time: 10 mins prep + 65 mins proving + 20 mins baking

1 Pour 150ml (5fl oz) lukewarm water into a large bowl. Crumble in the yeast, cover, and leave in a warm place to rest for about 10 minutes. Combine with a balloon whisk, then add the flour, olive oil, salt, and sugar and knead until it forms a supple dough. Cover and leave to prove in a warm place for 30–45 minutes, until doubled in size.

2 Preheat the oven to 200°C (400°F/Gas 6). On a floured work surface, shape the dough into a long log and roll this out until it is about a finger-width thick. To make the ciabatta rolls, cut this sheet into 8–10 equal-sized rectangles, cover, and leave to prove for a further 20 minutes.

3 Either dust the ciabatta rolls with flour or, if you prefer a smooth surface, brush with soya milk. Bake the rolls in the centre of the oven for 15–20 minutes. Remove and leave to cool slightly.

20g (¾oz) fresh yeast
300g (10oz) plain flour, plus extra for dusting
2 tbsp olive oil
1 tsp salt
½ tsp fine cane sugar
3½ tbsp soya milk, for brushing (optional)

CARROT AND WALNUT BREAD

This delicious bread is a huge hit thanks to the nutritious spelt, the vitamin-rich carrots, and the healthy fats in the walnuts.

380ml (13fl oz) soya milk, plus extra for brushing
1 cube fresh yeast
100g (3½oz) walnuts
50g (1¾oz) vegan margarine, plus extra for greasing the tin
500g (1lb 2oz) carrots
2 tbsp lemon juice
750g (1lb 10oz) spelt flour with a high gluten content, plus extra for dusting
½ tsp salt
1 pinch of fine cane sugar

1 Gently heat the soya milk in a small pan over a low heat. Pour into a bowl, crumble in the yeast, cover, and leave at room temperature for about 10 minutes. Then stir until smooth with a balloon whisk.

2 Roughly chop the walnuts and toast them in a dry pan. Add the margarine and let it melt. Peel and finely grate the carrots, then mix them with the lemon juice in a bowl.

3 In a large bowl, combine the flour, salt, and sugar. Work in the milk and yeast mixture, then add the walnut and margarine mix plus the grated carrot. Knead everything until it forms a smooth and supple dough. Shape it into a ball, cover, and leave to prove in a warm place for about 40 minutes, until doubled in size.

4 Knead the dough vigorously once more and shape into 2 small loaves. Put these into a well-oiled loaf tin dusted with flour. Cover and leave for a further 20 minutes. Preheat the oven to 190°C (375°F/Gas 5). Make diamond-shaped incisions in the top of the bread and brush the top with a bit of soya milk. Bake in the centre of the oven for 40–45 minutes. Remove and leave to cool slightly.

TIP
Fill a small, heat-resistant bowl with water and put it in the oven during baking — this will make the bread even more moist.

PUMPKIN AND BUCKWHEAT ROLLS

1 In a large bowl, combine the flour with the cream of tartar, guar gum, sea salt, allspice, and aniseed. Add the linseed oil and mineral water and work everything together until it forms a smooth dough. Knead in the pumpkin seeds.

2 Preheat the oven to 200°C (400°F/Gas 6) and line a baking tray with baking paper. Divide the dough into 12 equal-sized portions and shape these into oval rolls. Place the rolls on the baking tray and make several diagonal incisions in the surface of each one. Bake the rolls in the centre of the oven for about 30 minutes. Remove and leave to cool slightly. These rolls are also perfect for freezing.

500g (1lb 2oz) buckwheat flour
1 tsp cream of tartar
2 tbsp guar gum
1 tsp sea salt
½ tsp ground allspice
1 pinch of ground aniseed
3½ tbsp linseed oil
500ml (16fl oz) carbonated mineral water
100g (3½oz) pumpkin seeds

For a 30 x 40cm (12 x 15½in) baking trays
Time: 20 mins prep
+ 55 mins proving + 25 mins baking

For the dough:
½ cube fresh yeast
350g (12oz) spelt flour with a high gluten content, plus extra for dusting
1 tsp salt
1 pinch of fine cane sugar
2 tbsp olive oil

For the sauce:
400g (14oz) passata
100g (3½oz) tomato purée
1 tbsp olive oil
1 tsp sea salt
½ tsp ground white pepper
1 pinch of fine cane sugar
1 squeeze lemon juice
1 tsp dried oregano

For the topping:
125g (4½oz) smoked tofu or vegan ham
8 pineapple slices
oregano leaves, for scattering

For the "cheese":
5 tbsp cashew nut butter
2 tsp yeast flakes
½ tsp salt
¼ tsp ground white pepper
1 squeeze lemon juice

HAWAIIAN PIZZA

1 To make the dough, put 200ml (7fl oz) lukewarm water into a bowl and crumble in the yeast. Cover and leave at room temperature for about 10 minutes, then use a balloon whisk to mix to a smooth consistency.

2 In a separate large bowl, combine the spelt flour, salt, and sugar. Add the olive oil and the yeast and water mixture and knead everything until you have a smooth dough. Cover and leave to prove for about 45 minutes, until doubled in size.

3 Meanwhile, for the sauce, stir together the passata, tomato purée, and olive oil. Season to taste with the sea salt, pepper, sugar, lemon juice, and oregano.

4 For the topping, roughly dice the tofu or ham. For the "cheese", stir 3 tablespoons of water into the cashew nut butter. Add the yeast flakes, salt, pepper, and lemon juice to taste.

5 Preheat the oven to 200°C (400°C/Gas 6) and line a baking tray with baking paper. Knead the dough vigorously once more and roll it out on a work surface dusted with flour until it is the size of the baking tray. Spread the tomato sauce, topping, and then the "cheese" over the dough. Bake the pizza in the centre of the oven for 20–25 minutes until golden brown. Remove, slice into 12 portions, and scatter with oregano leaves before serving.

TIP
This pizza also tastes delicious with pickled tofu, strips of pepper and onion, cherry tomatoes, mushrooms, or pumpkin.

For a 28cm (11in) long loaf tin
Time: 25 mins prep
+ 35 mins baking

PUMPKIN AND AMARANTH BREAD

Packed with nutrients, full of flavour, and super quick to bake, this tasty bread is ideal for those with a gluten intolerance.

1 Combine the flour with the amaranth, sesame seeds, baking powder, sea salt, turmeric, and guar gum in a bowl. Add the olive oil and mineral water and knead everything swiftly to form a smooth dough. Work in the pumpkin seeds.

2 Preheat the oven to 200°C (400°F/Gas 6). Transfer the dough to a greased loaf tin dusted with flour and bake in the centre of the oven for 30–35 minutes, until an inserted skewer comes out clean. Remove and leave to cool completely in the tin before turning out the loaf.

300g (10oz) buckwheat flour, plus extra for dusting
70g (2¼oz) puffed amaranth
100g (3½oz) ground sesame seeds
1 tsp baking powder
½ tsp sea salt
1 tsp ground turmeric
2 tsp guar gum
2 tbsp olive oil
500ml (16fl oz) carbonated mineral water
100g (3½oz) pumpkin seeds
vegan margarine, for greasing the tin

TIP
If you can't find ground sesame seeds, you can also use the whole seeds. If so, reduce the quantity of liquid slightly or adjust the amount of flour accordingly.

For a 24cm (9½in) springform tin (12–14 pieces)
Time: 30 mins prep
+ 1 hr chilling + 35 mins baking

For the pastry:
300g (10oz) plain flour, plus extra
   for dusting
1 tsp salt
150g (5½oz) vegan margarine

For the filling:
150g (5½oz) smoked tofu
1 garlic clove
10 spring onions
250g (9oz) soya cream
150g (5½oz) vegan cheese, grated
1 tsp salt
½ tsp freshly ground black pepper
½ tsp ground turmeric
1 pinch of grated nutmeg

Also:
3 tbsp rapeseed oil, for frying

QUICHE LORRAINE

1 For the pastry, combine the flour with the salt. Add the margarine in little blobs and work it in with your fingers. Gradually add 8 tablespoons water and combine everything until you have a smooth shortcrust. Wrap in cling film and put in the fridge for about 1 hour.

2 Roll out the pastry on a surface dusted with flour and transfer it into a springform tin lined with baking paper, or a well-greased quiche tin dusted with flour. Shape the pastry to create a 5cm (2in) high edge, press it down firmly, and prick with a fork. Put the tin in the fridge to chill while you prepare the filling.

3 Cut the smoked tofu into little cubes and finely chop the garlic. Slice the spring onions into thin rings. Heat the oil over a high heat in a non-stick pan and briefly sear the tofu cubes. Then reduce to a moderate heat and sauté the cubes until brown on all sides. Add the spring onions and finally the garlic and continue to cook briefly. Tip the contents of the pan onto a large plate lined with kitchen paper and let the excess fat drain away.

4 Preheat the oven to 180°C (350°F/Gas 4). In a large bowl, combine the soya cream with the cheese and season with the salt, pepper, turmeric, and nutmeg. Fold in the tofu mixture and spread everything over the quiche base, smoothing the surface. Bake in the centre of the oven for 30–35 minutes. Remove and enjoy while still warm.

TIP
Instead of shop-bought vegan cheese you can also use the cashew nut "cheese" from the Hawaiian pizza (see p216).

SWEET SNACKS

little treats — cupcakes,
traybakes, brownies, and more

Makes 10
Time: 10 mins prep

TIP
Nougat rapidly goes soft at room temperature or in your hands, which is why you should shape the mixture with teaspoons and then just round it off with your hands.

85g (3oz) flaked almonds
150g (5½oz) firm vegan nougat
30g (1oz) hazelnut brittle
80g (2¾oz) vegan dark chocolate
½ tbsp coconut oil

SUPER CRUNCHY ALMOND NUT BALLS

1 Toast the flaked almonds in a dry pan until golden brown. At the same time, heat the nougat in a heatproof bowl over a saucepan of simmering water. Finely crumble the toasted almonds into a small bowl and mix with the crumbled brittle. Work them into the nougat until evenly distributed and leave the mixture to chill for 20 minutes.

2 As soon as the nougat mixture is firm, but still malleable, form it into 10 balls. Let the balls chill once again for 20 minutes to firm up. Melt the dark chocolate with the oil in a heatproof bowl over a saucepan of simmering water. Use a fork to help you dip each ball into the chocolate, then set each on a wire rack. Put into the fridge immediately and keep them there until ready to eat or pack up.

Makes 10
Time: 15 mins prep
+ 1–2 hrs chilling

20g (¾oz) coconut oil
15g (½oz) crunchy vegan chocolate cereal
100g (3½oz) date paste (from a health food shop)
50g (1¾oz) ground hazelnuts
50g (1¾oz) ground almonds
30g (1oz) desiccated coconut

ENERGY BALLS WITH CHOCO POPS

1 Heat the oil in a small pan over a low heat. Slightly crush the chocolate cereal and mix with the oil, date paste, hazelnuts, and almonds to create an even mixture which you can shape easily.

2 Spread the desiccated coconut on a plate. Shape 10 balls from the date and nut mixture and roll them in the coconut, pressing it in gently to make it stick. Chill the energy balls for 1–2 hours.

FRUITY
MACADAMIA CREAM

Mellow vanilla seeds enhance this exquisite dessert that is prepared using the queen of nuts, puréed with succulent courgette, orange juice, and maple syrup until creamy. Served with vitamin-rich fresh berries and vegan white chocolate, this is a feast for the eyes and the mouth.

200g (7oz) macadamia nuts
1 small courgette
3½ tbsp apple juice (optional)
25g (scant 1oz) goji berries
    (optional)
2–3 tbsp orange juice
4–5 tbsp maple syrup
scraped-out seeds from
    ½ vanilla pod
pinch of salt
50g (1¾oz) blueberries
50g (1¾oz) raspberries
a few mint leaves (optional)
50g (1¾oz) vegan white chocolate

1 Soak the macadamia nuts in cold water for 12 hours. Peel the courgette, slice in half lengthways, and remove the seeds. Chop the remaining vegetable into coarse chunks. Bring the apple juice to the boil and add the goji berries (if using), then remove the pan from the hob and set aside.

2 Purée the macadamias, courgette, orange juice, maple syrup, vanilla seeds, and salt in a food processor until you have a smooth, creamy consistency. Drain the goji berries in a sieve and fold into the cream. Transfer the cream into 2 containers or jars with lids.

3 Scatter the blueberries, raspberries, and mint (if using) on top of the cream, then grate over the chocolate. Seal the containers and store in the fridge until ready for eating or transporting.

TIP
For an even more chocolatey touch, add 50g (1¾oz) cocoa powder to the cream.

Makes 10–12 pieces
Time: 25 mins prep
+ 30 mins cooking
+ 12 hrs resting

BAKLAVA

This tempting exotic delicacy with walnuts and pistachios is available all over the world, so naturally our lunchbox couldn't be without it. We all know how sweet things lift your spirits, so why not bring a bit of joy to your lunch breaks? While you're at it, pack up some extra portions of this vegan treat and spread a bit of happiness among your work colleagues, too.

1 To make the syrup, bring 500ml (16fl oz) water and the sugar to the boil in a saucepan. Stir in the lemon juice and remove the pan from the heat. Preheat the oven to 200°C (400°F/Gas 6). For the filling, melt the margarine in a small pan over a low heat. Then, finely chop the walnuts and pistachios and mix with the cinnamon.

2 Grease a baking tray. Lay a pastry sheet on the tray and brush with some melted margarine. Loosely lay another sheet on top and scatter some of the chopped nuts evenly over it. Continue layering pastry and nuts in this way, brushing with margarine (reserving 1–2 tbsp), and finishing with an upper layer of pastry. Press together the pastry edges so the filling cannot leak out. Cut into rectangles about 4 × 2cm (1½ × ¾in) and brush with the reserved margarine.

3 Bake the baklava in the centre of the oven for around 30 minutes until golden brown. Remove from the oven and spoon the syrup evenly over, allowing it time to absorb until you have used it all. Leave to stand for about 12 hours.

350g (12oz) golden caster sugar
juice of ½ small lemon
125g (4½oz) vegan margarine,
   plus extra for the baking tray
200g (7oz) walnuts
100g (3½oz) pistachios
1 tsp ground cinnamon
225g (8oz) yufka pastry sheets
   (from a Turkish store, or online),
   or filo pastry

TIP
Baklava will keep for 2 weeks in a well-sealed container. Don't store the pieces on top of each other!

PEANUT BUTTER AND PUFFED RICE CRISPIES

In a bowl, stir together the peanut butter, margarine, cinnamon, and agave syrup until smooth. Stir in the puffed rice until evenly distributed. Chill for around 15 minutes, then use your hands to form 10–12 little balls from the mixture. Transfer the balls to a well-sealed container and leave to rest for around 12 hours in the fridge, to set fully.

Makes 10–12
Time: 10 mins prep
+ 12 hrs chilling

70g (2¼oz) soft, slightly salted
   crunchy peanut butter
1 tbsp soft vegan margarine
½ tsp ground cinnamon
1½ tbsp agave syrup
15g (½oz) puffed rice

REDCURRANT AND COCONUT TURNOVERS

1 Preheat the oven to 220°C (425°F/Gas 7). Line a baking tray with greaseproof paper. Combine the flour, sugar, baking powder, bicarbonate of soda, desiccated coconut, and salt in a bowl using a balloon whisk. Stir together the soya milk and lemon juice and leave to stand for 5 minutes. Meanwhile, remove the stalks from the redcurrants. Stir the lemon zest into the milk and juice mixture and add this to the flour mixture with the margarine. Knead everything together until you have a smooth dough.

2 Roll out the dough on a floured work surface to create a large rectangle measuring about 30 × 28cm (12 × 11in). Spread the redcurrants evenly across half the dough sheet and fold the other half over, pressing the edges together. Slice the filled pastry slab into 5 equal-sized triangles. Press the dough firmly together again at the edges. Lay the turnovers on the baking tray and bake in the centre of the oven for around 15 minutes until they are light brown on top. Leave to cool on a wire rack.

3 Make the glaze (if using) by cooking the redcurrants in a small saucepan with 1 tbsp water until the berries pop open. Press them through a sieve. Sift the icing sugar into a bowl and gradually stir in the redcurrant juice until smooth. Brush the pockets with the glaze and sprinkle with desiccated coconut, or coconut flakes.

Makes 5
Time: 25 mins prep
+ 15 mins cooking

For the pockets
300g (10oz) white spelt flour,
   plus extra for dusting
100g (3½oz) golden caster sugar
1 tsp baking powder
¾ tsp bicarbonate of soda
30g (1oz) desiccated coconut
pinch of sea salt
100ml (3½fl oz) soya milk, or other
   plant-based milk
1 tsp lemon juice
150g (5½oz) redcurrants
finely grated zest of 1 unwaxed
   lemon
60g (2oz) soft vegan margarine

For the glaze (optional)
50g (1¾oz) redcurrants
150g (5½oz) icing sugar
desiccated coconut or coconut
   flakes, for sprinkling

Makes a 20cm (8in) loaf cake
Time: 30 mins prep
+ 50 mins cooking

SUPER-CHOCOLATEY SNACKING CAKE

This loaf cake certainly deserves its name! It contains not only cocoa powder, but also chocolate chips, and two further types of melted chocolate poured on top. Because one thing is clear: chocolate makes you really happy. Good for a wet Wednesday at work.

For the cake
vegan margarine, for the tin
150g (5½oz) plain flour, plus extra for the tin
100g (3½oz) white spelt flour
130g (4¾oz) golden caster sugar
1 tbsp vanilla sugar, or 1½ tsp vanilla extract
1½ tsp bicarbonate of soda
40g (1¼oz) cocoa powder
60g (2oz) vegan dark chocolate, chopped
4 tbsp soya milk, or other plant-based milk
2 tsp white wine vinegar
4 tbsp vegetable oil
220ml (7½fl oz) carbonated mineral water

For the icing
60g (2oz) vegan dark chocolate
1 tbsp soya cream, or other plant-based cream
20g (¾oz) vegan white chocolate

Special equipment
20cm (8in) long loaf tin

1 Preheat the oven to 180°C (350°F/Gas 4). Grease the loaf tin with margarine and dust with flour. Combine both types of flour, the caster sugar, vanilla sugar or extract, bicarbonate of soda, and cocoa powder in a bowl with a balloon whisk.

2 In a separate bowl, stir together the soya milk and vinegar, leave to stand for 10 minutes, then stir in the oil. Add the soya milk mixture to the flour mixture, then pour in the mineral water, mixing everything swiftly but delicately with a spoon to create a smooth consistency. Fold in the chopped chocolate. Immediately transfer the mixture to a 20cm (8in) long loaf tin and bake in the centre of the oven for 50 minutes. Remove and leave to cool on a wire rack.

3 To make the icing, chop the dark chocolate, add it to a heavy-based saucepan with the cream, and let it melt over a low heat. Ice the cake with this mixture and let it dry. Melt the white chocolate in a heatproof bowl over a saucepan of simmering water. Transfer it to a freezer bag, carefully snip off a corner and, with swift movements, draw decorative lines across the cake. Leave to set, then slice and pack up to take with you.

Makes 15 cubes (depending on size)
Time: 35 mins prep
+ 55 mins baking

FRUIT PUNCH CUBES

For the cake mixture:
675g (1½lb) plain flour
300g (10oz) fine cane sugar
1 tsp baking powder
zest of 1 organic lemon
350ml (12fl oz) rapeseed oil
2–3 tsp vanilla extract
450ml (15fl oz) carbonated mineral
    water
vegan margarine, for greasing the
    baking tray

For the filling:
125g (4½oz) vegan dark chocolate,
    plus extra for decorating
12 tbsp apricot jam
6 tbsp fine cane sugar
1 splash of rum

For the glaze:
300g (10oz) icing sugar
6 tbsp red wine
4 tbsp rum

1 Preheat the oven to 200°C (400°F/Gas 6). To make the cake mixture, combine the flour, cane sugar, and baking powder in a bowl. Add the lemon zest, rapeseed oil, and vanilla extract. Stir in the mineral water with a spoon and combine everything swiftly to a smooth consistency – it doesn't matter if there are a couple of little lumps remaining. Spread the mixture over a greased baking tray and bake in the centre of the oven for about 15 minutes. Then lower the temperature to 150°C (300°F/Gas 2) and continue to bake for an additional 40 minutes, until the cake is golden brown and an inserted skewer comes out clean. Remove from the oven and leave to cool completely.

2 To make the filling, melt the dark chocolate in a bain-marie. Crumble one third of the cake into a bowl and combine with the apricot jam, sugar, rum, and chocolate until you have a firm consistency. Slice the remaining cake in half crossways. Spread the chocolate and fruit mixture over the lower section, replace the top section, and press down firmly. Use a sharp knife to slice the cake into little cubes.

3 For the glaze, stir the icing sugar into the red wine and rum until smooth, then dunk the little cake cubes into the glaze. If you wish, grate some dark chocolate on top.

TIP
The consistency of the glaze should not be too thin, so add the liquid gradually to the icing sugar and stir until smooth. You can also briefly freeze the cubes before glazing, spike them with a fork, dunk in the glaze, then leave to dry and in the fridge. The cubes can be glazed twice, if desired.

PUDDING PRETZELS

1 To make the dough, mix the flour, cane sugar, salt, and yeast in a bowl. Melt the margarine and add to the dry ingredients along with the soya milk. Knead everything to form a smooth dough, cover, and leave to prove in a warm place for about 45 minutes, until it has doubled in size.

2 Roll out the yeast dough to the same size as the puff pastry sheet (approx. 42 × 24cm/16 x 9½in). Place the dough sheet on top of the puff pastry sheet and prick all over with a fork. Fold the sheet over once and roll it out again. Then, cut into 2cm (¾in) wide strips. Twist each strip as tightly as possible and form a pretzel shape from it. Place the pretzels on a baking tray lined with baking paper, cover, and leave to prove in a warm place for 20 minutes. Preheat the oven to 180°C (350°F/Gas 4) and bake the pretzels on the middle shelf for 20 minutes. Remove from the oven and leave to cool completely.

3 For the filling, mix 200ml (7fl oz) of the soya milk with the custard powder until smooth. Place the remaining soya milk in a pan and bring to the boil over a moderate heat, adding the vanilla seeds, cane sugar, and salt. Remove the pan from the heat and add the custard powder mix, then bring to the boil again, stirring constantly. Take the pan off the heat once more, add the margarine, and stir until smooth. Leave it to cool.

4 To make the icing, sieve the icing sugar into a bowl then stir in a bit of water and lemon juice until you have a smooth, thick mixture. Coat the pretzels with the icing. Put the custard filling into a piping bag with a large star nozzle attached and pipe it into all the hollow spaces of the pretzels.

For the dough:

350g (12oz) plain flour
20g (¾oz) fine cane sugar
1 pinch of salt
2 tsp dried yeast
30g (1oz) vegan margarine
200ml (7fl oz) soya milk
270g (9½oz) puff pastry (ready-made, see pp364–65)

For the filling:

500ml (16fl oz) soya milk with vanilla flavouring
60g (2oz) instant custard powder
seeds scraped from ½ vanilla pod
85g (3oz) fine cane sugar
1 pinch of salt
20g (¾oz) vegan margarine

For the icing:

125g (4½oz) icing sugar
squeeze of lemon juice

BLUEBERRY CUPCAKES
WITH FRUITY FROSTING

These cupcakes are great to take to a garden party, or just enjoy
as a stunning and delicious treat.

For the cupcakes:

250g (9oz) spelt flour
¾ tsp baking powder
¾ tsp bicarbonate of soda
½ tsp salt
110ml (3¾fl oz) soya milk
juice and zest of 1 small organic
    lemon
130ml (4½fl oz) agave syrup
2 large, very ripe bananas
250g (9oz) blueberries (frozen or
    fresh), plus 100g (3½oz)
    blueberries, for decoration

For the frosting:

150g (5½oz) soft vegan margarine
450g (1lb) icing sugar
3–4 tbsp blueberry syrup

1 To make the cupcakes, mix the flour with the baking powder,
bicarbonate of soda, and salt in a bowl. In a separate bowl,
stir together the soya milk and the lemon juice and zest and leave
to thicken for about 5 minutes. Stir in the agave syrup. Peel the
bananas and mash well using a fork. Add the bananas to the soya
milk and agave syrup mixture and stir everything well. Stir the
liquid ingredients into the dry ingredients. Finally, carefully fold
in the blueberries.

2 Preheat the oven to 180°C (350°F/Gas 4). Put paper cases into
the moulds in a muffin tray and divide the mixture between the
cases. Bake the cupcakes in the centre of the oven for 20–25 minutes,
until an inserted skewer comes out clean. Remove from the oven
and leave to cool completely.

3 To make the frosting, use an electric mixer on its fastest setting
to beat the margarine until it is creamy. Sift over the icing sugar
and continue to beat until well combined. Then, carefully stir in the
blueberry syrup to create a smooth cream. Transfer into a piping bag
with a star nozzle attached. To do this, fold over the end of the piping
bag and hold the bag low down, then fill with the icing. Scrape down
the contents, making sure there is no air in the bag. Pipe swirls of
frosting onto the cupcakes. Decorate the
swirls with blueberries. If you prefer a
little less sweetness, reduce the
frosting ingredients by half.

TIP
You can also
make these
cupcakes with other
fruits, like
raspberries. Replace
the blueberry
syrup with
raspberry
syrup too.

For a 20 × 20cm (8 x 8in) tin
(12–16 bars)
Time: 15 mins prep
+ 1 day soaking

POWER BAR
WITH MORINGA

This healthy bar gives you an instant energy boost thanks to the nutritious goji berries, high-protein moringa powder, and sweet dried fruit.

1 Soak the almonds in cold water the previous day, and soak the apricots about 30 minutes before starting preparation, then drain. Purée the almonds, apricots, dates, agave syrup, and vanilla seeds in a food processor to create a paste. Scrape the paste from the sides of the container between blitzes with a spatula.

2 Transfer the paste to a bowl, stir in the goji berries, moringa powder, and sea salt, and combine everything to make a cohesive mixture. Transfer the mixture to a tin lined with baking paper and press the mixture flat. Leave to chill thoroughly, then cut into bars.

175g (6oz) whole almonds
90g (3¼oz) dried apricots
100g (3½oz) dates (ideally Medjool)
2 tbsp agave syrup
seeds scraped from ½ vanilla pod
50g (1¾oz) goji berries
1 tbsp moringa powder (from a
    health food or vegan shop)
¼ tsp sea salt

TIP

The power bars will keep for about 2 weeks if stored in an airtight container in the fridge, so they are ideal for preparing in larger quantities so that you can stock up on supplies.

Makes 12 cupcakes
Time: 35 mins prep
+ 30 mins baking

STRUDEL CUPCAKES

If you like cupcakes and strudel, you will fall in love with this exquisite creation, which combines juicy fruits, delicate spices, and soft vanilla cream.

For the cupcakes:
250g (9oz) filo pastry (ready-made; see pp364–65)
80g (2¾oz) vegan margarine
50g (1¾oz) wholemeal breadcrumbs
50g (1¾oz) fine cane sugar
500g (1lb 2oz) apples or pears, plus extra for decorating
rum (optional)

For the topping:
250ml carton soya cream, suitable for whipping, well chilled
2 sachets cream stiffener
seeds scraped from 1 vanilla pod
1 tsp vanilla extract (optional)

1 For the cupcakes, first put paper cases into the moulds of a muffin tray. Cut a total of 24 squares from the filo pastry. Melt the margarine in a small pan over a moderate heat and use this to brush the pastry pieces on all sides, leaving some margarine over. In each muffin tin mould, lay 2 squares on top of one another with the points angled so that it look a bit like a star. Carefully press the pastry right down into the base and sides of each mould.

2 Preheat the oven to 180°C (350°F/Gas 4). Add half of the remaining margarine to a pan, heat it once again and sauté the breadcrumbs in it. Transfer to a bowl and mix with the sugar, then set aside. Peel and core the apples or pears and chop into little cubes. Fold the diced fruit into the breadcrumb and sugar mixture and drizzle with rum, if using.

3 Divide the fruitevenly between the muffin moulds; it is fine to pile it up a bit. Fold the corners of the pastry over the top, press down, and brush with some margarine. Bake the cupcakes in the centre of the oven for about 30 minutes, until golden brown. Remove from the oven and leave to cool completely.

4 For the topping, beat the cream with the cream stiffener, vanilla seeds, and vanilla extract, if using. Top the cupcakes with the cream and decorate with a piece of apple or pear before serving.

TIP

To prevent the decorative fruit pieces from going brown, drizzle them with some lemon juice or brush with clear vegan jelly.

For a 25 × 25cm (10 x 10in) baking tin
Time: 25 mins prep
+ 1 day soaking + 3 hrs chilling

RAW ALMOND BROWNIES

Brownies taste great when prepared American-style with lots of cocoa powder, sugar and fat, but this quickly prepared chilled version is also fantastic. Try it out some time!

For the brownies:
400g (14oz) whole almonds
100g (3½oz) raisins
200g (7oz) cocoa nibs (from a
   health food shop or organic
   supermarket)
100g (3½oz) cocoa powder
4 tbsp maple syrup
2 tbsp baobab powder (from a
   health food shop, vegan
   supermarket, or online retailer)
6 tbsp coconut oil

Also:
finely flaked coconut, for sprinkling

1 A day in advance, soak the almonds in plenty of water. Drain the almonds thoroughly, then grind them coarsely in a food processor. Add the remaining ingredients and process everything until you have a homogeneous mixture.

2 Sprinkle the base of the cake tin with coconut flakes. Transfer the mixture to the tin and smooth it out. Leave to stand for about 2–3 hours in the fridge, then turn it out on to a cutting board and cut into 9–12 pieces.

TIP
If the mixture is too dry and heavy, add some more water.

BERRY CRUMBLE

For a 22cm (8½in) springform tin (12 pieces)
Time: 35 mins prep
+ 45 mins baking

1 To make the base, combine both types of spelt flour in a bowl. Add the cane sugar, baking powder, bicarbonate of soda, salt, vanilla, and chickpea flour and mix everything together thoroughly. In a separate bowl, stir the soya milk, soya yogurt, and rapeseed oil until smooth. Set both mixtures aside.

2 For the filling, trim and then halve or quarter the strawberries depending on their size. Mix with the vanilla extract and sugar and then set aside.

3 To make the crumble, combine the flours in a bowl. Mix together with the baking powder and the sugar. Work in some margarine using your fingers until the mixture is a crumbly consistency. Add the vanilla extract. If the mixture is too firm, add a bit of soya milk.

4 Preheat the oven to 180°C (350°F/Gas 4). Line the springform tin with baking paper. Combine the dry and liquid ingredient mixtures for the base until you have a smooth dough. Put three-quarters of the dough into the tin and smooth it out. Then spread the berries over the top and press down gently. Spread the remaining dough mix over the top and smooth it out again. Scatter the crumble over the top.

5 Bake the crumble cake in the centre of the oven for 40–45 minutes, until an inserted skewer comes out clean. Remove the tin from the oven and serve the crumble while still warm with vegan vanilla ice cream or chilled soya cream.

For the base:
125g (4½oz) spelt flour
125g (4½oz) wholemeal spelt flour
115g (4oz) fine cane sugar
1 tsp baking powder
½ tsp bicarbonate of soda
½ tsp salt
¾ tsp vanilla powder
1½ tbsp chickpea flour
60ml (2fl oz) soya milk with vanilla flavouring
60g (2oz) soya yogurt with vanilla flavouring
3 tbsp rapeseed oil

For the filling:
600g (1lb 5oz) strawberries (or other berries)
1–2 tsp vanilla extract
20g (¾oz) fine cane sugar

For the crumble:
40g (1¼oz) spelt flour
40g (1¼oz) wholemeal spelt flour
½ tsp baking powder
4 tbsp fine cane sugar
45g (1½oz) vegan margarine
1–2 tsp vanilla extract
some soya milk with vanilla flavouring

Also:
vegan vanilla ice cream or whipped soya cream, to serve

Makes 12 small cream puffs
Time: 25 mins prep
+ 30 mins baking

For the cream puffs:
50g (1¾oz) vegan margarine
150g (5½oz) plain flour
50g (1¾oz) cornflour
1 pinch of salt
2 tbsp soya cream

For the filling:
350g (12oz) jar sour cherries,
   drained, liquid reserved
3 tsp vanilla extract
15g (½oz) cornflour
250ml carton soya cream, suitable
   for whipping, well chilled
1 sachet cream stiffener

CREAM PUFFS
WITH CHERRY FILLING

1 Preheat the oven to 200°C (400°F/Gas 6). To make the cream puffs, put 250ml (9fl oz) water into a pan with the margarine and bring to the boil. Combine the flour, cornflour, and salt then add to the pan, stirring constantly with a wooden spoon. Next add the soya cream. Cook the mixture for 1–2 minutes, until it forms a smooth and supple ball and a brown coating forms on the base of the pan.

2 Transfer the ball of dough into a piping bag with a star nozzle attached. Pipe 12 spirals onto a baking tray lined with baking paper, leaving a gap between each one. Bake in the centre of the oven for 30 minutes until golden brown. Do not open the oven during baking.

3 While the cream puffs are baking, prepare the filling. Put the cherries with 100ml (3½fl oz) of the reserved marinating juice and the vanilla extract into a pan and simmer briefly. Add some of the cherry juice to the cornflour and stir until smooth, then add to the cherry mixture. Continue to simmer until the mix has begun to thicken. Remove from the hob and leave to cool. Whip the cream with the cream stiffener.

4 Remove the cream puffs from the oven, leave to cool, then slice them open with a bread knife. Spread some cherries onto the bottom halves, then add a layer of cream, and, finally, replace the tops.

TIP
In autumn you can also make a particularly delicious filling using chestnut purée and whipped soya cream.

Makes 8 mini cakes
Time: 35 mins prep
+ 50 mins baking + chilling

For the mini cakes:
250g (9oz) plain flour
225g (8oz) fine cane sugar
1 tsp vanilla powder
½ tsp ground cinnamon
½ tsp grated nutmeg
½ tsp ground ginger
1 tsp baking powder
1 tsp bicarbonate of soda
1 tsp salt
3 very ripe bananas
250ml (9fl oz) coconut milk
120ml (4fl oz) rapeseed oil
1 tbsp cider vinegar

For the peanut frosting:
250g (9oz) soft vegan margarine
300g (10oz) smooth peanut butter
250g (9oz) icing sugar

Also:
80g (2¾oz) peanuts
flaked coconut
vegan caramel sauce (ready-made)

MINI PEANUT AND COCONUT CAKES
WITH CARAMEL

1 Preheat the oven to 160°C (325°F/Gas 3). For the mini cakes, combine the flour, cane sugar, vanilla, cinnamon, nutmeg, ginger, baking powder, bicarbonate of soda, and salt in a bowl. Peel the bananas and mash them to a purée with a fork. In a separate bowl, whisk the coconut milk and rapeseed oil, add the cider vinegar, and stir in the mashed bananas. Quickly stir the liquid ingredients into the dry ingredients until you have a smooth mixture, but take care not to stir too vigorously.

2 Line a 24cm (9½in) springform tin with baking paper, then transfer the mixture into the tin and smooth it out. Bake in the centre of the oven for 45–50 minutes, until an inserted skewer comes out clean. Remove from the oven and leave to cool completely. Slice the cake in half horizontally and use a glass (about 7cm/2¾in in diameter) to stamp out 16 little round cake bases.

3 For the peanut frosting, use an electric mixer on the highest setting to beat the margarine until creamy, then stir in the peanut butter. Sift over the icing sugar and, with the mixer on its lowest setting, carefully combine everything. If the frosting is too soft, simply chill it briefly.

4 Transfer the frosting into a piping bag with a round nozzle attached. Pipe blobs of the frosting mixture onto half of the little bases, then carefully put the remaining cake sections on top and finish with more generous dollops of frosting. Leave to chill. Toast the peanuts and flaked coconut in a dry pan, leave to cool, then scatter over the mini cakes. Drizzle over some caramel sauce and chill the cakes until you are ready to serve.

Makes 12 cupcakes
Time: 40 mins prep
+ 25 mins baking time

HAZELNUT CUPCAKES
WITH CHESTNUT AND VANILLA TOPPING

1 Preheat the oven to 180°C (350°F/Gas 4). To make the cupcakes, combine the flour, ground hazelnuts, cane sugar, and baking powder in a bowl. In a separate bowl, whisk together the soya milk and rapeseed oil. Add the liquid ingredients to the dry ingredients and combine.

2 Put paper cases into the moulds of a muffin tray and fill evenly with the mixture. Bake the cupcakes in the centre of the oven for about 25 minutes.

3 Meanwhile, make the frosting by cooking the soya milk, cornflour, vanilla extract, and cane sugar in a pan over a moderate heat, stirring constantly until you have a custard, then leave to cool. Beat vigorously with an electric mixer, then stir in the margarine. Add the chestnut purée and rum, sift over the icing sugar, and stir everything together until you have a smooth topping.

4 For the filling – both the fruity and the nutty version – whip the cream with some cream stiffener. For the fruity version, stir in the jam; for the nutty version stir in the hazelnut praline and vanilla.

5 Use a tablespoon to scoop out a slight hole in each cake (ideally in a single piece), put in some of the filling, then pop the piece of cake you hollowed out back on top. Transfer the frosting into a piping bag with a round nozzle attached and pipe swirls on top of the cupcakes. Decorate each one with some jam or finely chopped hazelnut praline.

For the cupcakes:
250g (9oz) plain flour
150g (5½oz) ground hazelnuts
200g (7oz) fine cane sugar
1 tsp baking powder
250ml (9fl oz) soya milk with vanilla flavouring
120ml (4fl oz) rapeseed oil

For the frosting:
250ml (9fl oz) soya milk
25g (scant 1oz) cornflour
2–3 tsp vanilla extract
50g (1¾oz) fine cane sugar
100g (3½oz) soft vegan margarine, beaten until creamy
675g (1½lb) chestnut purée
3 tbsp rum
3–4 tbsp icing sugar

For the filling:
250ml carton soya cream, suitable for whipping, well chilled
1 sachet cream stiffener
100g (3½oz) cranberry jam or hazelnut praline, plus extra for decorating
some vanilla powder, for the nutty filling

Makes 1 strudel (10–12 portions)
Time: 10 mins prep
+ 25 mins baking

SPEEDY POPPY SEED STRUDEL
WITH RUM RAISINS

This simple strudel is perfect for when you need to rustle up something quickly, but without compromising on taste. It will even win over your granny.

1 Remove the puff pastry from the fridge 10 minutes in advance. Combine the ground poppy seeds with the cane sugar and breadcrumbs in a bowl. Pour in the rum, then gradually stir in just enough soya milk to create a spreadable paste. This can vary depending on how finely ground the poppy seeds are.

2 Lay the puff pastry on the work surface and spread the poppy seed mixture evenly over it, leaving a gap of 3cm (1½in) all around the edge. Scatter the rum-soaked raisins over the poppy seed filling.

3 Preheat the oven to 180°C (350°F/Gas 4). Roll up the strudel from the long edge then fold in the ends, pressing them together slightly. Lift carefully onto a baking tray with the seam facing down and brush with soya milk. Bake the strudel in the centre of the oven for about 25 minutes. Remove and dust with icing sugar. Leave to cool completely.

For the strudel:
1 ready-made roll puff pastry (250g/9oz); see pp364–65
250g (9oz) ground poppy seeds
150g (5½oz) fine cane sugar
25g (scant 1oz) breadcrumbs
5 tbsp rum
4–6 tbsp soya milk, plus extra for brushing
50g (1¾oz) raisins, soaked overnight in rum

Also:
icing sugar, for dusting

TIP
To make an almond strudel, replace the poppy seeds with ground almonds and the soya milk with almond milk. Simply leave out the rum and raisins.

For a 20 × 20cm (8 x 8in)
baking tin
Time: 30 mins prep
+ 45 mins baking

For the brownie mix:
100g (3½oz) soft vegan margarine
225g (8oz) fine cane sugar
175g (6oz) silken tofu
150g (5½oz) plain flour
seeds scraped from 1 vanilla pod
60g (2oz) vegan cocoa powder
1 tsp baking powder
1 pinch of salt
60ml (2fl oz) soya milk
8 tbsp crunchy peanut butter
4 tbsp maple syrup
5 tbsp roasted peanuts
60g (2oz) vegan dark chocolate

For the topping:
150g (5½oz) vegan dark chocolate
1 tsp coconut oil
3 tbsp smooth peanut butter

BROWNIES WITH A PEANUT KICK

Really sinful – that's how brownies should be! Wallow in the intense chocolate flavour and creamy consistency. When combined with peanuts, the result is an unrivalled little chocolate cake.

1 Preheat the oven to 180°C (350°F/Gas 4). Line the baking tin with baking paper. To make the brownie mixture, beat the margarine until creamy using an electric mixer on its highest setting, gradually adding the sugar while beating. Squeeze out the silken tofu slightly and dab dry with some kitchen paper, then stir into the margarine and beat everything until you have a cohesive mixture.

2 In a separate bowl, combine the flour, vanilla seeds, cocoa powder, baking powder, and salt, then fold this into the margarine and tofu mixture. Mix the soya milk with 3 tablespoons of the crunchy peanut butter and the maple syrup and gradually stir this into the brownie mixture. Finally, chop the peanuts and dark chocolate and fold these in, too.

3 Put half the mixture into the tin and smooth it out. Then, put little blobs of the remaining crunchy peanut butter over the mixture before covering with the rest of the brownie mix. Smooth the surface and bake in the centre of the oven for about 45 minutes. Remove from the oven, leave to cool completely, and cut into 6–9 brownies.

4 Transfer the brownies to a wire rack with greaseproof paper under it. To make the topping, melt the chocolate and coconut oil over a bain-marie, stirring carefully, then spread this over the brownies. Don't worry if the chocolate runs down the sides a bit. Gently heat the smooth peanut butter and use a teaspoon to carefully make 3 little blobs, spaced slightly apart, on the still-warm chocolate. Finally, take a fairly thick wooden skewer and pull it through each blob to create a heart shape.

Makes 1 strudel (10–12 portions)
Time: 35 mins prep
+ 30 mins resting
+ 35 mins baking

For the pastry:
300g (10oz) plain flour, plus extra
    for dusting
1 pinch of salt
2 tbsp rapeseed oil
20g (¾oz) vegan margarine, for
    brushing

For the filling:
1.5kg (3lb 3oz) apples (such as
    Bramley)
110g (3¾oz) vegan margarine
50g (1¾oz) breadcrumbs
juice and grated zest, 1 organic
    lemon
50g (1¾oz) raisins
2 tbsp rum
50g (1¾oz) ground almonds
80g (2¾oz) fine cane sugar
1 tsp ground cinnamon
salt

Also:
icing sugar, for dusting

TIP
Warm strudel
goes beautifully
with cold vanilla
ice cream or
a delicious
vanilla sauce
(see p369).

APPLE STRUDEL

1 Boil some water in a pan. To make the pastry, sift the flour into a pile on the work surface and create a well in the centre. Add the salt, rapeseed oil, and 120ml (4fl oz) lukewarm water to the well and use your hands to combine everything to a smooth consistency. Don't overwork the ingredients, otherwise the pastry will become tough and be liable to tear. Shape it into a ball, brush with margarine, and transfer to a plate. Pour away the boiled water, and leave the pastry to rest for 30 minutes under the upturned warm pan.

2 Meanwhile, for the filling, peel and core the apples, divide into 8 sections, then slice into 5mm (¼in) thick crescents. Melt half the margarine in a pan and cook the breadcrumbs until they are pale brown. Mix the apples with the lemon juice and zest, the raisins, rum, almonds, sugar, cinnamon, and salt.

3 Preheat the oven to 200°C (400°F/Gas 6). Melt the remaining margarine and set aside. Press the ball of strudel pastry flat on a tea towel dusted with flour, then roll it out with a rolling pin. Lift up the pastry with both hands and stretch it out over the backs of your hands until it is paper thin and measures around 60 × 60cm (24 x 24in).

4 Brush about half the margarine in a thin layer over the pastry. Spread the breadcrumbs over the lower quarter of the pastry sheet, leaving a gap of 3cm (1½in) around the edge. Put the filling on top of the crumbs. Fold the outer edges of the pastry over the filling. Roll up the strudel, using the towel to help you and place it with the seam edge facing down on a baking tray lined with baking paper. Use a brush to carefully remove any excess flour.

5 Brush the rest of the melted margarine over the strudel and bake on the middle shelf of the oven for 30–35 minutes. Remove, leave to cool briefly, and serve while it is still warm. Dust generously with icing sugar before serving.

For a 30 x 40cm (12 x 15½in) baking tray
Time: 20 mins prep
+ 35 mins baking

For the cake mix:

350g (12oz) soya cream, suitable for whipping, well chilled
200g (7oz) fine cane sugar
1–2 tsp vanilla extract
4 tbsp powdered egg substitute, such as Ener-g Egg Replacer
150g (5½oz) plain flour
150g (5½oz) spelt flour with a high gluten content
1 pinch of salt
1 tsp baking powder

For the topping:

175g (6oz) vegan margarine
200g (7oz) fine cane sugar
1–2 tsp vanilla extract
6 tbsp soya milk
300g (10oz) flaked almonds

Also:

vegan margarine, for greasing the baking tray

"BUTTER" CAKE

1 Preheat the oven to 200°C (400°F/Gas 6). For the cake mix, use a balloon whisk to combine the soya cream, sugar, vanilla extract, and egg substitute until you have a smooth consistency. In a separate bowl, combine the flours, salt, and the baking powder. Beat both mixtures together until light and creamy. Spread the mixture over a well-greased baking tray and bake in the centre of the oven for 10 minutes.

2 Meanwhile, for the topping, cream the margarine with the sugar and vanilla extract. Mix in the soya milk and almonds and spread the sugar and almond mixture evenly over the pre-baked base. Cook the cake for a further 20–25 minutes, until the topping is golden brown. Remove from the oven, leave to cool, and cut into 16 pieces.

SWEET BREADS & ROLLS

doughy delights — buns, rolls, stollen, and more

EASTER BUNS

Traditional Austrian yeasted buns (*pinzen*) have inspired this recipe for particularly handy lunchbox sweet rolls. The deliciously light dough contains rum-flavoured raisins and is finished off with an apricot jam glaze, scattered with pearl sugar. Traditionally, the buns are eaten at Easter... but something this delicious deserves to be enjoyed throughout the year.

500g (1lb 2oz) flour, plus extra
   for dusting
1½ tsp finely grated unwaxed
   lemon zest
pinch of sea salt
70g (2¼oz) vegan margarine
20g (¾oz) fresh yeast
80g (2¾oz) golden caster sugar
2 tsp vanilla sugar, or 1 tsp vanilla
   extract
260ml (9fl oz) soya milk, or other
   plant-based milk, plus extra
   for brushing
100g (3½oz) Rum Raisins (see p37)
2–3 tbsp apricot jam
pearl sugar, for sprinkling

1 Mix the flour, lemon zest, and salt in a bowl. Add the margarine in little blobs and work it in using your fingertips. Create a dip in the mix, crumble in the yeast, and add both the sugar and the vanilla sugar or extract. Warm the soya milk in a pan over a low heat and pour it in. Dust with some flour and leave this starter mix, covered, in a warm place for about 10 minutes to prove.

2 Add the Rum Raisins to the starter mix and knead everything for 10 minutes until you have a smooth, yeasty dough. If the dough is too moist, add a bit of flour – but take care the dough doesn't become too firm. Cover and leave to prove in a warm place for 1 hour.

3 Preheat the oven to 180°C (350°F/Gas 4). Line a baking tray with greaseproof paper. Knead the dough briefly once again on a floured work surface and divide it into 6 portions. Shape each piece into a long, thick sausage, lay it on the baking tray, and leave to prove for 30 minutes.

4 Snip into the buns several times (see photo). Brush with soya milk and bake in the centre of the oven for 18–20 minutes. Remove from the oven, transfer to a wire rack to cool, brush with the apricot jam, and sprinkle with pearl sugar.

For a 28cm (11in) long loaf tin
Time: 20 mins prep
+ 1 hr baking

BANANA BREAD

1 Preheat the oven to 180°C (350°F/Gas 4). In a large bowl, combine the flour, cornflour, baking powder, bicarbonate of soda, salt, cane sugar, vanilla, cinnamon, and nutmeg.

2 In a separate bowl, stir the soya milk with the rapeseed oil and sour cream until smooth. Peel the bananas and mash well with a fork until you have a creamy mixture with an even consistency. Stir the banana purée into the soya milk mixture. Quickly stir together the liquid and dry ingredients with a spoon until there are no lumps in the mix.

3 Grease a loaf tin with margarine and dust with flour. Transfer the mixture to the tin, smooth the surface, and bake the bread in the centre of the oven for 50–60 minutes, until an inserted skewer comes out clean.

For the dough:
300g (10oz) plain flour, plus extra for dusting
2 tbsp cornflour
1 heaped tsp baking powder
1¼ tsp bicarbonate of soda
½ tsp salt
250g (9oz) fine cane sugar
1 tsp vanilla powder
½ tsp ground cinnamon
¼ tsp grated nutmeg
100ml (3½fl oz) soya milk
75ml (2½fl oz) rapeseed oil
200g (7oz) vegan sour cream (or soya yogurt with a squeeze of lemon)
4 medium, very ripe bananas

Also:
vegan margarine, for greasing the tin
icing sugar, for dusting

TIP
Banana bread tastes great plain or spread with some vegan margarine. To decorate, you can also make an icing by stirring together some icing sugar and banana juice. Spread this on top of the bread and scatter over some chopped banana chips to decorate.

For a 30cm (12in) springform tin
(16 pieces)
Time: 35 mins prep
+ 55 mins proving + 30 mins baking

SWEET RASPBERRY FLOWER

This sweet flower always creates a bit of a sensation at the breakfast table
or at a picnic with friends.

For the dough:
1 cube fresh yeast
50g (1¾oz) vegan margarine
600g (1lb 5oz) spelt flour, plus extra
    for dusting
100g (3½oz) fine cane sugar
2 tsp salt

For the filling:
300g (10oz) raspberries (frozen)
20g (¾oz) fine cane sugar
50g (1¾oz) flaked almonds
2 mint leaves

1 To make the dough, put 300ml (10fl oz) lukewarm water into a
bowl and crumble in the yeast. Cover and leave to prove at room
temperature for about 10 minutes, then use a balloon whisk to mix to
a smooth consistency. Melt the margarine in a small pan over a low
heat. Combine the flour, sugar, and salt in a bowl.

2 Add the water and yeast mixture to the dry ingredients along
with the margarine, and knead everything to create a smooth
dough. Cover and leave to prove in a warm place until it has
doubled in size.

3 Meanwhile, for the filling, heat the raspberries with the sugar over
a low heat. Purée, leave to cool briefly, then fold in the almonds.
Finely chop the mint leaves and add these, too.

4 Knead the dough through once more and divide into 3 equal-
sized portions. Roll these out on a floured work surface to create
roughly 1cm (½in) thick discs with a diameter of about 30cm (12in).
Place the first disc into the springform tin, cover it with half the
raspberry and almond mixture, then place the second disc on top
and cover with the remaining raspberry and almond mixture. Place
the third disc of dough on top to form the final layer – this does not
get a raspberry topping.

5 Preheat the oven to 180°C (350°F/Gas 4). Use a glass (about
8cm/3¼in in diameter) to create an indentation in the centre of the
dough disc. Cut the dough just as far as this glass indentation to create
16 equal sections. Now take hold of each piece (grasping the top and
bottom layers together) and twist it 3 times. Finally, fold over the outer
edges of 2 adjacent pieces, shaping them to be nice and round, and
join them together to create a "flower petal". Repeat to create 7 more
petals. Bake the flower in the centre of the oven for 30 minutes.

Makes 4 small 25cm (10in) loaves
Time: 35 mins prep
+ 12 hrs steeping
+ 90 mins baking

MUM'S SPICE BREAD

This traditional spiced loaf is wonderfully moist and nutty, with Christmassy flavours that smell delicious before it's even cooked.

1 One day ahead, grate the apples, including the skin, into a bowl. Add the walnuts, raisins, rum, cocoa powder, and sugar and combine everything thoroughly. Cover the bowl with cling film and leave to steep overnight in the fridge.

2 The following day, add the flour, baking powder, salt, and spices. Stir 3 tablespoons of water into the linseed, leave to swell for a few minutes, then add this to the mix. Knead everything until you have a smooth dough. The dough is very heavy, so it's important to knead in the flour vigorously with your hands to prevent lumps forming.

3 Preheat the oven to 180°C (350°F/Gas 4). Transfer the dough into four 25cm (1in) loaf tins and bake in the centre of the oven for 80–90 minutes. If the bread starts to go too brown, cover the surface with baking paper. Remove the loaves and leave to cool completely.

750g (1lb 10oz) apples
200g (7oz) walnuts
500g (1lb 2oz) raisins
2 tbsp rum
1 tbsp vegan cocoa powder
250g (9oz) fine cane sugar
500g (1lb 2oz) plain flour
½ tsp baking powder
¾ tsp salt
1½ tsp ground cloves
1½ tsp ground cinnamon
1½ tsp ground allspice
2 tbsp ground linseed

TIP
This spice bread tastes even more sophisticated if you combine two or three types of apple. If stored in a cool place, it will keep for several weeks and it can also be frozen very successfully.

Makes 1 Swiss roll (10–12 pieces)
Time: 30 mins prep
+ 15 mins baking

SWISS ROLL
WITH RASPBERRY CREAM

1 Preheat the oven to 180°C (350°F/Gas 4) and line a baking tray
with baking paper. To make the sponge for the Swiss roll, sift the
flour, cornflour, and baking powder into a large bowl. In a separate
bowl, stir together the soya yogurt, soya milk, soya flour, rapeseed oil,
and cane sugar until the sugar has dissolved as much as possible. Stir
the liquid ingredients into the dry ingredients and spread the mixture
over the baking paper. Bake the sponge in the centre of the oven for
12–15 minutes.

2 In the meantime, sprinkle sugar over a clean tea towel. Turn the
sponge out onto the towel while it is still hot and carefully pull
off the baking paper. Use the towel to carefully roll up the sponge
to create a Swiss roll shape, then leave to cool completely.

3 To make the raspberry cream, whip the soya cream using
an electric mixer on its highest setting for at least 3 minutes,
gradually adding the cream stiffener at the end as you whisk. Then
stir in the soya yogurt. Carefully fold in the raspberries and leave to
chill briefly. Unroll the sponge and spread with the raspberry cream,
leaving a 2cm (¾in) gap around the edges. Then roll it up again and
refrigerate. Serve dusted with icing sugar.

For the sponge mix:

225g (8oz) plain flour
2 tbsp cornflour
1 tsp baking powder
150g (5½oz) soya yogurt with vanilla
  flavouring
100ml (3½fl oz) soya milk
4 tbsp soya flour
2 tbsp rapeseed oil
150g (5½oz) fine cane sugar, plus
  extra for sprinkling

For the raspberry cream:

200g (7oz) soya cream, suitable for
  whipping, well chilled
1 sachet cream stiffener
150g (5½oz) soya yogurt with vanilla
  flavouring
150g (5½oz) raspberries

Also:

icing sugar, for dusting

TIP
If you prefer a
firmer consistency
for your cream
filling, let the yogurt
drain overnight in a
sieve lined with a tea
towel. The resulting
"cheese" can be folded
into the soya cream,
as described
above.

Makes 1 large Christmas stollen (15–20 slices)
Time: 25 mins prep
+ 55 mins proving
+ 70 mins baking

CHRISTMAS STOLLEN

For the stollen mix:

600g (1lb 5oz) plain flour
75g (2½oz) ground almonds
100g (3½oz) fine cane sugar
2 heaped tbsp soya flour
1 pinch of salt
250ml (9fl oz) soya milk
1–2 tsp vanilla extract
1 cube fresh yeast
1 tsp rum
50g (1¾oz) candied lemon peel
50g (1¾oz) candied orange peel
125g (4½oz) soft vegan margarine
100g (3½oz) raisins
100g (3½oz) marzipan

Also:

3 tbsp vegan margarine
250g (9oz) icing sugar

1 Combine the flour, almonds, cane sugar, soya flour, and salt in a large bowl. Heat the soya milk in a pan over a low heat, add the vanilla extract, then pour it into a separate bowl. Crumble in the yeast, cover, and leave to prove in a warm place for 10 minutes. Then stir until smooth with a spoon and add to the dry ingredients along with the rum, candied lemon peel, candied orange peel, margarine, raisins, and marzipan. Knead everything until well combined, cover, and leave to prove in a warm place for 45 minutes.

2 Preheat the oven to 180°C (350°F/Gas 4). Line a baking tray with a double layer of baking paper to prevent the stollen from becoming too dark on the bottom. Create a loaf shape from the dough using both hands, making a shallow depression lengthways down the centre. Bake the stollen in the centre of the oven for 60–70 minutes, turning it halfway through the baking time, until an inserted skewer comes out clean. Leave to cool completely on a wire rack.

3 To create the icing sugar coating, melt the margarine over a low heat and brush the stollen all over with it. First, dust the base of the stollen liberally with icing sugar, then do the same on the top. The stollen tastes best if left for a week to allow the flavours to develop.

TIP
Instead of working marzipan into the dough, you can give the stollen a marzipan filling. Roll 200g (7oz) marzipan into a log shape and place it in the centre of the stollen during the shaping process. Proceed as described in the recipe.

Makes a 24cm (9½in) tart / 12 pieces
Time: 40 mins prep
+ 50 mins proving
+ 45 mins cooking

For the dough

450g (1lb) strong white flour, plus extra for dusting
50g (1¾oz) cocoa powder
pinch of sea salt
½ tsp finely grated zest of 1 unwaxed lemon
180g (6oz) golden caster sugar
70g (2¼oz) soft vegan margarine, plus more for the tin
220ml (7½fl oz) soya milk, or other plant-based milk
20g (¾oz) fresh yeast

For the custard

380ml (13fl oz) soya milk, or other plant-based milk
50g (1¾oz) golden caster sugar
75g sachet of vegan vanilla custard powder

For the filling

60g (2oz) vegan dark chocolate
250g (9oz) raspberries
20g (¾oz) cornflour
20g (¾oz) icing sugar

For the decoration (optional)

50g (1¾oz) vegan dark chocolate
1 tsp coconut oil
50g (1¾oz) raspberries

Special equipment

24cm (9½in) springform cake tin

RASPBERRY AND CHOCOLATE
"WINDMILL"

1 To make the dough, mix the flour, cocoa powder, salt, lemon zest, and half the sugar in a bowl using a balloon whisk. Add blobs of margarine and rub it in with your fingers. Make a dip in the centre of the mix. Heat the soya milk in a pan over a low heat, pour it into the dip, and crumble in the yeast. Sprinkle the remaining sugar over the milk and yeast mixture and dust with a bit of flour. Cover and leave this starter mix to prove in a warm place for around 10 minutes. Stir once again and knead for 10 minutes until you have a smooth dough. Cover and leave to prove in a warm place for 40 minutes.

2 Meanwhile, make the custard by bringing half the soya milk to the boil with the sugar in a pan over a high heat. Stir the custard powder into the remaining milk until smooth. As soon as the milk boils, remove the pan from the heat and add the custard powder and milk mixture, stirring constantly. Return the pan to the heat and bring everything to the boil once again, continuing to stir all the time. Remove from the heat and leave to cool. Give it a stir every so often to prevent a skin forming.

3 Grease a 24cm (9½in) springform cake tin. Roughly chop the chocolate for the filling. Roll out the dough on a floured work surface to form a rectangle measuring about 40 × 30cm (16 × 12in). Spread the vanilla custard over the dough and then sprinkle over the chocolate chunks and raspberries. Mix together the cornflour and icing sugar and sift over.

4 Preheat the oven to 180°C (350°F/Gas 4). Cut the slab of dough into 4cm (1½in) wide strips. Roll one of the strips into a snail shape and place this in the centre of the tin. Arrange the other strips around it, working out in a spiral towards the edge of the tin. Bake in the centre of the oven for 40–45 minutes. If it looks too dark after 15 minutes, cover with a sheet of baking parchment. Remove and leave to cool on a wire rack.

5 Chop the chocolate for decorating (if using), and melt it with the coconut oil in a heatproof bowl suspended over a saucepan of simmering water. Stir well. Decorate the cake with the melted chocolate and raspberries.

For a 28cm (11in) long loaf tin
Time: 20 mins prep + 50 mins
baking + 10 mins cooling

DELICIOUS
ALMOND BUTTER
WHOLEGRAIN BREAD

A bread or a cake? Who cares, it's fun to make, healthy, and it tastes
great plain, with a dollop of soya cream, or spread with almond butter.

350g (12oz) wholemeal flour, plus
    extra for dusting
250g (9oz) fine cane sugar
1 pinch of salt
1 pinch of ground cinnamon
200g (7oz) ground almonds
1½ tsp bicarbonate of soda
1½ tsp baking powder
60ml (2fl oz) soya milk
1 tbsp cider vinegar
2–3 tsp vanilla extract
60ml (2fl oz) almond milk
60ml (2fl oz) rapeseed oil
5 tbsp almond butter
grated zest of 1 small organic lemon
250ml (9fl oz) carbonated mineral
    water
vegan margarine, for greasing the
    tin

1 Preheat the oven to 180°C (350°F/Gas 4). Combine the flour,
sugar, salt, cinnamon, almonds, bicarbonate of soda, and
baking powder in a bowl. In a separate bowl, whisk the soya milk
with the cider vinegar, add the vanilla extract, and leave to thicken
for 5 minutes. Stir in the almond milk, rapeseed oil, almond butter,
and lemon zest until smooth. Quickly combine the liquid and dry
ingredients with a large spoon. Then slowly add the mineral
water and stir the mix again (not too vigorously) with the
spoon until smooth.

2 Grease a loaf tin with margarine and dust with flour.
Transfer the mixture to the tin, smooth the surface, and bake in
the centre of the oven for about 50 minutes, until an inserted skewer
comes out clean.

3 Remove from the oven
and leave the bread
to cool in the tin for
about 10 minutes.
Use a knife to gently
loosen the loaf
around the edges,
knock it out of
the tin, and leave
to cool completely
on a wire rack.

TIP
Transform the
bread into more of a
cake by topping it with an
almond butter and dark
chocolate glaze. To do this,
spread the bread with almond
butter and leave to dry
a little. Melt 150g (5½oz)
vegan chocolate with 1 tbsp
coconut oil and spread this
over the almond butter layer.
Optionally, toast a
handful of flaked almonds
in a dry pan and
scatter over
top.

For a 30cm (12in) long loaf tin
Time: 12 hrs soaking
+ 30 mins prep + 75 mins proving
+ 1 hr baking

PUMPKIN STOLLEN

1 Soak the raisins overnight in rum. Dice the pumpkin and cook it in a pan with the soya milk over a moderate heat until soft. Process it to a purée with a hand blender and leave to cool slightly. In a large bowl, combine the flour, sugar, dried yeast, lemon zest, vanilla, ginger, allspice, and salt.

2 Melt the margarine in a small pan and stir it into the pumpkin purée. Use floured hands to work the purée into the dry ingredients, kneading everything to create a supple dough. Incorporate the rum-raisins and, depending on how moist or dry the dough is, add some extra soya milk or flour, as required. Cover and leave to prove for about 45 minutes in a warm place.

3 Preheat the oven to 180°C (350°F/Gas 4). Knead the dough once again. Grease a large loaf tin, put the dough inside, and leave to prove for about another 30 minutes. Bake the stollen in the centre of the oven for about 1 hour. If the stollen begins to go too brown, cover it with foil. Remove and leave it to cool completely.

100g (3½oz) raisins
rum
300g (10oz) Hokkaido pumpkin, or small red squash
130ml (4½fl oz) soya milk
500g (1lb 2oz) plain flour, plus extra for your hands
180g (6¼oz) fine cane sugar
1 sachet dried yeast
grated zest of 1 organic lemon
1 tsp vanilla powder
½ tsp ground ginger
½ tsp ground allspice
1 pinch of salt
100g (3½oz) vegan margarine, plus extra for greasing the tin

TIP

You can leave the skin of the Hokkaido pumpkin on as it tastes really delicious. Eat the stollen plain, dusted with icing sugar, or spread with vegan margarine.

CAKES & TARTS

delicious bakes for an afternoon
treat or a decadent dessert

For a 22cm (8½in) springform tin
Time: 35 mins prep
+ 1 hr chilling + 45 mins baking

MARBLED CHOCOLATE CHEESECAKE

This dark shortcrust pastry with a hint of coffee, delicious vanilla yogurt filling, and a delicate crumble is pretty hard to resist.

1 For the base, combine the flour, sugar, baking powder, cornflour, cocoa powder, instant coffee, and salt in a bowl. Add the margarine in little blobs and work it in with your fingers, then add the vanilla extract. If the pastry is too firm, add a few drops of water. Wrap the pastry in cling film and chill for 1 hour in the fridge.

2 Preheat the oven to 160°C (325°F/Gas 3) and line the springform tin with baking paper. Thinly cover the base of the tin with three quarters of the pastry – press it down slightly and bring up the sides so it stands about 4cm (1½in) high. Prick the pastry with a fork and chill it again.

3 To make the filling, stir together the cornflour and soya milk with a balloon whisk until smooth. Stir in the soya yogurt, sugar, vanilla extract, and lemon juice and zest. In a small pan, melt the margarine over a low heat and, when it is lukewarm (not hot), combine it with the soya and sugar cream. Spread the mixture smoothly over the pastry. From the remaining pastry, use your fingers to pull off little crumble pieces and distribute these over the filling mixture.

4 Bake in the centre of the oven for 45 minutes, until an inserted skewer comes out clean. Remove the tin from the oven and leave to cool completely.

For the base:
200g (7oz) plain flour
100g (3½oz) fine cane sugar
2 tsp baking powder
2 tbsp cornflour
4 tbsp vegan cocoa powder
1 tbsp instant coffee granules, finely ground
1 pinch of salt
125g (4½oz) vegan margarine
1–2 tsp vanilla extract

For the filling:
40g (1¼oz) cornflour
5 tbsp soya milk with vanilla flavouring
500g (1lb 2oz) soya yogurt with vanilla flavouring
110g (3¾oz) fine cane sugar
1–2 tsp vanilla extract
juice and zest of 1 organic lemon
125g (4½oz) vegan margarine

TIP
For a really lavish cake, double the ingredients for the topping and use a larger springform (24 or 26cm/8 or 10½in in diameter), and bake for about 1 hour.

For a 30cm (12in) long loaf tin
Time: 25 mins prep
+ 1 hr baking + 15 mins cooling

QUICK MARBLE CAKE

Hey presto – and it's ready! Enjoy this easy-to-make sponge cake with an attractive striped appearance.

1 Carefully grease a large loaf tin and dust with flour. To make the pale cake mix, combine the flour, sugar, and bicarbonate of soda in a bowl. In a separate bowl, whisk the soya milk, lemon zest, and corn oil, add the vanilla extract, then fold these into the dry ingredients. Take care not to stir too vigorously.

2 Preheat the oven to 180°C (350°F/Gas 4). For the dark cake mix, combine the flour, sugar, bicarbonate of soda, and cocoa powder. In a separate bowl whisk the corn oil and soya milk, add the vanilla extract, and fold these into the dry ingredients.

3 Put 3 tablespoons of the pale mix into the centre of the tin, then add 3 tablespoons of the dark mix on top and continue in this manner until all the cake mix has been used up. Bake the cake in the centre of the oven for 50–60 minutes, until an inserted skewer comes out clean. Leave the cake in the tin and put it on a wire rack to cool for about 15 minutes before turning it out of the tin.

For the pale cake mix:
250g (9oz) plain flour, plus extra
    for dusting
100g (3½oz) fine cane sugar
1 tsp bicarbonate of soda
290ml (9½fl oz) soya milk
grated zest of 1 organic lemon
150ml (5fl oz) corn oil
2–3 tsp vanilla extract

For the dark cake mix:
250g (9oz) plain flour
90g (3¼oz) fine cane sugar
1 tsp bicarbonate of soda
25g (scant 1oz) vegan cocoa powder
150ml (5fl oz) corn oil
340ml (11½fl oz) soya milk
2–3 tsp vanilla extract

Also:
vegan margarine, for greasing
    the tin

For a 30 x 40cm (12 x 15½in) baking tray
Time: 35 mins prep
+ 30 mins baking

DANUBE WAVE CAKES

For the cake mix:
250g (9oz) soft vegan margarine
1–2tsp vanilla extract
250g (9oz) fine cane sugar
500g (1lb 2oz) plain flour
1 tsp baking powder
4 tbsp soya flour
300ml (10fl oz) soya milk
4 tbsp vegan cocoa powder
675g (1½lb) sour cherries, pitted
    and drained

For the cream:
750ml (1¼ pints) soya milk with
    vanilla flavouring
80g (2¾oz) instant custard with
    vanilla flavouring
75g (2½oz) fine cane sugar
250g (9oz) soft vegan margarine

Also:
200g (7oz) vegan dark chocolate

1 To make the cake, use an electric whisk to cream the margarine with the vanilla extract and sugar. In a separate bowl, combine the flour, baking powder, and soya flour, then fold this into the margarine and sugar mixture. Finally, stir in the soya milk.

2 Preheat the oven to 200°C (400°F/Gas 6). Spread half the mixture over a baking tray lined with baking paper. Fold the cocoa powder into the remaining mixture and spread this over the pale cake mix. Draw a fork through both mixtures to create a slightly marbled effect. Scatter the sour cherries evenly over the cake, pressing them down slightly. Bake the cake in the centre of the oven for 25–30 minutes. Remove and leave to cool completely.

3 Meanwhile, for the cream, take a few tablespoons of the soya milk and mix this with the custard powder, then stir in the sugar. Bring the remaining soya milk to the boil over a moderate heat, remove the pan from the hob, stir in the custard paste, then bring everything back to the boil, stirring constantly. Leave the custard to cool to room temperature.

4 Beat the margarine until it is fluffy, then stir in the custard a spoonful at a time. Spread this creamy mixture over the cake and smooth the surface. Melt the dark chocolate in a bain-marie, let it cool slightly, and swiftly spread it over the creamy layer. Keep the cake chilled until ready to serve, then cut into 12 pieces.

For a 24cm (9½in) springform tin (12 pieces)
Time: 45 mins prep
+ 65 mins baking
+ at least 12 hrs chilling

BLACK FOREST GATEAU

Enjoy the vegan version of this classic recipe. Black Forest gateau is renowned for its delicate shortcrust, flavour-packed cherries, dark sponge, and delicious cream.

1 For the filling, whip the soya cream with an electric whisk on its highest setting for 2 minutes. Beat in the cream stiffener, 100ml (3½fl oz) of the kirsch, and the vanilla. Set in the fridge to chill. Preheat the oven to 180°C (350°F/Gas 4). For the shortcrust, combine the flour, hazelnuts, and sugar. Use your fingers to work in the margarine then mix in the vanilla extract. Transfer to a springform tin lined with baking paper. Smooth out the pastry and prick all over with a fork. Bake in the oven for 20–25 minutes. Leave to cool completely.

2 For the sponge mixture, combine the flour, sugar, baking powder, salt, and bicarbonate of soda. Sift in the cocoa powder. Stir the cider vinegar into the soya milk, leave to thicken for 5 minutes, then stir in the rapeseed oil. Quickly combine the liquid and dry ingredients with a large spoon. Transfer to a springform tin lined with baking paper and bake in the centre of the oven for 40 minutes. Leave to cool completely, then slice in half horizontally. Put a cake ring securely around the shortcrust base.

3 For the filling, drain the cherries but retain the juice. Mix half the juice with the cornflour, sugar, and vanilla extract. Bring the other half to the boil, remove the pan from the hob, stir in the cornflour and juice mixture, then return to the boil, while stirring. Remove from the heat again. Stir in the cherries. Once the mixture has cooled slightly, spread it over the pastry base.

4 Place one of the sponge layers on top of the cherries and press down slightly. Drizzle the sponge with 2 tablespoons kirsch, then spread one third of the cream on top. Cover with the second sponge layer, drizzle with 2 tablespoons kirsch, spread with cream, and chill briefly. Release from the cake ring and cover the sides with cream. Transfer the remaining cream to a piping bag with a star nozzle attached and pipe 12 swirls on top. Top each swirl with an Amarena cherry. Scatter chocolate flakes over top and chill overnight.

For the filling and decoration:
900ml (1½ pints) soya cream, suitable whipping, well chilled
10 tbsp cream stiffener
140ml (4¾fl oz) kirsch
1 tbsp ground vanilla
720g jar of cherries
30g (1oz) cornflour
2 tbsp fine cane sugar
1–2 tsp vanilla extract
12 Amarena cherries
vegan dark chocolate flakes

For the shortcrust:
70g (2¼oz) plain flour
80g (2¾oz) ground hazelnuts
50g (1¾oz) fine cane sugar
70g (2¼oz) vegan margarine
1–2 tsp vanilla extract

For the sponge mix:
300g (10oz) plain flour
200g (7oz) fine cane sugar
2 tsp baking powder
½ tsp salt
2 tsp bicarbonate of soda
30g (1oz) vegan cocoa powder
1½ tbsp cider vinegar
400ml (14fl oz) soya milk
150ml (5fl oz) rapeseed oil

For a 24cm (9½in) springform tin
Time: 35 mins prep
+ 65 mins baking

CARROT CAKE
WITH CHOCOLATE AND CREAM CHEESE TOPPING

Here, the carrots go beautifully with the sweet white chocolate and cream cheese in the topping. Pistachios add the perfect finishing touch to the whole combination.

For the cake:
400g (14oz) plain flour
2 tsp bicarbonate of soda
350g (12oz) fine cane sugar
seeds scraped from 1 vanilla pod
1 tsp salt
2 tsp ground cinnamon (slightly heaped)
2 tsp baking powder
400g (14oz) soya yogurt
200ml (7fl oz) corn oil
400g (14oz) carrots, very finely grated

For the topping:
100g (3½oz) vegan white chocolate
80g (2¾oz) soft vegan margarine
125g (4½oz) vegan cream cheese
50g (1¾oz) icing sugar
grated zest of 1 organic lemon

Also:
100g (3½oz) pistachios, chopped

1 Preheat the oven to 180°C (350°F/Gas 4). To make the cake, combine the flour, bicarbonate of soda, cane sugar, vanilla seeds, salt, and cinnamon in a medium-sized bowl. Sift in the baking powder and stir everything together again.

2 In a separate larger bowl, use a balloon whisk to mix the soya yogurt and corn oil, then vigorously stir in the grated carrot using a spoon. Add the dry ingredients in two stages, using a large spoon to mix everything to an even consistency and only stirring as much as required to combine the carrot mixture with the flour.

3 Line the springform tin with baking paper. Transfer the cake mixture into the tin and smooth the surface. Bake the cake in the centre of the oven for 65 minutes. Remove and leave to cool completely.

4 To make the topping, melt the white chocolate in a bain-marie then leave to cool to room temperature. Use an electric whisk on its fastest setting to beat the margarine and the cream cheese. Sift over the icing sugar and mix this in along with the lemon zest, using the whisk on a moderate setting. Gradually pour in the chocolate, incorporating it into the mixture with the whisk on a low setting. The result should be a smooth, creamy, soft topping, which will firm up in the fridge. Spread the topping over the carrot cake and smooth the surface. Scatter with the chopped pistachios and chill the carrot cake until ready to serve.

For a 23 × 23cm (9 x 9in) baking tin
Time: 30 mins prep
+ 40 mins baking

CHOCOLATEY FRUIT CAKE

Chocolate lovers and fruit fans both get their money's worth here. This chocolate cake can be made with almost any type of fruit or berries. Enveloped in a delicate chocolate glaze and topped with toasted almonds, this is a truly special creation.

For the cake:
500g (1lb 2oz) seasonal fruit
470ml (15½fl oz) soya milk
3 tsp cider vinegar
200g (7oz) fine cane sugar
1–2 tsp vanilla extract
270g (9½oz) wholemeal spelt flour
60g (2oz) vegan cocoa powder, sifted
1½ tsp bicarbonate of soda
1 tsp baking powder
½ tsp salt
130ml (4½fl oz) sunflower oil

Also:
150g (5½oz) vegan dark chocolate
1 tbsp coconut oil
flaked almonds, for scattering

1 Preheat the oven to 180°C (350°F/Gas 4). To make the cake, first chop the fruit into pieces. In a bowl, whisk the soya milk with the cider vinegar and leave to thicken for 5 minutes. Stir in the sugar and vanilla extract with a balloon whisk. In a separate bowl, combine the flour, cocoa powder, bicarbonate of soda, baking powder, and salt. Fold the dry ingredients into the liquid mixture and combine until you have a smooth consistency. Next, stir in the sunflower oil and combine well with the mixture. Finally fold in the fruit.

2 Transfer the mixture to a tin lined with baking paper, smooth the surface, and bake in the centre of the oven for about 40 minutes, until an inserted skewer comes out clean. Remove and leave to cool completely.

3 Melt the chocolate with the coconut oil in a bain-marie, stir until smooth, and cover the cake all over. Carefully toast the flaked almonds in a dry pan and scatter them over the still molten chocolate. Slice the cake into about 16 pieces to serve.

TIP
It is important to wash and chop the fresh fruit at the start, because the mix shouldn't be left to stand for too long. If you use tinned or frozen fruit, this will need to be thoroughly drained or squeezed so the cake doesn't go soggy. If necessary, reduce the quantity of fruit slightly.

For a 30 x 40cm (12 x 15½in) baking tray
Time: 40 mins prep
+ 1 hr proving + 50 mins baking

PEAR CAKE
WITH MARZIPAN CRUMBLE

Juicy pears on a pale base, covered with a delicate marzipan crumble – a really luxurious tray bake!

1 Prepare the filling by peeling and quartering the pears, then remove the cores and chop the pears into cubes. Place the fruit in a pan, add the sugar and vanilla extract, and cook for 8–10 minutes over a moderate heat initially, then reducing to a low heat. Leave to cool.

2 For the base, combine the flour, sugar, and salt in a bowl. Gently heat the soya milk in a small pan over a low heat and add the vanilla extract. Pour this into a separate bowl, finely crumble the yeast into the milk, and leave to stand for about 10 minutes.

3 In the meantime, add blobs of the margarine to the flour mixture and swiftly work them in until the flour has completely absorbed the fat. Stir the milk and yeast mixture until smooth, then knead this in; the yeast dough should be nice and smooth. Cover and leave to prove in a warm place for about 30 minutes.

4 Line a baking tray with baking paper and roll the dough out on it, creating a slight rim around the edge. Leave the dough to prove for about 20 minutes.

5 Preheat the oven to 180°C (350°F/Gas 4). To make the crumble, mix the flour with the sugar. Add the margarine, and marzipan in little pieces, working them in with your fingers to create a crumbly texture. Add the vanilla extract. Spread the pear compote evenly over the base. Scatter the crumble over the filling and bake the cake in the centre of the oven for 40–50 minutes. Remove from the oven and leave to cool. Cut into 12 pieces.

For the filling:
1.5kg (3lb 3oz) pears
4 tbsp fine cane sugar
2–3 tsp vanilla extract

For the base:
400g (14oz) spelt flour
90g (3¼oz) fine cane sugar
1 pinch of salt
200ml (7fl oz) soya milk
1–2 tsp vanilla extract
½ cube fresh yeast
80g (2¾oz) vegan margarine

For the marzipan crumble:
180g (6¼oz) spelt flour
3 tbsp cane sugar
100g (3½oz) vegan margarine
200g (7oz) marzipan
1–2 tsp vanilla extract

TIP
Try sprinkling with icing sugar to serve. This cake tastes delicious served warm with some vegan vanilla ice cream.

For a 26cm (10½in) springform tin (12 pieces)
Time: 40 mins prep
+ 1 hr chilling + 1 hr baking

For the base:
250g (9oz) plain flour
125g (4½oz) fine cane sugar
½ tsp baking powder
150g (5½oz) vegan margarine
1–2 tsp vanilla extract

For the filling:
800g (1¾lb) pears
900ml (1½ pints) pear juice
85g (3oz) cornflour
6 tbsp fine cane sugar
1–2 tsp vanilla extract

Also:
250ml carton soya cream, suitable
   for whipping, well chilled
ground cinnamon, for dusting

PEAR JUICE TART
WITH CINNAMON CREAM

1 To make the base, combine the flour, sugar, and baking powder in a bowl. Work in the margarine using your fingers, add the vanilla extract, and bring everything together to create a smooth shortcrust pastry. Line a springform tin with baking paper. Put the pastry into the tin, pressing it down and smoothing it out with a tablespoon. Create a rim of 7cm (2¾in) up the sides. Prick the base with a fork and leave to chill for 1 hour.

2 Meanwhile, to make the filling, peel and quarter the pears, remove the cores, and dice the pears finely. Put the pear juice into a pan. In a bowl, mix the cornflour with the sugar, add a bit of the pear juice and vanilla extract, and stir until the mixture is smooth and there are no visible lumps.

3 Preheat the oven to 180°C (350°F/Gas 4). Bring the pear juice to the boil over a moderate heat, remove the pan from the hob, and stir in the cornflour mixture. Bring the mixture back to the boil, stirring constantly, then swiftly fold in the diced pear. Pour over the shortcrust base and bake the tart in the centre of the oven for 1 hour. Remove and leave to cool completely in the tin.

4 Whip the soya cream and then chill until ready to serve. Cut the tart into pieces, put a generous blob of cream on each portion, and dust with plenty of cinnamon.

TIP
This recipe
also tastes
fantastic made with
apples and apple
juice. Drizzle the
diced fruit with
lemon juice to
prevent it going
brown.

For a 28cm (11in) springform tin
(12–14 pieces)
Time: 20 mins prep
+ 3 hrs chilling

"CHEESECAKE" WITH MANGO CREAM

1 Melt the coconut oil for both the base and the filling in a small pan over a low heat. To make the base, finely grind the cashew and macadamia nuts in a food processor. Add 2 tablespoons coconut oil and the remaining base ingredients, plus the salt and process everything until you have a homogeneous mixture. Transfer to a springform tin lined with baking paper, smooth the surface, then chill for 30 minutes.

2 To make the filling, combine the remaining coconut oil with the other ingredients in a food processor on its top setting until it forms a well-combined, smooth paste. If this is too thick, add a bit of water and mix again. Spread the filling over the base and transfer to the freezer for 30 minutes.

3 In the meantime, make the mango cream by mixing all the ingredients in a food processor on its highest setting until you have a smooth consistency. Spread this quickly over the frozen surface of the cheesecake (it will set rapidly). Put the cheesecake in the fridge for at least 2 hours and scatter with mango chips before serving.

TIP
If you are short of time, you can simply put the cheesecake in the freezer for 1 hour before serving.

For the base:
2 tbsp coconut oil
200g (7oz) cashew nuts
150g (5½oz) macadamia nuts
100g (3½oz) fine coconut flakes
1 tbsp lemon juice
1 tsp grated organic lemon zest
1 tbsp agave syrup
1 pinch of salt

For the filling:
150g (5½oz) coconut oil
750g (1lb 10oz) cashew nuts
150ml (5fl oz) lemon juice
85ml (2¾fl oz) agave syrup
seeds scraped from ½ vanilla pod

For the mango cream:
300g (10oz) mango chips, plus extra
   for decorating (from an organic or
   health food shop)
1 tbsp psyllium husks
2 tbsp agave syrup
1 tbsp lemon juice

For a 30 x 40cm (12 x 15½in) baking tray
Time: 40 mins prep
+ 40 mins baking

POPPY SEED AND REDCURRANT CAKE
WITH A MERINGUE TOPPING

Fruity on the bottom, fluffy on the top: this moist poppy seed and redcurrant cake is topped with a vegan version of fluffy meringue. This cake looks absolutely stunning.

For the cake:
350g (12oz) wholemeal flour
1 tbsp cornflour
1 slightly heaped tsp baking powder
1 slightly heaped tsp bicarbonate of
   soda
70g (2¼oz) ground poppy seeds
225g (8oz) fine cane sugar
2 tsp vanilla powder
250ml (9fl oz) soya milk
1 tbsp cider vinegar
110ml (3¾fl oz) rapeseed oil
350g (12oz) redcurrants

For the meringue topping:
2 tbsp powdered egg substitue,
   such as Ener-g egg Egg Replacer
250g (9oz) fine cane sugar
1 tbsp agar-agar
1 generous splash rum
some icing sugar, for dusting

1 Preheat the oven to 180°C (350°F/Gas 4). To make the cake, combine the dry ingredients in a large bowl. In a separate bowl, whisk the soya milk with the cider vinegar and leave to thicken for 5 minutes. Add the rapeseed oil and 175ml (6fl oz) water and whisk everything together. Stir the liquid mixture into the dry ingredients – a couple of lumps here and there won't matter.

2 Line a high-sided baking tray with baking paper. Smooth the cake mixture out over the tray. Scatter the redcurrants over and press them down slightly. Bake the cake in the centre of the oven for 30–40 minutes, until an inserted skewer comes out clean. Remove and leave to cool completely.

3 Preheat the oven to 240°C (475°F/Gas 9) with the grill setting enabled. To make the meringue, put the egg substitute and 300ml (10fl oz) water into a container and beat with an electric mixer on its highest setting for 5 minutes, then sprinkle in 150g (5½oz) of the sugar and continue to beat.

4 In a pan bring 200ml (7fl oz) water to the boil with the remaining 100g (3½oz) sugar and the agar-agar, stirring constantly, then add the rum. As soon as the sugar has dissolved, stir this quickly into the meringue mixture.

5 Spread the mixture over into waves and dusting with icing sugar. Bake the cake for 1–2 minutes under the grill until the topping has browned slightly. Remove from the oven, leave to cool, and refrigerate. To serve, slice into 12 pieces.

For a 23 × 23cm (9 x 9in) square springform tin
Time: 40 mins prep
+ 40 mins baking

RASPBERRY AND GOOSEBERRY CAKE

This fruity treat is topped with an exquisite creamy layer of icing and delicate flowers. It looks impressive, but is super quick to make.

1 Preheat the oven to 180°C (350°F/Gas 4). Line a square springform tin with baking paper. To make the cake, whisk the rapeseed oil with 150ml (5fl oz) water in a bowl, then use an electric whisk to beat in the chickpea flour. Add the icing sugar with the whisk on its highest setting.

2 In a separate bowl, combine the plain flour, baking powder, bicarbonate of soda, vanilla, and salt. Stir this into the chickpea mix by the spoonful, then swiftly combine everything with the spoon until smooth.

3 Stir the cider vinegar into the soya milk, leave to thicken for about 5 minutes, stir it all through again, then fold into the cake mix using a spoon. Transfer the mixture into the tin and smooth the surface. Mix the berries and scatter them over the cake, pressing down slightly. Bake in the centre of the oven for about 40 minutes, until an inserted skewer comes out clean. Remove and leave to cool completely.

4 To make the icing, combine the cornflour with the vanilla in a pan. Stir in the raspberry juice until smooth and bring to the boil over a moderate heat, stirring constantly. As soon as the mixture has thickened, remove the pan from the heat and allow the mixture to cool to room temperature, stirring occasionally.

5 Use an electric whisk on its highest setting to cream the margarine in a bowl. Sift over the icing sugar and mix it in with the whisk on a moderate setting. Then fold the vanilla and raspberry cream into the margarine and sugar mixture, one spoonful at a time. Stir it all together until smooth then spread over the cake. If desired, decorate the cake with edible flowers, before slicing into 12 pieces.

For the cake:
3 tbsp rapeseed oil
100g (3½oz) chickpea flour
190g (6½oz) icing sugar
200g (7oz) plain flour
2 tsp baking powder
1 tsp bicarbonate of soda
1 tsp vanilla powder
1 pinch of salt
2 tsp cider vinegar
85ml (2¾fl oz) soya milk
150g (5½oz) raspberries
100g (3½oz) gooseberries

For the topping:
40g (1¼oz) cornflour
½ tsp ground vanilla
250ml (9fl oz) raspberry juice (available online)
150g (5½oz) soft vegan margarine
40g (1¼oz) icing sugar
edible flowers, such as pink and white daisies, for decorating (optional)

TIP
Lots of other seasonal berries will also taste great — you could try combining the raspberries with blackcurrants.

For a 24cm (9½in) springform tin (12 pieces)
Time: 35 mins prep
+ 12 hrs draining
+ 2 hrs cooling and baking

OREO "CHEESECAKE"

These lovely cream-filled double biscuits are vegan – so they don't just play a supporting role in this "cheesecake", they are given star billing.

For the filling:
1kg (2¼lb) soya yogurt
juice and zest of 1 organic lemon
3½ tbsp rapeseed oil
120ml (4fl oz) soya milk
70g (2¼oz) cornflour
150g (5⅕oz) fine cane sugar
1 pinch of salt
1 tsp vanilla powder (or the seeds
   from 1 vanilla pod)

For the base:
60g (2oz) vegan margarine
16 Oreo cookies, plus 4 cookies
   reserved for decoration

1 Line a sieve with a clean tea towel and place it over a large bowl. Pour in the soya yogurt and leave to drain overnight. The following day, squeeze out any excess water from the yogurt.

2 To make the base, melt the margarine in a pan over a low heat. Use a food processor to blitz the Oreo cookies to make crumbs. Gradually add the margarine and work until everything is combined. Line a springform tin with baking paper. Cover the base with a thin layer of the cookie mixture, press it down slightly with a spoon, and smooth the surface. Leave to chill in the fridge for at least 1 hour.

3 Preheat the oven to 180°C (350°F/Gas 4). To make the filling, put the soya yogurt into a bowl and stir in the lemon juice, lemon zest, and rapeseed oil until smooth. In a separate bowl, stir the soya milk and cornflour until smooth, then mix in the sugar, salt, and the vanilla. Finally, stir everything into the soya yogurt and lemon mixture until you have a smooth and creamy consistency. Spread this mixture over the biscuit base.

4 Carefully twist apart the 2 layers of the Oreo cookies you saved for decoration and arrange them on the cheesecake, creamy side down, pressing them slightly into the mixture. Bake in the centre of the oven for 50–60 minutes. Remove from the oven, leave to cool slightly, then transfer to the fridge to cool completely.

For a 24cm (9½in) springform tin (12–14 pieces)
Time: 40 mins prep
+ 35 mins baking

APRICOT STRUDEL TART
WITH ALMONDS AND SESAME SEEDS

1 Remove the filo pastry from the fridge 10 minutes before preparation.

2 Preheat the oven to 180°C (350°F/Gas 4). Halve, stone, and dice the apricots. Peel, core, and finely dice the apples. Melt 2 tbsp margarine in a pan over a moderate heat and toast the breadcrumbs in the fat. Stir in the sugar and vanilla extract. Briefly cook the chopped almonds with the sesame seeds in a dry pan until pale brown. Combine these with the ground almonds. Mix the cinnamon with the cardamom and ginger. Melt the remaining margarine.

3 Place 2 sheets of filo on top of each other, brush with a thin layer of margarine, top with one fifth each of the fruit, breadcrumbs, almond and sesame seed mixture, and the spices. As you work, leave a gap of about 3cm (1½in) free around the edges. Finally, drizzle with 1 tablespoon maple syrup. Fold in the sides and roll up the strudel lengthways. Repeat four more times with the remaining ingredients.

4 Line a springform tin with baking paper and place the strudels inside, one beside the other in a spiral formation (it doesn't matter if the filo tears a bit at the top). Finally, brush the strudel tart with margarine.

5 Toast the sesame seeds and flaked almonds in a dry pan and scatter them over the strudel tart. Drizzle with maple syrup, and bake in the centre of the oven for 35 minutes. Remove and leave to cool completely.

TIP
Optionally, take 500ml (16fl oz) well-chilled soya cream, suitable for whipping, add 2 sachets of cream stiffener and 2 tsp ground vanilla then beat with an electric whisk for 3 minutes until stiff. Spread over the tart.

For the strudel tart:
1 pack filo pastry (10 sheets, measuring 30 × 30cm/12 x 12in)
10 apricots
400g (14oz) apples
60g (2oz) vegan margarine
100g (3½oz) wholemeal breadcrumbs
25g (scant 1oz) cane sugar
1–2 tsp vanilla extract
50g (1¾oz) chopped almonds
25g (scant 1oz) sesame seeds
50g (1¾oz) ground almonds
1 tsp ground cinnamon
½ tsp ground cardamom
1 pinch of ground ginger
5 tbsp maple syrup

Also:
25g (scant 1oz) sesame seeds
25g (scant 1oz) flaked almonds
3 tbsp maple syrup

For a 24cm (9½in) springform tin (12 pieces)
Time: 35 mins prep
+ 40 mins baking
+ at least 13 hrs chilling

MOLEHILL CAKE

This edible "molehill" has a dark base, lots of cream, shards of chocolate, and a sweet little mound of cream covered in large crumble pieces.

For the crumble:
300g (10oz) plain flour
150g (5½oz) fine cane sugar
1 tbsp vegan cocoa powder, sifted
150g (5½oz) vegan margarine
1 tsp vanilla extract

For the base:
150g (5½oz) plain flour
2 tbsp cornflour
125g (4½oz) icing sugar, sifted
1 tbsp vegan cocoa powder, sifted
1½ tsp baking powder
½ tsp vanilla powder
1 pinch of salt
120ml (4fl oz) soya milk
5 tbsp rapeseed oil

For the filling:
2 x 250ml cartons soya cream, suitable for whipping, well chilled
2 sachets cream stiffener
6 medium bananas
80g (2¾oz) vegan dark chocolate
3 tbsp apricot jam

1 Preheat the oven to 180°C (350°F/Gas 4). To make the crumble, combine the flour, cane sugar, and cocoa powder in a bowl. Add the margarine in blobs with the vanilla extract and work into the mix with your fingers to create a rough crumble. Spread the crumble over a baking tray lined with baking paper, and bake in the centre of the oven for about 20 minutes.

2 For the base, combine the flour, cornflour, icing sugar, cocoa powder, baking powder, vanilla, and salt in a bowl. In a separate bowl, whisk the soya milk and rapeseed oil. Stir the liquid and dry ingredients together quickly with a large spoon. Line a springform tin with baking paper, spoon in the mixture, smooth the surface, and bake in the centre of the oven for about 20 minutes, until an inserted skewer comes out clean. Remove from the oven and leave to cool completely.

3 Meanwhile, for the filling, beat the soya cream with an electric whisk on its highest setting; after about 2 minutes add the cream stiffener and continue to beat for a further 2–3 minutes. Peel 3 of the bananas, mash them to a pulp with a fork, and fold into the cream. Chop the dark chocolate, fold this into the banana and cream mixture, and transfer to the fridge to chill for at least 1 hour.

4 Gently heat the apricot jam in a small pan over a low heat and spread it over the base of the cake. Peel the remaining bananas, slice into discs, and place them on the base. Spread the banana cream over the top and return the cake to the fridge to chill for a few minutes. Cover the creamy topping with crumble pieces and leave the cake to firm up in the fridge overnight.

TIP
You can also make the crumble finer and pile up the cream in a dome shape on top of the cake to make it look even more like a molehill.

For a 24cm (9½in) springform tin (12–14 pieces)
Time: 45 mins prep
+ 1 hr baking + 12 hrs chilling

BANANA CAKE
WITH SOUR CREAM AND CHOCOLATE FROSTING

1 Preheat the oven to 180°C (350°F/Gas 4). For the cake, combine the flour, baking powder, cane sugar, vanilla, cornflour, and lemon zest. Whisk the corn oil with the rice milk and add to the dry ingredients. Slowly stir in the mineral water with a spoon until all the lumps in the mixture have gone.

2 Line a springform tin with baking paper, put the mixture into the tin, and bake in the centre of the oven for about 1 hour. When an inserted skewer comes out clean, the cake is ready. Leave to cool completely.

3 To make the frosting, break the chocolate into pieces and melt with the margarine in a bain-marie. Stir the vanilla into the sour cream and fold this into the chocolate mixture. Sift over the icing sugar and mix it in with an electric whisk. Slice the cake horizontally into 3 layers. Place one of the pieces on a cake plate, put a cake ring around it and spread with a thin layer of the frosting.

4 Peel the bananas for the filling and slice thinly. Distribute half of the slices over the frosting and press down slightly. Place the second cake layer on top and drizzle with rum. Cover with a thin layer of frosting and top with sliced banana. Put the third cake layer on top and likewise drizzle with rum before spreading over the frosting. Run a knife between the edge of the cake and the ring to release it. Cover the sides of the cake with the remaining frosting and decorate the cake with grated chocolate, if using. Ideally, put it in the fridge overnight to let the flavours develop.

For the cake:
450g (1lb) plain flour
1 tsp baking powder
250g (9oz) fine cane sugar
1 tsp vanilla powder
2 tbsp cornflour
lemon zest
100ml (3½fl oz) corn oil
100ml (3½fl oz) rice milk
350ml (12fl oz) carbonated mineral water

For the frosting:
350g (12oz) vegan dark chocolate
115g (4oz) vegan margarine
½ tsp vanilla powder
300g (10oz) vegan sour cream (at room temperature)
750g (1lb 10oz) icing sugar

For the filling and decoration:
5 medium bananas
rum
dark and white vegan chocolate, grated (optional)

For a 24cm (9½in) springform tin (12–14 pieces)
Time: 45 mins prep
+ 70 mins baking
+ at least 1 hr chilling

ALMOND "CHEESECAKE"
WITH BLUEBERRIES

For the base:
250g (9oz) plain flour
½ tsp baking powder
125g (4½oz) fine cane sugar
150g (5½oz) vegan margarine, chilled
1–2 tsp vanilla extract

For the filling:
350g (12oz) blanched whole almonds (alternatively, ground almonds)
500g (1lb 2oz) soya yogurt
200g (7oz) fine cane sugar
1–2 tsp vanilla extract
juice and zest of 2 organic lemons
80g (2¾oz) cornflour
175ml (6fl oz) almond milk
125g (4½oz) coconut oil
250g (9oz) blueberries

Also:
1 sachet clear cake glaze, vegan
50g (1¾oz) fine cane sugar

1 To make the base, combine the flour, baking powder, and sugar in a bowl. Add the margarine and vanilla extract and use your fingers to quickly work the ingredients to create a smooth shortcrust texture. Transfer to a springform tin lined with baking paper, making sure the pastry comes about 7cm (2¾in) up the sides. Prick the base with a fork and leave to chill.

2 Preheat the oven to 180°C (350°F). For the filling, finely grind the almonds in a food processor on its highest setting. Mix the almonds, soya yogurt, sugar, vanilla extract, and lemon juice and zest and leave to rest briefly. Stir the cornflour into the almond milk until smooth and add this to the main mixture.

3 Melt the coconut oil in a small pan over a low heat. Then swiftly stir it into the almond and yogurt mixture with a balloon whisk and pour this into your shortcrust base. Bake the cheesecake in the centre of the oven for 70 minutes. Remove from the oven and leave to cool for about an hour.

4 Top the "cheesecake" with the blueberries. In a saucepan, mix the cake glaze with the sugar and 250ml (9fl oz) cold water, stirring until smooth. Bring briefly to the boil and let it cool slightly while stirring. Then carefully distribute it over the blueberries using a spoon. The cheesecake tastes best if the flavours are left to develop overnight.

TIP
You can also use frozen blueberries instead of fresh. To make sure the filling doesn't go soggy, you should spread 2 tbsp vegan cream stiffener over the surface before you add the berries.

For a 24cm (9½in) springform tin (12 pieces)
Time: 45 mins prep + 40 mins baking + at least 3 hrs chilling

CHESTNUT LAYER CAKE
WITH HAZELNUT NOUGAT

1 Preheat the oven to 180°C (350°F/Gas 4). For the base, combine the flour, sugar, baking powder, bicarbonate of soda, and salt. Sift over the cocoa powder and fold it in. Whisk together the soya milk and cider vinegar, leave to thicken for 5 minutes, then stir in the rapeseed oil. Quickly mix the liquid and dry ingredients with a large spoon.

2 Line a springform tin with baking paper, transfer the cake mix into the tin, and bake in the centre of the oven for about 40 minutes, until an inserted skewer comes out clean. Leave to cool completely. Place the base on a cake plate and surround with a cake ring.

3 For the topping, bring 300ml (10fl oz) of the soya cream to the boil over a moderate heat with the agar-agar and the chocolate and simmer for a few minutes, stirring carefully until the chocolate melts. Leave the cream to cool slightly, remembering to stir occasionally.

4 Whip the remaining soya cream for 3 minutes using an electric whisk on its highest setting. Use a hand blender to combine the chestnut purée with the warm chocolate and cream mixture. Once the chocolate cream mixture has cooled, fold in the whipped cream and spread swiftly over the base of your cake. Smooth the surface with a spoon and chill thoroughly in the fridge for 3 hours.

5 To decorate, first melt the hazelnut spread in a bain-marie. Spread most of the melted spread over the surface of your cake, then spread the remaining spread over a board. Leave the cake and the spread to cool. Whip the cream with the chestnut purée and transfer to a piping bag with a star nozzle attached. Cut the solidified spread into pieces. Carefully release the cake from the ring, pipe on 12 generous swirls, and top each one with a square of the cooled spread.

For the base:
300g (10oz) plain flour
200g (7oz) fine cane sugar
2 tsp baking powder
2 tsp bicarbonate of soda
½ tsp salt
30g (1oz) vegan cocoa powder
400ml (14fl oz) soya milk
1½ tbsp cider vinegar
150ml (5fl oz) rapeseed oil

For the topping:
600ml (1 pint) soya cream suitable for whipping, well chilled
1 slightly heaped tsp agar-agar
125g (4½oz) vegan dark chocolate, roughly chopped
150g (5½oz) chestnut purée

Also:
190g (6½oz) hazelnut spread, vegan
150ml (5fl oz) soya cream, suitable for whipping, well chilled
80g (2¾oz) chestnut purée

For two 24cm (9½in) springform tins (12 pieces)
Time: 45 mins prep
+ 40 mins baking
+ at least 12 hrs chilling

NEAPOLITAN WAFER CAKE

A cake for special occasions and courageous bakers! A bit of effort is required here, but it is well worth it. Make sure you invite some friends over to eat it, or hold a party as soon as the cake is ready!

For the cake layers:
500g (1lb 2oz) plain flour
300g (10oz) ground hazelnuts
400g (14oz) fine cane sugar
30g (1oz) baking powder
1 tsp ground vanilla
500ml (16fl oz) soya milk with vanilla flavouring
240ml (8fl oz) rapeseed oil

For the filling:
1.2 litres (2 pints) soya cream, suitable for whipping, well chilled
4 packs of Neapolitan wafer biscuits (each weighing 75g/2½oz)
100g (3½oz) apricot jam

Also:
1 pack Neapolitan wafers
50g (1¾oz) vegan dark chocolate, melted

1 Preheat the oven to 180°C (350°F). For the cake layers, combine the flour, hazelnuts, sugar, baking powder, and vanilla in a bowl. In a separate bowl, mix the soya milk and rapeseed oil, then stir these into the dry ingredients until thoroughly combined. Line 2 springform tins with baking paper and put half the mixture into each. Bake in the centre of the oven for about 40 minutes, until an inserted skewer comes out clean. Remove from the oven and leave to cool completely.

2 For the filling, whip the cream, with an electric whisk on its highest setting, for at least 3 minutes until stiff. Put the Neapolitan wafers into a freezer bag and bash them with a rolling pin to create fine crumbs. Gradually fold the crumbs into the cream, then whisk on the highest setting until well combined. Refrigerate.

3 Slice both of the cakes horizontally with a sharp knife or cheese wire to create 4 cake sections. Place one of these sections on a cake platter. Heat the apricot jam in a small pan, then spread a quarter of it on the cake followed by a quarter of the cream, smoothing the surface to finish. Continue layering up cake, jam, and cream in this manner with the remaining sections finishing with a mound of cream on top.

4 To decorate, chop the Neapolitan wafers into pieces and scatter them over the centre of the cake, then drizzle with melted chocolate. Put the cake in the fridge and leave the flavours to develop overnight.

TIP
If you'd like the cake to be even nuttier and sweeter, replace the apricot jam with vegan hazelnut spread.

For one 26cm (10½in) diameter ring mould
Time: 25 mins prep
+ 70 mins baking
+ at least 2 hrs chilling

FRANKFURT CROWN CAKE

1 Preheat the oven to 180°C (350°C/Gas 4). To make the cake, combine the flour, sugar, baking powder, lemon zest, and salt. Use a large spoon to quickly stir in the rapeseed oil, then add the mineral water until you have a homogeneous mixture. Grease a ring mould with margarine and dust with flour. Transfer the cake mix into the tin and bake in the centre of the oven for 70 minutes, until an inserted skewer comes out clean.

2 Meanwhile, for the buttercream, measure out about 150ml (5fl oz) of the hazelnut drink and stir in the custard powder and sugar until smooth. Bring the rest of the drink to the boil in a pan over a moderate heat. Remove from the hob, stir in the custard powder mixture, then bring everything back to the boil before leaving to cool, stirring occasionally. Cream the margarine until light and fluffy and fold it into the custard spoon by spoon. Whip the cream and fold this into the mixture.

3 For the praline, melt the margarine in a pan, add the sugar and let this dissolve, then cook until it turns brown. Stir in the almonds. Spread the mixture out over baking paper and leave to cool, then crumble it up to create your praline. Press the cherry jam through a sieve and stir until smooth.

4 Turn the cake out from the tin and slice it to create 3 layers. Spread the bottom section with cherry jam and cover this with some of the "buttercream". Place the middle section on top and, likewise, spread with jam and buttercream. Add the final layer and cover the cake completely with the remaining buttercream, setting some aside for the final decoration.

5 Sprinkle praline all over the ring cake, pressing some of the praline carefully into the sides. Transfer the remaining buttercream into a piping bag with a star nozzle attached and use this to pipe 12 stars on top. Decorate each star with a cherry, then chill for at least 2 hours.

For the cake:
600g (1lb 5oz) plain flour, plus extra for dusting
350g (12oz) fine cane sugar
2 tsp baking powder
grated zest of 1–2 organic lemons
1 tsp salt
300ml (10fl oz) rapeseed oil
525ml (17fl oz) carbonated mineral water
vegan margarine, for greasing the mould

For the buttercream:
500ml (16fl oz) vegan hazelnut drink
40g (1¼oz) instant custard powder
75g (2½oz) fine cane sugar
250g (9oz) soft vegan margarine
200ml (7fl oz) soya cream, suitable for whipping

For the praline:
10g (¼oz) vegan margarine
50g (1¾oz) fine cane sugar
125g (4½oz) chopped almonds

Also:
3 tbsp cherry jam
12 glacé cherries

For a 24cm (9½in) springform tin (12–14 pieces)
Time: 45 mins prep + 1 hr baking

GINGER BISCUIT CREAM CAKE
WITH A FRUITY NOTE

For the base:
100g (3½oz) vegan ginger biscuits
350g (12oz) plain flour
200g (7oz) fine cane sugar
2 tsp baking powder
75ml (2½fl oz) rapeseed oil
2–3 tsp vanilla extract
450ml (15fl oz) carbonated mineral
  water

For the filling:
600ml (1 pint) soya cream, suitable
  for whipping, well chilled
100g (3½oz) vegan ginger biscuits
2 small tins of mandarin oranges,
  including juice (about 450g/1lb)
20g (¾oz) agar-agar

For the topping:
250ml carton soya cream, suitable
  for whipping, well chilled
1 sachet cream stiffener
50g (1¾oz) vegan ginger biscuits

1 Preheat the oven to 160°C (325°C/Gas 2). For the base, blitz the ginger biscuits in a food processor to create fine crumbs, or bash them in a freezer bag. Combine the biscuit crumbs, flour, sugar, and baking powder in a bowl. Mix the dry ingredients with the rapeseed oil, vanilla extract, and mineral water using a large spoon until you have a smooth consistency.

2 Line a springform tin with baking paper, transfer the cake mix into the tin, and bake in the centre of the oven for about 1 hour, until an inserted skewer comes out clean. Remove from the oven, leave to cool completely, and slice in half horizontally. Place the bottom half on a cake platter and put a cake ring around it.

3 For the filling, whip the soya cream until it is stiff. Finely crumble the ginger biscuits in a freezer bag and fold the crumbs into the cream. Spread half the cream on the base and let it firm up slightly. Drain the mandarins in a sieve, catching the juice in a pan. Then bring the juice to the boil with the gelling powder, stirring constantly. Lower the temperature and leave to simmer for a further 2 minutes. Allow to cool slightly, spread the mandarins and juice over the cream layer, and cover with the remaining cream. Place the upper section of your cake on top.

4 For the topping, whip the soya cream with the cream stiffener and spread this all over the cake. There should be some cream left over. Break the ginger biscuits into rough chunks and use these along with the remaining cream to add the finishing decorative touches to the cake. Chill the cake until ready to serve.

For a 28cm (11in) long loaf tin
Time: 30 mins prep
+ at least 2–3 hrs chilling time

CHOCOLATE BISCUIT CAKE

250g (9oz) coconut oil
240g (8½oz) icing sugar
100g (3½oz) vegan cocoa powder
1 tsp vanilla extract
50 vegan plain biscuits
100g (3½oz) white vegan chocolate
   (optional)

1 Melt the coconut oil in a small pan over a low heat. Combine the icing sugar and cocoa powder and add these to the coconut oil in the pan. Add the vanilla extract and use a balloon whisk to mix these ingredients into the coconut oil.

2 Line a loaf tin with cling film and put in a thin layer of the chocolate mixture, smoothing the surface. Top with a layer of biscuits, followed by a layer of chocolate mixture, and continue in this manner until all the biscuits and mixture have been used. The final layer should be a chocolate layer smoothed out to create a nice even finish.

3 Put the chocolate biscuit cake into the fridge to chill for at least 2–3 hours, until it is completely firm. Turn it out onto a board or flat plate and pull off the cling film. If using, melt the white chocolate in a bain-marie and spoon over the cake to decorate. Return the chocolate biscuit cake to the fridge until ready to serve.

For a 24cm (9½in) springform tin (12 pieces)
Time: 30 mins prep
+ 4 hrs chilling

MOUSSE AU CHOCOLAT
RASPBERRY CAKE

Uncooked but nonetheless spectacular! The biscuit base is topped with a layer of enticing chocolate mousse and jewel-like raspberries.

1 To make the base, blitz the biscuits in a food processor until you have fine crumbs. Melt the margarine and mix with the crumbs until well combined. Line a springform tin with baking paper and spread the biscuit mixture over the base, using a spoon to press it down firmly and smooth the surface. Chill for at least 2 hours.

2 For the topping, melt the dark chocolate in a bain-marie and leave to cool slightly. Whip the cream with an electric mixer on its highest setting for 3 minutes then add the chocolate. It is important for the cream to combine well with the chocolate. If required, use a spatula to scrape the chocolate from the base and sides of the bowl and stir it all through thoroughly. Flavour the mousse with the rum and beat everything again vigorously.

3 Spread half of the mousse over the biscuit base. Scatter the raspberries evenly over the surface and cover with the remaining mousse, smoothing the surface. Leave to chill for a few hours.

4 Whip the cream for decorating, decant into a piping bag with a nozzle of your choice attached, and pipe 12 large swirls of cream onto the cake. Put 1 raspberry on top of each swirl of cream. Chill until ready to serve.

For the base:
225g (8oz) vegan caramel cookies
125g (4½oz) vegan margarine

For the filling:
400g (14oz) vegan dark chocolate
900ml (1½ pints) soya cream, suitable, for whipping, well chilled
2–3 tbsp rum
175g (6oz) raspberries, plus 12 raspberries for decoration

Also:
100ml (3½fl oz) soya cream, suitable for whipping, well chilled

TIP
Soya cream whips more easily when it is extremely well chilled. Chill the cream the previous day and, if you prefer a firmer consistency, stir in 1 sachet of cream stiffener. If children are going to be eating this cake, simply leave out the rum.

For a 28cm (11in) tart tin (12 pieces)
Time: 20 mins prep
1 day soaking + 2 hrs chilling

For the base:
100g (3½oz) whole blanched
  almonds
300g (10oz) dates, pitted
150g (5½oz) walnuts
2 tbsp vegan cocoa powder

For the chocolate cream:
2 avocados (Hass variety)
2 very ripe bananas
7 dates, pitted
5 tbsp vegan cocoa powder
1 tsp orange juice, freshly squeezed

Also:
40g (1¼oz) fine coconut flakes, for
  sprinkling

CHOCOLATE TART

1 For the base, soak the almonds in plenty of water the day before. Leave the almonds to drain well then chop roughly in a food processor. Add all the ingredients for the base and process everything until you have a homogeneous mixture. Sprinkle the tart tin with coconut flakes. Transfer the almond mixture into the tart tin, spreading it out to 1–2cm (½–¾in) thick and creating a slight rim around the edge. Leave it to chill in the fridge.

2 For the chocolate cream, halve the avocados, remove the stones, and use a tablespoon to scoop out the flesh. Add to a food processor. Peel the bananas and roughly break into pieces. Add the bananas, dates, cocoa powder, and orange juice to the avocados and process everything to a smooth and creamy consistency. Spread this over the base and smooth the surface. Before serving, chill the tart for about 2 hours in the fridge or, if you're short of time, about 1 hour in the freezer.

BEE STING CAKE

The classic German "bee sting cake" consists of a light yeast dough, a fine custard and cream filling, and a sweet layer of almonds – there is nothing else quite like it.

1 To make the base, combine the flour, yeast, salt, and sugar in a bowl. Melt the margarine in a small pan and stir it into the dry ingredients. Then heat the soya milk and 200ml (7fl oz) water over a low heat and add these to the mix. Knead everything together until you have a smooth, supple dough. Cover the dough and leave to prove in a warm place for about 45 minutes.

2 Preheat the oven to 180°C (350°F/Gas 4). Roll out the dough and place it on a baking tray lined with baking paper.

3 To make the topping, heat the margarine with the sugar in a pan over a moderate heat, stirring constantly until melted, then mix in the flaked almonds. Spread the mixture evenly over the base using a dough scraper. Bake in the centre of the oven for 25–30 minutes. Remove from the oven and allow it to cool.

4 Meanwhile, make the filling by beating the rice cream, using an electric mixer on its highest setting, and leave to chill. Take 200ml (7fl oz) of the soya milk and stir together with the custard powder until smooth. Put the remaining soya milk, the vanilla seeds, sugar, and salt into a pan and bring to the boil over a moderate heat. Remove the pan from the hob and stir in the custard paste made earlier. Bring the mixture back to the boil, stirring constantly. Remove the pan from the hob once again and stir in the margarine. Leave the custard to cool then fold in the rice cream.

5 Once the base is cool cut it into 12 pieces. Slice each piece in half horizontally and fill with the cream.

For the base:
750g (1lb 10oz) spelt flour with a
    high gluten content, plus extra to
    work with
1½ sachets dried yeast
1 pinch of salt
125g (4½oz) fine cane sugar
100g (3½oz) vegan margarine
200ml (7fl oz) soya milk

For the topping:
150g (5½oz) vegan margarine
150g (5½oz) fine cane sugar
200g (7oz) flaked almonds

For the filling:
300g (10oz) rice cream, suitable for
    whipping, well chilled
1 litre (1¾ pints) soya milk with
    vanilla flavouring
125g (4½oz) instant custard powder
seeds scraped from ½ vanilla pod
80g (2¾oz) fine cane sugar
1 pinch of salt
20g (¾oz) vegan margarine

Serves 12–14
Time: 1 hr

PANCAKE LAYER CAKE

A quick, gluten-free alternative to a cake or gateau. Using fresh seasonal fruit with a soft coconut cream creates a colourful and tasty treat.

For the batter:
250g (9oz) buckwheat flour
1 tsp baking powder
seeds scraped from ½ vanilla pod
2 tbsp fine cane sugar
1 pinch of sea salt
600ml (1 pint) cold carbonated
   mineral water

Also:
600ml (1 pint) coconut cream,
   suitable for whipping, well chilled
400g (14oz) strawberries
60ml (2fl oz) rapeseed oil, for
   cooking
100g (3½oz) strawberry jam
coconut flakes, for decorating

1 In a large bowl, combine the buckwheat flour and baking powder. Stir in the vanilla seeds, sugar, and sea salt. Add the mineral water and mix to create a batter. Leave to stand for 20 minutes.

2 Meanwhile, whip the coconut cream and then chill it in the fridge. Trim and quarter the strawberries.

3 Heat some rapeseed oil in a pan. Add a ladle of pancake batter to the pan, spreading it out slightly. As soon as the edges have cooked firm and turned golden, flip the pancake and cook until golden on the other side. Continue in this manner until all the batter has been used.

4 Leave the pancakes to cool completely. Layer them up spreading each one with jam, whipped cream, and then topping it with strawberries. Finish with a scatter of flaked coconut over the top layer.

TIP
Coconut cream
tastes particularly
delicious if you fold
in a few tablespoons of
toasted flaked coconut.
To do this, toast the
coconut flakes in a dry
pan over a moderate heat
until golden. Take
care, as coconut
flakes burn very
quickly.

CHOCOLATE CAKE WITH BANANA

For a 24cm (9½in) springform tin (12–14 pieces)
Time: 40 mins prep
+ 12 hrs draining + 40 mins baking

1 For the banana cream, put the soya yogurt into a sieve lined with a thick paper towel and leave to drain overnight into a bowl. For decorating, whip the cream until stiff. Melt the chocolate in a bain-marie and fold it into the cream. Refrigerate overnight.

2 To make the base, first preheat the oven to 180°C (350°F/Gas 4). Combine the flour, sugar, baking powder, bicarbonate of soda, and salt. Sift over the cocoa powder and fold it in. Stir the cider vinegar into the soya milk, leave to thicken for 5 minutes, then stir in the rapeseed oil. Quickly stir together the liquid and dry ingredients with a spoon. Transfer to a springform tin lined with baking paper and bake for about 40 minutes. Leave to cool, transfer to a cake plate, and surround with a cake ring.

3 For the filling, peel the bananas, slice thickly, and spread them over the base. In a small pan, prepare the banana juice with the cake glaze, following the instructions on the glaze pack. As soon as it has thickened, spread the mixture over the bananas and transfer the cake to the fridge to chill.

4 For the banana cream, squeeze out the drained soya yogurt and put it into a bowl. Whip the soya cream using an electric mixer on its highest setting, then stir in the sugar, vanilla extract, and cream stiffener. Peel the bananas, mash with a fork to a fine purée, and fold this into the cream. Add the yogurt and stir everything to a smooth, firm consistency. Spread this over the glazed bananas and smooth the surface. Chill the whole cake again.

5 Transfer the chocolate cream into a piping bag with a star nozzle attached , pipe swirls around the edge of the cake and sprinkle them with banana chips. Carefully release the cake ring with the help of a sharp knife and chill the cake until ready to serve.

For the banana cream:
1kg (2¼lb) soya yogurt
300ml (10fl oz) soya cream, suitable for whipping, well chilled
2 tbsp fine cane sugar
1–2 tsp vanilla extract
3 tbsp cream stiffener
2 medium-sized ripe bananas

For decorating:
100g (3½oz) soya cream, suitable for whipping, well chilled
80g (2¾oz) vegan dark chocolate, chopped banana chips, roughly chopped

For the base:
300g (10oz) plain flour
200g (7oz) fine cane sugar
2 tsp baking powder
2 tsp bicarbonate of soda
½ tsp salt
30g (1oz) vegan cocoa powder
1½ tbsp cider vinegar
400ml (14fl oz) soya milk
150ml (5fl oz) rapeseed oil

For the filling:
4 medium bananas
450ml (15fl oz) banana juice drink
2 sachets vegan clear cake glaze

For a 24cm (9½in) springform tin (12 pieces)
Time: 40 mins prep
+ 40 mins baking
+ at least 3 hrs chilling

DARK CHOCOLATE AND RASPBERRY GATEAU

This thoroughly chocolatey gateau with its dark sponge cake, delicate chocolate cream, and sublime raspberries will add a touch of extravagance to any dessert table.

For the base:
300g (10oz) plain flour
200g (7oz) fine cane sugar
2 tsp baking powder
2 tsp bicarbonate of soda
½ tsp salt
30g (1oz) vegan cocoa powder
400ml (14fl oz) soya milk
1½ tbsp cider vinegar
150ml (5fl oz) rapeseed oil

For the filling:
450g (1lb) vegan dark chocolate
600ml (1 pint) soya cream, suitable
  for whipping, well chilled
450g (1lb) raspberries (fresh or
  frozen), plus 60g (2oz) fresh
  raspberries, for decorating

Also:
vegan chocolate flakes

1 Preheat the oven to 180°C (350°C/Gas 4). For the base, combine the flour, sugar, baking powder, bicarbonate of soda, and salt in a bowl. Sift over the cocoa powder and fold it in. In a separate bowl, stir the cider vinegar into the soya milk and leave to thicken for 5 minutes, then stir in the rapeseed oil with the balloon whisk. Quickly combine the liquid and dry ingredients with a large spoon.

2 Line a springform tin with baking paper, transfer the cake mix into the tin, and bake in the centre of the oven for about 40 minutes, until an inserted skewer comes out clean. Remove from the oven and leave to cool completely.

3 Meanwhile, prepare the filling. Roughly chop the dark chocolate, melt it in a bain-marie, and stir until smooth. Whip the soya cream using an electric mixer on its highest setting. Quickly beat in the chocolate until you have a homogeneous cream, then chill for 2–3 hours.

4 Slice the sponge in half and place the lower section on a cake plate, surrounded by a cake ring. Spread a thick layer of the cream mixture on top and cover with the raspberries followed by about half of the remaining cream mixture. Put the second cake layer on top and press down slightly. Cover the surface of the cake with the cream mixture, leaving some left over for the sides.

5 Remove the cake ring and spread the remaining cream over the sides of the gateau. Scatter with chocolate flakes. Distribute the remaining raspberries on top and refrigerate.

For a 24cm (9½in) tart tin (12 pieces)
Time: 25 mins prep
+ 15 mins baking + chilling time

COCONUT TART
WITH CHOCOLATE

This delicious gluten-free tart is simple to prepare and it tastes absolutely heavenly, so it will be popular with everyone, not just fans of coconut and chocolate.

1 Preheat the oven to 180°C (350°F/Gas 4). For the base, melt the coconut oil in a small pan over a low heat then set aside. Use a spoon to stir the coconut flakes and agave syrup together in a bowl. Knead in the slightly cooled coconut oil with your fingers.

2 Grease a tart tin with margarine. Transfer your mixture to a tin, creating a thick rim about 3cm (1½in) high. Smooth the base with a spoon, pressing everything down firmly. Bake in the centre of the oven for about 15 minutes, until the sides and base are pale brown – but not too dark. Remove from the oven and leave to cool slightly until the base is firm.

3 For the filling, roughly chop the dark chocolate. Bring the coconut milk to the boil in a pan over a moderate heat and stir in the chocolate, until you have a smooth consistency and there are no more lumps. Pour the chocolate cream into the base and chill the tart in the fridge for several hours, until set.

4 Toast the flaked coconut in a dry pan and scatter over the tart. Whip the soya cream, if using, with an electric mixer on its highest setting. Use the cream to decorate the tart. Serve well chilled.

For the base:
100g (3½oz) coconut oil
280g (9½oz) coconut flakes
200ml (7fl oz) agave syrup

For the filling:
300g (10oz) vegan dark chocolate
225g (8oz) coconut milk

Also:
vegan margarine, for greasing the tin
flaked coconut
soya cream, suitable for whipping, well chilled (optional)

TIP
This tart is made without any flour and also contains very little sugar. Dark chocolate with a cocoa content of at least 70% is ideal for this recipe.

For a 24cm (9½in) tart tin (12 pieces)
Time: 30 mins prep
+ 30 mins chilling + 45 mins baking

For the base:
250g (9oz) wholemeal spelt flour, plus extra for dusting
80g (2¾oz) fine cane sugar
1 tsp vanilla powder
1 tsp baking powder
1 pinch of salt
grated zest of 1 small organic lemon
1 tbsp ground linseed
100g (3½oz) vegan margarine, plus extra for greasing the tin

For the crumble:
150g (5½oz) wholemeal spelt flour
100g (3½oz) fine cane sugar
1 tsp vanilla powder
125g (4½oz) vegan margarine

For the filling:
60g (2oz) ground almonds
500g (1lb 2oz) seasonal fruit, washed and chopped

Also:
icing sugar, for dusting

WHOLEMEAL TART
WITH SEASONAL FRUIT

This splendid tart is incredibly versatile! The base can be combined with any fruit for a delicious treat; whether you use apples and pears or a thick layer of berries – this is a tart for all seasons.

1 For the base, combine the flour, cane sugar, vanilla, baking powder, salt, and lemon zest in a bowl. Stir the linseed together with 3 tablespoons of water and leave to swell for 5 minutes. Add little blobs of margarine to the flour mixture and use your fingers to rub it in, then add the linseed to create a smooth pastry mixture. Grease a tart tin and dust with flour. Transfer your pastry into the tin, pressing it out to cover the bottom and create a rim around the edge, and prick all over with a fork. Chill the pastry for at least 30 minutes.

2 Preheat the oven to 180°C (350°C/Gas 4). Meanwhile, for the crumble, combine the flour, cane sugar, and vanilla in a bowl and carefully rub in the margarine. Use your fingers to create rough crumble pieces.

3 For the filling, spread the almonds over the base and cover with the fruit. Top with the crumble and bake the tart in the centre of the oven for 35–45 minutes. Remove, leave to cool, and dust with icing sugar.

TIP
This tart tastes delicious with a custard layer. Prepare a custard made from 350ml (12fl oz) soya milk, 3 tbsp cane sugar, 2–3 tsp vanilla extract, and 40g (1¼oz) cornflour. Spread the custard over the base of the tart instead of the almonds then add the fruit layer on top. Scatter over the crumble and bake as described.

BISCUITS & COOKIES

Little baked goodies — cookies, spirals, wedges, and more

MUESLI COOKIES

1 Preheat the oven to 180°C (350°F/Gas 4). In a large bowl, combine the flour, sugar, cinnamon, allspice, and aniseed. Stir together the rapeseed oil and almond milk and add the vanilla extract. Add these to the dry ingredients and mix until you have a smooth consistency. Carefully fold in the muesli.

2 Line a baking tray with baking paper. Use 2 tablespoons to scoop out the mixture into roughly 3cm (1½in) large dollops on the baking tray, pressing each one down slightly. Bake the biscuits in the centre of the oven for 15–20 minutes. Remove and leave to cool completely on a wire rack.

200g (7oz) strong wholemeal flour
50g (1¾oz) fine cane sugar
1 tsp ground cinnamon
1 pinch of ground allspice
1 pinch of ground aniseed
90ml (3fl oz) rapeseed oil
100ml (3½fl oz) almond milk
1–2 tsp vanilla extract
200g (7oz) muesli of your choice

TIP
A fan oven is not suitable for this recipe as the cookies can easily become too dry and the dried fruit in the muesli is liable to burn.

Makes 50 cookies
Time: 20 mins prep
+ 30 mins resting + 15 mins baking

"LEBKUCHEN" COOKIES

1 To make the dough, combine the flour, cane sugar, cocoa powder, spices, and baking powder in a bowl. In a separate bowl, combine the soya cream, rapeseed oil, vanilla extract, and amaretto, then add these to the dry ingredients. Knead everything until you have a supple dough, adding a bit more liquid if required, then leave to rest for about 30 minutes.

2 Preheat the oven to 180°C (350°F/Gas 4). Roll out the dough to about 1cm (½in) thick on a work surface dusted with flour and stamp out stars, hearts, and other shapes. Place these on a baking tray lined with baking paper and brush with soya milk. Bake the cookies in batches in the centre of the oven for 12–15 minutes. Remove and leave to cool completely.

3 Make a thick glaze by stirring together icing sugar, 2 tablespoons of water, and the orange juice. Brush this over the cookies. Put one almond on each cookie and leave to dry on a wire rack. Store in a biscuit tin.

For the dough:
500g (1lb 2oz) strong wholemeal flour, plus extra for dusting
225g (8oz) fine cane sugar
4 tbsp vegan cocoa powder
2 tbsp mixed spices (cinnamon, ground cloves, allspice, ginger, mace, and ground cardamom)
1 tsp baking powder
250ml (9fl oz) soya cream
3 tbsp rapeseed oil
2–3 tsp vanilla extract
1 tbsp amaretto

For the glaze:
125g (4½oz) icing sugar
½ tsp orange juice
50 whole blanched almonds

Also:
soya milk, for brushing

TIP
You can also use lemon juice to make the icing sugar glaze, and the almonds can be replaced with hazelnuts.

Makes 6 dough figures
Time: 25 mins prep
+ 70 mins proving
+ 20 mins baking

"WECKMÄNNER" DOUGH FIGURES

Different German regions have different names for these traditional dough figures, including "Weckmann", "Stutenkerl", and "Krampus". Whichever name, they are usually baked and eaten around the time of Saint Nicholas' Day in Germany.

For the dough:
350ml (12fl oz) soya milk
1 cube fresh yeast
675g (1½lb) plain flour
1½ tsp salt
100g (3½oz) fine cane sugar
100g (3½oz) soft vegan margarine
1–2 tsp vanilla extract

Also:
raisins, to decorate
soya milk, for brushing

1 To make the dough, warm the soya milk over a low heat and remove from the heat. Crumble in the yeast, cover, and leave to stand at room temperature for 10 minutes. Combine the flour with the salt and sugar in a bowl. Add the margarine in little blobs and work it in slightly with your fingers until the lumps are no longer visible. Add the vanilla extract. Make a well in this mixture and pour in the milk and yeast mixture. Slowly work the ingredients together to form a supple dough. Knead the dough for 5 minutes, cover, and leave to prove in a warm place for 30 minutes, until it has doubled in size. Then knead it once again.

2 Line a baking tray with baking paper and shape little dough figures from the mixture. To do this, split the dough into 6 equal portions, roll each piece into a fairly thick sausage shape, and flatten it slightly. Snip the top of the dough at the sides slightly and round it off to make the head. To make the legs, make a vertical incision at the bottom and pull the two sections apart. Make the arms in a similar manner.

3 Lay the little figures on a baking tray, press in raisins for the eyes, mouth, and buttons, and brush the dough with soya milk. Cover and leave to prove in a warm place for about 30 minutes. Meanwhile, preheat the oven to 200°C (400°F/Gas 6). Bake in the centre of the oven for 15–20 minutes. Remove and leave to cool completely.

TIP
To make your dough figures a consistent size and shape, it helps to create a paper template to guide you when shaping the dough.

Makes 35–40 cookies
Time: 35 mins prep
+ 30 mins chilling + 15 mins baking

CHRISTMAS BISCUITS

For the dough:
2 tbsp chickpea flour
300g (10oz) wholemeal flour, plus
   extra for dusting
75g (2½oz) fine cane sugar
1 tsp baking powder
juice of ½ lemon
1–2 tsp vanilla extract
2 drops bitter almond oil
200g (7oz) vegan margarine

Also:
3 tbsp soya milk
250g (9oz) strawberry jam
1 tbsp icing sugar, plus extra for
   dusting (optional)

1 Stir the chickpea flour together with 2 tablespoons of water until smooth. In a large bowl, combine the wholemeal flour, cane sugar, and baking powder. Add the chickpea flour paste, lemon juice, vanilla extract, and almond oil. Then add the margarine in blobs and knead everything until it forms a supple dough. Wrap in cling film and leave to rest in the fridge for at least 30 minutes.

2 Dust the work surface with flour and roll the dough out thinly. Use circular or Christmas biscuit cutters to stamp out shapes. In half of these shapes, use a smaller cutter to stamp out a design in the centre, making sure you leave a border of about 5mm (¼in). Keep re-rolling any remaining dough and stamping until the dough has all been used. You should have equal numbers of solid bases and tops with patterns cut in them.

3 Preheat the oven to 200°C (400°F/Gas 6). Line a baking tray with baking paper, place the biscuits on it, and brush the tops with soya milk. Bake the biscuits in the centre of the oven for 12–15 minutes. Remove and leave to cool completely.

4 Press the jam through a sieve into a small pan. Bring the jam to the boil briefly over a low heat. Remove from the heat and then use a spoon to spread it over the biscuit bases. If desired, dust the cut out biscuit tops with icing sugar before setting them on the bases. Leave to dry.

Makes about 30 cookies
Time: 35 mins prep
+ 1 hr chilling + 15 mins baking

SPICED COOKIES

Spiced cookies are a traditional German recipe made using shortcrust. In the past, wooden moulds were used to stamp Christian motifs on the biscuits. Nowadays you will find all sorts of other decorative patterns, too.

1 tbsp chickpea flour
250g (9oz) plain flour
1 tsp baking powder
80g (2¾oz) fine cane sugar
1 pinch of ground cardamom
1 pinch of ground cloves
½ tsp ground cinnamon
100g (3½oz) vegan margarine
1–2 tsp vanilla extract
50g (1¾oz) ground almonds

1 Stir the chickpea flour with 2 tablespoons of water until smooth. Sift the plain flour into a large bowl. Add the baking powder, sugar, and spices and mix everything together thoroughly. Add the chickpea flour paste, the margarine in little blobs, and the vanilla extract. Using the dough hook on an electric mixer, combine everything into a smooth dough, gradually adding the almonds. Wrap the dough in cling film and chill in the fridge for at least 1 hour (see below).

2 Preheat the oven to 180°C (350°F/Gas 4). Roll the dough out thinly and stamp out shapes with a cookie cutter. Place the little cookies on a baking tray lined with baking paper and bake in the centre of the oven for 10–15 minutes. Remove them from the oven and leave to cool completely.

TIP

These spiced cookies taste even better if you prepare the dough the previous evening and leave it to chill overnight.

Makes 30–35 crescents
Time: 25 mins prep
+ 1 hr chilling + 20 mins baking

VANILLA CRESCENTS

Vanilla crescents are a great addition to the festive season – there should be some in every cookie jar. It's important to make them with real vanilla, as that is what gives them their fabulous flavour.

For the dough:
300g (10oz) plain flour
100g (3½oz) fine cane sugar
90g (3¼oz) ground almonds
seeds scraped from 1–2 vanilla pods
1 splash of lemon juice and some
    lemon zest
200g (7oz) vegan margarine, chilled

Also:
60g (2oz) icing sugar
1 tsp vanilla powder

1 In a large bowl, combine the flour, cane sugar, almonds, and vanilla seeds. Add the lemon juice and zest, then add the margarine in little blobs. Work everything together swiftly with your fingers until you have a supple, well-combined dough. Wrap in cling film and leave in the fridge for about 1 hour.

2 Preheat the oven to 190°C (375°F/Gas 5) and line a baking tray with baking paper. Shape little rolls from the dough, bend and taper them into crescent shapes, and lay them on the baking tray. Bake the crescents in the centre of the oven for 15–20 minutes. Remove them from the oven, leave to cool briefly, then dust them with a combination of icing sugar and ground vanilla while they are still warm.

TIP

The scraped out vanilla pod can be used to make delicious vanilla sugar. Just fill a preserving jar with fine sugar and add the vanilla pod. After 7 days the sugar will have absorbed the flavour.

CHOCOLATE CHIP COOKIES
THE SALTY WAY

1 In a large bowl, beat the margarine with an electric mixer until creamy. Add the white and brown cane sugar and beat everything on the highest setting for several minutes, then stir in the vanilla seeds.

2 In a separate bowl, combine the flour, salt, bicarbonate of soda, and almonds. Gradually stir this into the fat and sugar mixture until you have a consistent dough. Finally, fold in the chocolate with a spoon so that it is evenly distributed.

3 Preheat the oven to 180°C (350°F/Gas 4). Using 2 teaspoons, cut off little portions of the dough and put them on a baking tray lined with baking paper. Take care to leave a gap between them as the dough will spread out slightly as it bakes.

4 Bake the cookies in the centre of the oven for about 10 minutes. When the edges are golden brown, remove the cookies from the oven.

75g (2½oz) vegan margarine
75g (2½oz) fine white cane sugar
75g (2½oz) fine brown cane sugar
seeds scraped from 1 vanilla pod
100g (3½oz) plain flour
½ tsp salt
½ tsp bicarbonate of soda
40g (1¼oz) ground almonds
80g (2¾oz) vegan dark chocolate, finely chopped

TIP
Leave the cookies to cool down completely before lifting them off the tray as they will still be very soft after baking. Cookies keep best in a tin, but even then they never stay around very long.

Makes 8–10 nut wedges
Time: 25 mins prep
+ 30 mins baking + 30 mins cooling

NUT WEDGES

1 To make the base, combine the flour, sugar, soya flour, and baking powder in a large bowl. Add the margarine in little blobs, then add the vanilla extract and quickly knead everything to a smooth consistency. Roll out the dough onto a baking tray lined with baking paper. Bring the apricot jam to the boil with 2–3 tablespoons of water in a small pan over a low heat, stir until smooth, and brush this over the base.

2 Preheat the oven to 180°C (350°F/Gas 4). For the topping, combine the margarine with the sugar, vanilla extract, and the chopped and ground hazelnuts, until it forms a coherent mixture. Spread this evenly over the base and smooth the surface.

3 Bake in the centre of the oven for 25–30 minutes. Remove the baking tray from the oven and leave to cool for about 30 minutes. Slice into ten 10cm (4in) squares then divide these in half diagonally to create triangles.

4 Chop the dark chocolate into pieces and melt in a bain-marie. Dip the tips of the nut wedges into the chocolate and leave on a wire rack to dry.

For the base:
300g (10oz) plain flour
100g (3½oz) fine cane sugar
2 tsp soya flour
2 tsp baking powder
175g (6oz) vegan margarine
2–3 tsp vanilla extract

For the topping:
200g (7oz) soft vegan margarine
200g (7oz) fine cane sugar
2–3 tsp vanilla extract
100g (3½oz) chopped hazelnuts
300g (10oz) ground hazelnuts

Also:
4 tbsp apricot jam
200g (7oz) vegan dark chocolate

TIP

Nut wedges taste great with any kind of nut, for instance, a mixture of walnuts, hazelnuts, and almonds. The combination of ground and chopped nuts gives the biscuits their crunchy bite.

225g (8oz) soft vegan margarine
110g (3¾oz) icing sugar, well sifted
½ tsp vanilla powder
1 pinch of salt
250g (9oz) spelt flour
50g (1¾oz) cornflour
1 jar good-quality raspberry jam
    (about 350g/12oz)
250g (9oz) vegan dark chocolate

PIPED SPIRALS
WITH RASPBERRY JAM

These shortbread biscuits are usually made with lots of eggs, but it's not hard to make a vegan version. Most of the ingredients will already be in your store cupboard.

1 Preheat the oven to 180°C (350°F/Gas 4). Cream the margarine and icing sugar in a bowl with an electric whisk on its highest setting until light and fluffy. Stir in the vanilla powder and salt. Combine the spelt flour and cornflour, then stir these in, too.

2 Transfer the mixture to a piping bag with a star nozzle attached. Line a baking tray with baking paper and pipe 16 spiral rings. Bake in the centre of the oven for about 15 minutes, until the biscuits just turn slightly golden, but are not too dark. Remove and leave to cool completely.

3 In a small pan, warm the jam over a low heat. Remove from the heat and spread a generous quantity of jam over half of the biscuit rings. Place the remaining halves on top and leave to set. Melt the dark chocolate in a bain-marie. Dip the rings into the chocolate to decorate as desired, then leave to dry on a wire rack. Store in a tin in a cool, dry location.

TIP

The dough may vary in consistency depending on the flour. If it is too firm, a bit of soya cream can be added to make it softer. If it is too soft, some extra flour will make it stiffer. These spiral biscuits are also delicious with a vegan chocolate and hazelnut spread.

BAKING PRODUCT INFORMATION

Agar-agar is a plant-based alternative to gelatine made from algae and mainly available in powder form. Agar-agar is absolutely tasteless.

Agave syrup is a sweetener that is free from commercial industrial sugar and can be used as a 1:1 substitute for honey. Agave syrup has a slightly less intense flavour than maple syrup.

Bicarbonate of soda (sodium hydrogen carbonate) is a leavening agent that is an ingredient in baking powder (which also contains an additional acidifier). Bicarbonate of soda only takes effect when it is combined with acidic ingredients, such as vinegar or lemon, and it helps to make cakes light and fluffy.

Cheese is often used in savoury baking recipes. Vegan cheese varieties with good melting properties include MozzaRisella, Nutcrafter Creamery, and No-Moo Melty from Vegusto.

Egg substitute products are powders you can buy made from starch and thickening agents.

Fine cane sugar has the best baking properties; it has a subtle caramel flavour and is pleasantly sweet. It is produced by squeezing out the sugar cane and boiling the juice to make a syrup to which tiny sugar crystals are added. These are then cleaned and dried. Alternatively, coconut sugar, birch sugar, or stevia can be used. The important thing to remember is: don't just substitute sugar 1:1 with agave syrup or maple syrup. The mixture would end up having quite different properties if you did this.

Flour is plain in most recipes. Wholemeal plain flours have more vitamins, fibre, and minerals than more refined white flours. However, you shouldn't simply use wholemeal flour as a substitute for white flour because wholemeal flour generally requires about 10 per cent more liquid. Some people cannot tolerate the gluten that is present in spelt, einkorn, emmer, green spelt, barley, oats, kamut, rye, triticale, or wheat. Gluten-free flour mixtures are available in well-stocked supermarkets and stores.

Guar gum is used in vegan baking and cooking as an egg substitute, a gelling agent, and a plant-based thickening agent. It is obtained from the seeds of the guar bean.

Linseeds are the mature seeds from the flax plant (also known as flaxseed) and should always be freshly ground as they easily go rancid if stored for long periods. Linseed is very high in fat, so it shouldn't be ground in a flour mill. It is also available for sale ready ground.

Maple syrup is another sweetener that is a good substitute for honey. Maple syrup is primarily used in American recipes, for example, for brownies or pancakes.

Margarine that is suitable for vegans is produced using palm oil, coconut oil, sunflower oil, or soya. Most vegan varieties of margarine have excellent baking properties, but some have a very high water content and should not be used for baking. A good margarine should have an original buttery taste and a nice consistency. Here, again, it's important to pay attention to the information on the package.

Oils, particularly organic oils, often have a very intense flavour. For baking you should use high-quality, flavourless baking oils so that the taste of the oil doesn't overpower the other flavours in the cake. Ideal choices for baking include rapeseed oil, sunflower oil, and corn oil.

Psyllium husks are the husks of the small, dark, shiny seeds of the Indian psyllium plantain. The husks contain high levels of swelling agents and mucilage, so they are used as a plant-based swelling agent.

Silken tofu has a soft, gel-like consistency and is ideal for combining with other ingredients for baking.

Soya and soya products should be purchased carefully. Select organic soya products made from European soya beans. These are guaranteed to be GMO-free and haven't been transported over huge distances.

Soya cream/soya cream substitutes, like rice or oat creams, are not generally suitable for whipping, but used for spreading or making a ganache. Cream substitutes specifically for whipping are also available made from soya, rice, or coconut. After whipping, rice cream has a slightly less firm consistency than soya or coconut cream, so we recommend the addition of some cream stiffenerhere. In contrast to the animal products, plant-based creams cannot be "over beaten".

Soya flour is a dried product obtained from the soya bean and cannot simply be replaced by other flours as none have the binding capacity of soya flour. Choose soya flour that is labelled "full fat" and never store it beyond the specified use-by date because it can easily go rancid.

Soya milk, nowadays, come in numerous varieties; some unsweetened, others sweetened or with vanilla or chocolate flavouring, and many more besides. You can use any of these, but it is important to avoid the baked product ending up too sweet or with overly dominant flavours. Savoury baked items are always prepared with unsweetened soya milk. Often for successful vegan baking it is essential to thicken the soya milk using vinegar; on no account substitute other milks for the soya milk in this case. If you are just starting out on a vegan diet, it is best to chill soya milk well before drinking and select a slightly sweetened version to get used to the rather different milk flavour.

Soya yogurt is best unsweetened for baking. If you are using already-sweetened soya yogurt or a variety with added vanilla flavouring, you will need to be careful that your mix doesn't end up too sweet and that the vanilla flavour is not too dominant.

Starch is used in some recipes for binding. Unless specified otherwise, cornflour (corn starch) is intended.

Vanilla can be bought in different forms. You can buy vanilla pods, which are slit open lengthways and the seeds scraped out using a knife. Vanilla pods are very expensive so the seeds should be used sparingly. The pods can also be ground and finely pulverised then added to your baking ingredients. Ground vanilla can be bought as a ready-made product, and vanilla pods can be stored in a jar of sugar to create "vanilla" sugar. You can also buy vanilla flavouring – vanilla essence –in liquid form.

PASTRY, DOUGH & TOPPINGS EXPLAINED

Batter: The ingredients in these mixtures are simply stirred together. If desired, you can then fold in fruit or berries, or some vegetables for savoury cakes.

Biscuit dough: Biscuit dough is usually made with lots of eggs. In vegan baking, it is made without eggs, but still manages to be fluffy and moist. Pale biscuits usually contain mineral water plus vanilla as a flavouring; darker biscuits contain soya milk and cocoa powder for colouring. Baking powder and bicarbonate of soda work in conjunction with acids (for example, from a lemon) to act as leavening, or raising, agents.

Chocolate ganache: A chocolate ganache is made from a combination of chocolate and cream. Dark chocolate is finely chopped, melted, and stirred into a plant-based cream until smooth. The ganache is then spread over the cake or tart. A tip here: tilt the tray or baking tin so that the ganache can run evenly over the surface, this avoids leaving visible spoon marks when you are finished. Moist substances, such as a cream layer, should be thoroughly chilled before spreading the ganache and the chocolate ganache itself should not be too hot when it is applied.

Cupcakes: In contrast to muffins, these usually have a sugary sweet, creamy topping. They can be decorated creatively and are a great dish to bring along to an event.

Filo pastry: Filo pastry consists mainly of finely sieved flour, water, and fat. Ideally the filo pastry should be extremely thin so that you can almost see through it. The art is in working with the pastry without ripping it. You can also buy ready-made filo pastry, which is often vegan.

Frosting: Margarine, icing sugar, and a liquid are the main components in the frosting found on cupcakes or larger cakes. It is crucial that the individual ingredients are all the same temperature when being prepared. The margarine is beaten until fluffy, then icing sugar is sieved and beaten into the mix, and finally a liquid (such as syrup, or even a jam or fruit purée) is gradually added and carefully folded in.

Icing: For icing or a glaze, sieved icing sugar is stirred into a liquid. This works best with lemon juice. In order to produce a viscous, opaque, beautifully white icing, the lemon juice should only be added to the icing sugar one spoon or drop at a time and stirred until smooth. If the icing is going to be scattered with nuts or other decorations, this needs to be done relatively soon after the icing has been spread because it dries quickly.

Puff pastry: Puff pastry is a laminated dough consisting of multiple layers which puff up on baking (hence the name). The main ingredients are flour, salt, and water, then butter (or margarine for vegan baking) is incorporated in several stages. Ready-made puff pastry from the supermarket is usually vegan and is excellent for baking strudel dishes.

Shortcrust pastry: Shortcrust is often used when making biscuits, cheesecakes, or pies that have a filling. It can be pale or dark and is usually made from flour, sugar, baking powder, margarine, and possibly some water.

Yeast doughs: Consisting of flour, some salt and sugar, water or soya milk, yeast, and sometimes some oil or margarine. Temperature plays an important role when preparing yeast doughs: the temperature of the liquid that the yeast is dissolved in should be around 32°C (90°F) to enable the yeast to dissolve and let the dough rise properly. Working with dried yeast is slightly easier, as this can be stirred straight into the flour mixture.

BASIC BAKING RECIPES

YEAST DOUGH

For a 30 x 40cm (12 x 15½in) baking tray
Prep: 20 mins + 55 mins proving time + baking time

½ cube fresh yeast | 350g (12oz) spelt flour with a high gluten content | 1 tsp salt | pinch of fine cane sugar | 2 tbsp olive oil

Pour 200ml (7fl oz) lukewarm water into a bowl and crumble in the yeast. Cover and leave to ferment in a warm place for 10 minutes. Meanwhile, combine the flour, salt, sugar, and olive oil. Whisk the yeast and water mixture, add to the other ingredients, and knead everything until you have a supple dough. Cover and leave to prove in a warm place for about 45 minutes, until doubled in size. Knead it once again, roll out the dough, place it on the baking tray, and proceed as described in your recipe.

SWEET YEAST DOUGH

For a 30 x 40cm (12 x 15½in) baking tray
Prep: 20 mins + 55 mins proving time + baking time

500g (1lb 2oz) strong wheat flour | 3 tbsp fine cane sugar | ¼ tsp salt | 100ml (3½fl oz) soya milk, plus about 8 tbsp lukewarm soya milk | 1–2 tsp vanilla extract | ½ cube fresh yeast zest of ¼ organic lemon | 80g (2¾oz) soft vegan margarine

Sift the flour into a large bowl. Add the sugar and salt and combine. Create a well in the centre. Gently heat 100ml (3½fl oz) soya milk in a small pan, then pour it into the well. Add the vanilla extract. Crumble the yeast into the milk, then cover the mixture and leave to stand in a warm place for about 10 minutes. Stir this yeast mix into the dry ingredients, add the lemon zest and margarine in little blobs, and knead everything until you have a smooth dough. Depending on how the dough turns out, you may need to add more lukewarm soya milk or flour, the result should be a soft, but not sticky, dough. Cover the dough and leave to prove for 45 minutes, until it has doubled in size. Knead vigorously once again, then proceed as described in your recipe.

PUFF PASTRY

For a 30 × 40cm (12 x 15½in) baking tray
Prep: 1 hr + about 1½ hrs chilling time

550g (1¼lb) plain flour, plus some more for dusting | 5g salt | pinch of fine cane sugar | 500g (1lb 2oz) vegan margarine

To make the basic pastry, combine 500g (1lb 2oz) flour, the salt, sugar, 50g (1¾oz) margarine, and 300ml (10fl oz) water, and knead until smooth with the dough hook of an electric mixer. Wrap in cling film and chill for 30 minutes. For the margarine layer, quickly knead 450g (1lb) margarine into 50g (1¾oz) flour, making sure your hands are cold, and shape into an 18 × 18cm (7 x 7in) slab. Wrap in cling film and chill for 30 minutes. Roll out the basic pastry on a floured work surface to create a 1cm (½in) thick slab. Place the margarine layer on top of this slab of pastry. Fold the corners of the pastry in like an envelope towards the centre, enclosing the fat layer inside as you do so and pressing the edges firmly together. Roll it out to a size of approximately 60 × 20cm (24 x 8in) and 1cm (½in) thick. Fold one-third of the pastry towards the centre, then fold a third of the pastry over this from the other side. Gently press the slab of pastry flat with the rolling pin, first crossways then lengthways. Chill for about 20 minutes. Roll out the pastry again to create a 60 x 20cm (24 x 8in) slab. Fold the two narrow sides in to the centre, then fold once again to get 4 layers. Roll it out and repeat the initial fold-roll operation. Chill the pastry for 20 minutes. Then repeat the second fold-roll operation. Chill for 30 minutes and roll out to create 10 slabs of pastry, each roughly 5mm thick and 15 x 15cm (6 x 6in). If well wrapped, these will keep in the fridge for about 7 days.

TIP

To make pizza, try putting the dough in the fridge for 24 hours to rise slowly, which results in a particularly light texture.

SHORTCRUST PASTRY

For a 28cm (11in) springform tin
Prep: 20 mins + 1 hr chilling time + baking time

300g (10oz) plain flour | 1 tsp salt | 150g (5½oz) vegan margarine

In a large bowl, combine the flour with the salt and add the margarine in little blobs. Work the ingredients together with 8 tbsp water until you have a smooth pastry. Wrap in cling film and chill for 1 hour. Line the springform tin with baking paper. Roll out the pastry and lay it in the tin; if required, pull the edges up the sides to create a rim. Follow the instructions in your recipe for working with the pastry.

SIMPLE CAKE MIX

For a 28cm (11in) springform tin
Prep: 10 mins + 40 mins baking time

300g (10oz) plain flour | 2 tbsp cornflour | 125g (4½oz) fine cane sugar | 15g (½oz) baking powder | pinch of salt | 120ml (4fl oz) rapeseed oil | 140ml (4¾fl oz) soya milk | 2–3 tsp vanilla extract | 150ml (5fl oz) carbonated mineral water

Preheat the oven to 180°C (350°C/Gas 4). In a large bowl, combine the flour, cornflour, sugar, baking powder, and salt. Stir the rapeseed oil into the soya milk until smooth, add the vanilla extract, and mix into the dry ingredients. Add the mineral water and swiftly stir all the ingredients with a large spoon until you have a smooth consistency. Follow your recipe, adding any spices required. Transfer the mixture to your tin and bake for about 40 minutes. Proceed as described in the recipe, maybe topping with some fruit.

PALE SPONGE MIX

For a 30 × 40cm (12 x 15½in) tray or a 28in (11in) springform tin
Prep: 10 mins + 50 mins baking time

450g (1lb) plain flour | 240g (8½oz) fine cane sugar | 15g (½oz) baking powder | some zest from 1 organic lemon | 1 tsp ground vanilla | 2 tbsp cornflour | 100ml (3½fl oz) rice milk | 100ml (3½fl oz) corn oil | 350ml (12fl oz) carbonated mineral water

Preheat the oven to 180°C (350°C/Gas 4). In a large bowl, combine the flour, sugar, baking powder, lemon zest, vanilla, and cornflour. Mix the rice milk and corn oil and stir into the dry ingredients. Finally, carefully fold in the mineral water with a large spoon. Spread the mixture over the tray or transfer it into the tin and bake for about 50 minutes.

DARK SPONGE MIX

For a 30 × 40cm (12 x 15½in) tray or a 28cm (11in) springform tin
Prep: 10 mins + 40 mins baking time

300g (10oz) plain flour | 200g (7oz) fine cane sugar | 30g (1oz) vegan cocoa powder | 2 tsp baking powder | 2 tsp bicarbonate of soda | ½ tsp salt | 400ml (14fl oz) soya milk | 1½ tbsp cider vinegar | 150ml (5fl oz) rapeseed oil

Preheat the oven to 180°C (350°C/Gas 4). In a large bowl, combine the flour, sugar, cocoa powder, baking powder, bicarbonate of soda, and salt. In a separate bowl, whisk the cider vinegar into the soya milk and leave to thicken for about 5 minutes. Then stir in the rapeseed oil until smooth. Swiftly combine the dry and liquid ingredients with a large spoon. Spread the mixture over the tray or transfer it into the tin and bake for about 40 minutes.

BATTER

For 1 portion
Prep: 15 mins

350g (12oz) wholemeal flour | 1 sachet baking powder | 1 tbsp olive oil | 250ml (9fl oz) beer or other carbonated liquid | 1 tsp salt | fine cane sugar | ½ portion vegan whipped "egg whites" (see p368 for the recipe)

Combine the flour and baking powder in a large bowl. First add the olive oil, then the beer (or other liquid) and stir everything swiftly with a large spoon until smooth. Add the salt and sugar. Carefully fold in the vegan whipped egg white. Proceed as described in the recipe. For example, for apple fritters, dip the apple rings in the batter, fry in plenty of fat, and leave to drain on kitchen paper.

MERINGUES

For 8–15 meringues (depending on size)
Prep: 30 mins + 2 hs baking time

1 portion vegan whipped "egg whites" (200ml/7fl oz, see recipe, right) | 125g (4½oz) icing sugar | 1 tsp guar gum | 1 tsp vanilla extract

Preheat the oven to 130°C (250°F/Gas ½). Follow the recipe for vegan "egg whites", right. Sift the icing sugar into a bowl, add the guar gum and vanilla sugar and mix. Fold the mixture spoon by spoon into the egg whites and beat using an electric whisk on its highest setting. Transfer to a piping bag with a star nozzle and pipe equal-sized blobs onto a baking tray lined with baking paper. Let the meringues dry out in the centre of the oven for 1½–2 hours. Remove the meringues and leave to cool completely. Store in an airtight container.

COOKIE DOUGH

For 25–30 cookies
Prep: 35 mins + 1 hr chilling time + 15 mins baking time

300g (10oz) strong wheat flour, plus some more for dusting | 90g (3¼oz) fine cane sugar | 1 tsp chickpea flour | 1–2 tsp vanilla extract | 200g (7oz) vegan margarine | 125g (4½oz) icing sugar | juice of ½ lemon | colourful sugar strands, to decorate

In a large bowl, combine the flour and cane sugar. Stir 2 tsp water into the chickpea flour to create a paste, add the vanilla extract, then add to the dry ingredients. Add blobs of margarine and combine everything quickly to make a smooth mixture. Wrap the dough in cling film and chill for about 1 hour. Preheat the oven to 180°C (350°F/Gas 4). Generously dust a work surface with flour (or line it with baking paper), roll out the cookie dough, and stamp out shapes. Place these on a baking tray lined with baking paper. Bake in the centre of the oven for 10–15 minutes. Remove and leave to cool completely. To make the icing, sift the icing sugar into a bowl. Stir in a teaspoon of lemon juice at a time, stirring it into the icing sugar until smooth. The aim is to create a thick glaze. Spread it over the biscuits and decorate with sprinkles.

LINSEED "EGG WHITES"

For 1 portion
Prep: 5 mins + 30 mins cooking time + 1 hr chilling time

40g (1¼oz) linseed

Bring the linseed and 500ml (16fl oz) water to the boil in a pan. Simmer over a low heat for 20–25 minutes, until it forms a gel-like consistency. Strain the contents of the pan into a bowl through a fine sieve to separate the gel from the linseed granules. Chill the gel for 1 hour, then beat it for several minutes with an electric whisk or a food processor on its highest setting to create a neutral-tasting plant-based foam.

GLACÉ ICING

For 1 round cake (24cm/9½in springform) or 1 loaf cake (26cm/10½in long tin)
Prep: 5 mins

125g (4½oz) icing sugar | 2–3 tbsp lemon juice, water, or some other liquid (juice, syrup, milk, tea, liqueur, coffee, red wine, rum) | nuts, grated chocolate, colourful sugar strands, to decorate (optional)

Sift the icing sugar into a bowl and add the liquid a few drops at a time – the quantity will depend on the desired consistency of your icing. Stir with the balloon whisk until you have a smooth, very viscous mixture. For icing with a stronger flavour and which is more "opaque", add less liquid. Apply the icing as soon as possible because it sets quickly. Using hot liquid to make the icing helps it bind successfully and gives it a particularly wonderful sheen after it has dried. If you want to add any decorations, this needs to be done soon after the icing has been applied.

FROSTING

For 1 round cake (24cm/9½in springform) or 1 loaf cake (26cm/10½in long tin) or 12 cupcakes
Prep: 15 mins

200g (7oz) soft vegan margarine | about 400g (14oz) icing sugar | about 4 tbsp juice, jam, or fruit compote, as desired and at room temperature

Cream the margarine in a bowl until light and fluffy, then sift in the icing sugar and combine. Add teaspoonful's of the juice, jam, fruit compote, or other flavouring, stirring carefully. The quantity can vary depending on the desired consistency – very runny ingredients need more icing sugar; more viscous and cohesive ingredients, such as fruit purées, need less. Spread the cake with the frosting.

APRICOT GLAZE

For 1 round cake (24cm/9½in springform tin) or 1 loaf cake (26cm/10½in long tin)
Prep: 10 mins

4 tbsp apricot jam | 1 tbsp orange juice

Purée the jam and press it through a fine sieve. Stir it into the orange juice in a pan and simmer for about 2 minutes over a low heat. Spread the hot glaze over your cake with a pastry brush and leave to dry. Using an apricot glaze gives cakes, tarts, and other baked items a great flavour and keeps them fresh for longer. The icing on creamy gateaux stays in place better if you use an apricot glaze.

VANILLA CUSTARD

For about 500g (1lb 2oz) custard
Prep: 15 mins

500ml (16fl oz) soya, rice, or oat milk | 40g (1¼oz) cornflour | 2–3 tsp vanilla extract

Stir the cornflour and a little milk until smooth. Put the remaining milk into a pan and bring to the boil with the vanilla extract over a moderate heat. Remove from the heat and stir in the cornflour paste with a whisk. Bring it back to the boil, stirring constantly, until you have a thick custard – the longer it cooks, the thicker it will become.

VANILLA SAUCE

For about 600ml (1 pint) sauce
Prep: 15 mins

500ml (16fl oz) almond milk | 2 heaped tbsp cornflour | seeds from 1 vanilla pod, plus the pod itself | 3 tbsp fine cane sugar | pinch of salt | 200g (7oz) coconut cream

Take 4 tbsp of the almond milk and stir in the cornflour with a whisk until smooth. Put the remaining milk into a pan and bring to the boil over a moderate heat. Add the vanilla seeds, vanilla pod, sugar, salt, and coconut cream and return to the boil, stirring constantly. Remove from the heat and quickly stir in the cornflour paste with a whisk. Continue to cook until the sauce has thickened. Warm vanilla sauce goes well with strudel and other dishes.

BUTTERCREAM TOPPING

For 1 round cake (24cm/9½in springform)
Prep: 15 mins

350g (12oz) vanilla custard (see left, cooked until thick) | 200g (7oz) soft vegan margarine | 80g (2¾oz) icing sugar

Allow the thick, cooked custard to cool to room temperature. Meanwhile, cream the margarine in a bowl, sift over the icing sugar, and stir it in. Carefully stir the custard into the margarine and icing sugar mixture. Spread a thick layer over your cake and leave to chill.

CREAM TOPPING

For 1 round cake (24cm/9½in springform) or 1 loaf cake (26cm/10½in long tin)
Prep: 10 mins

1 pack soya cream, suitable for whipping (300g/10oz), well chilled | 1 sachet cream stiffener | extra ingredients to add flavour and/or colour as desired (vanilla extract, cinnamon, vegan food colouring, etc.)

Whip the soya cream using an electric whisk on its highest setting for at least 3 minutes, sprinkling in the cream stiffener as you do so. Beat in any additional ingredients. Use the topping to add the finishing touches to a cake then leave the cake to cool completely.

TIP

It's easy to make your own piping bag for decorating: just cut out a triangle of baking paper, roll it up into a cone (with the point sealed), and fold over the top edge. Fill it half full of melted chocolate, snip off the tip, and decorate your baked goods in whatever style you like.

INDEX

THE AUTHORS ...

Jérôme Eckmeier has worked at numerous prestigious restaurants both in Germany and abroad since training as a chef and food technician. For several years he has been cooking vegan food and following a vegan lifestyle. His internet cooking show and blog with his new vegan creations are a source of constant inspiration.

Photo: © Boris Seifert

Jérôme Eckmeier

Thank you to my wife Melanie (for her patience with me), our kids, our unborn veggie baby and also my parents. Thanks must also go to: Franz and Traute, Marius and Frauke, the Keller family, Dr. Norbert Knitsch, the Eckmeier clan from the Ruhr region, the guys at Budo Nüttermoor, my sensei Hardwig Tomic, Markus at Little Harbour Tattoo, the German Vegetarian Association (VEBU), Bernd Drosihn at tofutown, Sebastian Bete from the OZ, Erwin and Sandra, Ingo Jäger, Tatjana and Boris Seifert, Brigitte "sunshine" Kelly, Nicole Bader, Andreas Kessemeier and the staff at Pool Position, Mike Beuger at the law firm WBS in Cologne, Vik and Tina, the team at VHS Leer, the magazine "Vegetarisch Fit", cinemadirekt Berlin, Keimling Naturkost healthfood store, Jan Bredack and his family, the team at Veganz, Baola in Munich, Chris from myey.info, Roadhouse Herbrum and all you rock 'n' roll guys who have supported me in my work.

Daniela Lais is a freelance journalist and author living between Portland, Oregon, USA, and Hoerbranz in Austria. She has worked for many years in the bakery of the oldest vegetarian–vegan restaurant in Austria and has been vegan for more than fifteen years.

Photo: personal

Daniela Lais

My thanks go to my parents and all the friends who appreciate my creations and support me. Thanks to Joel, from whom I learned so much American food culture, proverbs, and wisdom, my friends Janet, Steven, Chris, David, and Denise, who have inspired many of my recipes and supported me in so many ways. I thank my community and many friends in Portland, Oregon, the most beautiful city in the world, and in my homeland. Thanks to my friend Janine Favia, from whom I learned a lot. You are a role model for me with your zest for life! Thanks to my publisher DK, to my co-author Jérôme Eckmeier and the VEBU, now proVeg. I thank all people who are committed to herbal nutrition. Last but not least, a very big thank you to the people who support me in everyday life and on my way, no matter in what way. I am infinitely grateful to each of you – without you, this book would not exist.

We are grateful to the following companies for their kind support:
Soyatoo! cream, Viana – smoked tofu, Baola, Keimling Naturkost healthfood store, myey.info, Veganz – we love life, www.alles-vegetarisch.de